THE LEGENDARY CUISINE
OF PERSIA

THE LEGENDARY
CUISINE OF PERSIA

Margaret Shaida

Interlink Books
An imprint of Interlink Publishing Group, Inc.
New York • Northampton

First American edition published in 2002 by
INTERLINK BOOKS
An imprint of Interlink Publishing Group, Inc.
99 Seventh Avenue, Brooklyn, NY 11215 and
46 Crosby Street, Northampton, MA 01060
www.interlinkbooks.com

Originally published by Grub Street, London, England
Text copyright © Margaret Shaida 2000, 2002
Preface copyright © Alan Davidson 2002
Foreword copyright © Gregory Lima 2002
Copyright © Grub Street, London 2000, 2002

Library of Congress Cataloging-in-Publication Data

Shaida, Margaret.
  The legendary cuisine of Persia / Margaret Shaida.-- 1st American ed.
    p. cm.
Includes bibliographical references and index.
  ISBN 1-56656-413-1
  1. Cookery, Iranian. I. Title.
  TX725.I7 S44 2001
  641.5955--dc21

                                        2001003657

Printed and bound in Korea

Author's Note
Spelling and Transliteration
The transliteration of Persian words in this book has been
simplified as far as possible. For instance, the difference
between Persian letters "gh" and "q" are minimal in
English pronunciation and I have opted to use "gh" for both
letters. However, there are two versions of the Persian "a,"
the long "a" (as in "calm") and the short "a" (as in "pat").
In this book, the long "a" is denoted with an accent "â."

CONTENTS

ACKNOWLEDGEMENTS

The number of people who have contributed to the appearance of this book are beyond count. Many of them I have never met. Many others are long dead. They are the generations of Iranian men and women who have created these recipes of such originality and enduring delight. They are the true authors of this book and I am happy to be able to acknowledge their inspiration and contribution.

My thanks must also go to a great number of people whom I have had the privilege of meeting. To Mrs. Shamsi Rast who brought her skills and laughter to my kitchen in Iran and to the late Mrs. Maria Tajaddod who brought her wide knowledge to my kitchen in England; to Mrs. Fatimeh Khorsandi whose awareness of both the history and the techniques of fine Persian food inspired me; to Mrs. Maheen Fatehi for her "southern" skills and Mrs. Simeen Bahram for her "northern" skills; to Mrs. Pouran Ataie who was especially generous with her time and knowledge—she tested many of the recipes and suggested many others; to a great number of friends who shared with me the hints and myths that form an integral part of the Persian kitchen; and to the many people who so shared with me their knowledge and love of Persian food.

I should also like to express my thanks to Professor Theodore Zeldin and Mr. Alan Davidson for their quiet encouragement. It was through them that I was able to widen my awareness of culinary history at the Oxford Symposia of Food and Cookery. I also received great assistance from Mrs. Hilary Laurie who gave me the benefit of her time and considerable experience.

Special thanks go to Mr. Nasser Engheta for his invaluable assistance and to Mr. A. Ghoreishi, both of whom imparted to me their deep love and extensive knowledge of the history and languages of ancient Persia.

Above all, my thanks go to my long-suffering and patient family who put up with my moods and experiments with great equanimity; to my mother-in-law who taught me the first lessons of love and skill that are such important ingredients of Persian food; to Batul for her advice and recipes, and, most especially, to my husband, Hassan, without whom I would never have become aware of the legendary cuisine of his homeland. His devotion, interest, and generous spirit have sustained me over many years.

FOREWORD

The title "Legendary" strikes the right note for this book. Time and again over the last twenty years, while I have been working on food and cooking, mainly from a historical viewpoint, I have been struck by the number of roads that lead back to Persia. This is not, of course, a completely new idea; there have been scholars in the past who have discerned the Persian influence in many other cuisines. Laufer's great work *Sino-Iranica* has served as a beacon to illuminate for such scholars the paths that led from Persia to China and back again. But in my belief it is only now that people are beginning to realize the full extent of these ancient influences, and how much of what is familiar on our own tables may be traced back, ultimately, to the land of Persia.

Margaret Shaida's book, with its wealth of historical matter, will intensify this realization. But this is not all it will do. Since it is the work of a marvelously skilled cook, with a gift for explaining to others how they can emulate her exploits in the kitchen, the recipes with which the book is studded will spread enjoyment far and wide. I speak from experience. She has for some time had the pleasant custom of providing a small banquet before the annual Oxford Food and Cookery Symposium, inviting some of the participants from overseas. Each of these banquets has been a masterpiece; a spectrum of delicate flavors and textures, a visual delight.

This combination, to which I thus emphatically draw attention, of historical illumination with practical recipes for delicious food is something that invites a little more explanation. I recently found myself discussing a medieval cookbook with a man who saw it purely and simply as a source of recipes that might (or might not) work if adapted for use today. When I speculated about the true date of the recipes, he displayed with vigor his lack of interest in this. "After all," he said, "it's the recipes themselves that count, isn't it? Do they work? Do the dishes taste good? There aren't any other questions."

Perhaps he was only seeking to condemn, by a venial exaggeration of his own attitude, any contrary one, on the lines that the important questions that pose themselves over a plateful of food are historical, sociological, etc., rather than how it tastes.

But, I thought to myself, the ideal situation is surely to have it both ways: not only to have delicious food on the table, but also to get the facts right about where the recipes came from and what their geographical and social contexts originally were, and what changes have taken place in them and why, and so on. The history of a dish is, to my mind, a romantic thing, and although it would be absurd, every time one eats a piece of bread, to insist that the whole panorama of the history of wheat and indeed of the other cereals used for bread and of the evolution of the myriad different kinds of loaf should flit through one's mind—although, I say, this would be carrying things much too far, the fact is that a considerable enhancement of the pleasures derived from good food may be had by being aware of and alert to such aspects when the setting makes this appropriate. (And, I would add, if any setting makes it appropriate it must surely be a Persian setting. For what other country can claim for its cuisine such a long history and one so rich in fructifying effects both westwards and eastwards?)

Here, anyway, is a book that follows, and with great success, what seems to me the right prescription for a really good cookbook; and Margaret Shaida is to be warmly congratulated on her achievement.

ALAN DAVIDSON, London

INTRODUCTION

In those long gone days when the trade caravans carrying the silks of China, the saffron of India, the frankincense of Araby, and most of the gold of Rome criss-crossed Iran from every direction, the question might rise in the caravanserais: Where was the center of the world? The answer, the Persians might argue, is Iran, where you can bask in the fragrance of the most temperate of climates, fill your flasks with the finest wines, listen to the profoundest poets, and enjoy the most delicious food. He might concede that as to the wine, the climate, and the poetry his judgment could be subjective, but the total centrality and superiority of the food would be too obvious for argument.

These notions are hard to disprove. To the north is the frozen tundra of the Russian steppes, to the south the blazing sands of Arabia, east are the monsoons of India. Iran, with its four distinct seasons, could seem perfectly temperate by such comparisons, the more so by its remarkable invention: the *qanat*. This enabled most of the population to live in the sunshine virtually every day of the year. The towering mountains tore apart the rain clouds, keeping the bad weather in other countries and making Iran almost a desert but for the *qanat* that brought the perennial waters of the stormy, snow-capped mountains through hand-dug channels deep beneath the soil dozens of miles to the otherwise arid, sandy plain below, and made it bloom in literally tens of thousands of oasis villages. Often brilliantly, with orchards, diverse crops, and *qanat*-fed drinking water to quench the thirsts of cities. The same often-forested mountains provided the pasture for the flocks—the meat and dairy, as well as the wool for the Persian carpets upon which woven gardens the meals were served. Aside from the sturgeon and caviar fisheries, rice paddies, and citrus groves of the Caspian littoral where the rainfall is heavier than England, most of the land is under cloudless skies. At night the stars fall down, almost into your lap, they are so bright and seemingly near. Which may account for some of Persia's more celebrated poets being highly accomplished astronomers, as was Omar Khayyam, or for the Star of Bethlehem to rise in these skies, for between dusk and dawn the Magi hardly had to use their magic to find the road.

But, if as some now sadly believe, Persia is no longer at the center of the world, if Hafez, Saadi, and Rumi's nightingales no longer sing as sweetly among the rose bushes to the strings of the *târ*, if the vineyards of Shiraz that Gibbon believed "always triumphed over the laws of Mohammed" have become fallow fields, and storm now rages over Persia's sunshine and shadows, it leaves the country only with the most delicious food.

There are some that might dispute even that. But they have not yet read this wonderful book.

For Margaret Shaida has achieved an elusive task that has slipped by other compilers of cookbooks dealing with Persian cuisine. She has defined the space within which the Persian cook finds her freedom and her limits, enabling her to cook Persian, as opposed to Chinese, Italian, French, or Indian. To cook Persian involves certain principles in combining ingredients, a host of traditions and a living sense of what is sufficient and what is right, as it is with Chinese or any other major cuisine. Once you are at home with the fundamentals, Persian cooking, within its own idiomatic expression, can offer remarkable variety, adaptability to the foods of the season and the limits of the market. But Persian cooking is only food if taken out of its social context. It is in the social context where it thrives and gains its stature among the greater of the living arts. For Persian cooking is inextricable from the greatest of all the Persian arts: hospitality.

Many of the recipes in this volume have been refined over the centuries, surviving virtually every joy and every calamity known to woman and to man. They survived while lizards crawled over shattered antiquities, not because someone saved them in a book of secrets, but precisely because they were widely shared and prized as a way to prepare nourishing food deliciously, and above all, worthy to be set before one's own guests, be they poets, philosophers, or the very king among kings.

It was as a bedazzled recipient of Persian hospitality over a period of more than twenty years as a journalist in Iran that I was introduced to the delights of the Persian kitchen, and no hospitality was warmer nor any Persian kitchen more venturesome than Shaida's. Margaret is one of the better cooks among very good cooks, and what she has done in the following pages is to evoke the true character of the food, not simply as a treasure trove of recipes that each of us can bring into our kitchens in whatever country we may live, but she gives us the ability to share in the culture in which each dish is deeply rooted. For the Persian cuisine, she shows convincingly, is the product of very intimate relationships between the land, the people, their customs, and their beliefs. She shows how the Persian kitchen on a quotidian level can be as much a work of the common genius as the brilliant work on the Persian loom.

The proof of all this, however, is in the taste. Can this cuisine that for centuries defied export now be re-created abroad? Perhaps some things can never happen just that way anywhere else than in the heart of Iran. How can you export the breads in cellophane leaving behind the oven and the baker? How can you take the spices one by one in little pinches without the overwhelming aroma of the spice seller's stalls in the bazaar? But to a remarkable degree, Margaret Shaida in the following pages makes this cuisine happen here, wherever you may be. And God be praised, *alhamdollilah*, she has done it just in time.

GREGORY LIMA, New York

THE HERITAGE OF PERSIA

Looking at the history of Persia is like looking through several panes of shattered glass. It is always just out of focus, distorted, and fractured behind the broken shards of the histories of Greece and Rome, half-hidden beyond the eastern reaches of the Muslim and Ottoman empires. It is a distant land, remote and mysterious; a land of ancient culture and often elegant ritual. It is also a land of remarkably good food.

The cuisine of Persia is unique. The origins of many dishes are shrouded in its long history of more than 3,000 years and in the reciprocal influences involved in that history. Still, many of its dishes can be traced back a thousand years, some even more. While it is not unusual in many countries for the food of kings and courtiers to be recorded, it is rare indeed to have knowledge of the food of the poor. We know, however, that the recipe for the simple onion soup (*eshkeneh*) is believed to be the same as that used to sustain the Persian foot soldiers on their campaigns under King Arsaces more than 2,000 years ago.

The survival of the Persian way of cooking is largely due to the enduring appeal of its delicate blend of flavors and to its ability successfully to absorb and adapt the foods of other nations. Persian food is nutritionally balanced and visually attractive. But above all, it has survived because it is delicious.

When the Persians first conquered the ancient world, they extended their civilization from the valley of the Indus in the east to Egypt and Greece in the west. They influenced religion and philosophy in Greece and Rome, but not the least influence was the introduction of their food.

Many Greeks had long followed the doctrine of Aristippus who believed in the nourishment of the spirit as well as the body; simple meals were accompanied by poetry, music, and philosophy. To such people, used to plain fare spiced with little more than hexameters, the sophisticated eating habits of the Persians proved fascinating and sometimes irresistible.

The Persian believed in the satisfaction of the eye as well as of the palate and they found little to gratify either in the fare of the ancient Greeks. Even Herodotus, the Greek traveler and writer who could find little good to say about his Persian enemies, commended the remarkable skills of the Persian bakers and cooks who accompanied the generals on their campaigns. He noted the magnificent variety of "good things" to be seen on their "richly accoutr'd" tables, and he recalled the astonishment of one of the Greek generals at the "folly" of the Persians who, though they "enjoyed such fare," had felt the need to come to Greece "to rob us of our penury."

1

Indeed, the Persians thought the Greeks remained hungry much of the time because of the dreariness of their food. Desserts were unknown to the Greeks, and the Persians thought "they left off hungry, having nothing worth mention served up to them after the meats." King Croesus himself advised Cyrus the Great that the Persians could defeat many of the troublesome tribes by luring them with "the good things on which the Persians live."

Some 200 years later, Alexander defeated the Persians, but he himself was one of the first to succumb to the refinements of the Persian court. The Macedonians absorbed many of the customs of their defeated former foe and in their returning baggage was no small measure of the food and formalities of the Persians. It was at this time that the lemons and saffron, pomegranates and pistachios of the Iranian plateau first became familiar in the Mediterranean region.

Saffron was an immediate success. Its delicate flavor and costly rarity were a great attraction to the Greeks and later to the Romans. There was less enthusiasm for the lemon, it being rather acid to the Greek palate, while the Romans initially used it only as a mothball. But there was no such confusion about the delights of the Persian pomegranates and pistachios.

It is of course next to impossible to trace the history of many dishes in the world today, particularly those classics that are found all over the Middle East. Each country lays claim to some dishes but proof is rare. The earliest reference is often taken as evidence of origin. Sometimes it depends where the traveler or writer has first tasted a dish or a sweetmeat: for instance, a famous Persian sweet, *râhal al-hoqum* (an Arabic phrase), is known as Turkish Delight in the West.

The earliest known cookbooks, from Athens and Rome, were mostly written by physicians concerned with the medical properties of food, or clerics defining the dietary laws of religion. No cookbooks have survived from the ancient Persians, most of whose libraries and records were destroyed by successive conquerors. It should be remembered too that the production and preparation of food has usually been a domestic and female chore of little interest to most historians. In any case,by definition, the best cook leaves the least evidence.

But there are a few scattered facts, an occasional reference, a poetic hint, or proverbial wisdom that can lead a lover of Persian food into some educated speculation. After all, the grudging praise of Herodotus cannot be entirely dismissed.

When the Persians re-established themselves following Alexander's death, they once more ruled over a country that was considerably more extensive than it is today. For over a thousand years their empire was the center of civilization in the eastern half of the known world. Baghdad and eastern Iraq, Afghanistan, and parts of Pakistan were all part of the Persian Empire, as was the eastern half of present-day Turkey. The Greeks ruled over the western half, and the boundaries of the Persian and Greek empires rubbed against each other for centuries, sometimes sparking into open conflict and sometimes melting into union against a common enemy. By about AD100, the common enemy was undoubtedly Rome, which was expanding eastwards with a steady determination.

It wasn't long before Persia and Rome were in direct contact. They had known of each other long before this, however. Apicius, the Roman author of a cookbook, has a recipe for lamb "cooked in the Parthian (Iranian) manner." It calls for a whole lamb stuffed with prunes and herbs, not unlike a dish made today in many parts of Iran.

At the same time, China made some exploratory moves toward the West. The first Chinese mission got as far as Persia, which it described as a very great country where rice, wheat, and grapevines were cultivated. Up until then, Persia had been the bridge between the West and India only. Now the final links were made between the West and the Far East, with Persia trading regularly with China from AD200 up to the middle of the seventh century and beyond.

By AD620, the Romans were in rapid decline, and a new power was whirling up in the southern Arabian deserts. The Muslims exploded on to the scene, and the conquest of Iran was as sudden as it was unexpected. But while the Arabs overpowered Iran with their religious fervor, they were in turn overwhelmed by the cultural and culinary artistry of Persia. When they swept back along the southern Mediterranean coast and up into Spain with their religion, they also took Persia's cuisine with them. There is a clear etymological trail.

The Old Persian *bâdangân* became *al-badinjan* in Arabic, *alberjinera* in Spanish, and finally aubergine in French and British English. Spinach, too, is derived from the Old Persian *espenâj*, orange from *nârang*, lemon from *limoo*, tarragon from *tarkhoon*.

Initially in Iran there was considerable social resistance to the Arab invaders. The culture and language of Persia, unlike those of Egypt and Syria, held firm against the Islamic conquerors, but the ancient Zoroastrian religion did not. Those who refused to submit to Islam were obliged to withdraw to refuges deep in Iran's great salt deserts. Some settled in the towns of Yazd and Kerman, where the descendants still live according to the tenets of Zoroaster. Others fled eastward, finding ultimate asylum in the state of Gujarat in India. For more than five centuries they were completely cut off from their brethren in Iran, but throughout they maintained their ancient religion—and their cuisine.

They have survived to this day and are now known as the Parsees (i.e., Persians) of India. Many Indian restaurants in the West today have a selection of "Persian" food on their menus. Of course, after nearly 1,000 years, Parsee food today is more Indian than Persian, though it retains a milder and more sour flavor than the spicier food of the Indian subcontinent.

The Arabs adopted many of the Persian dishes. Indeed, as they established themselves firmly in their new capital in Baghdad (the site of Ctesiphon, the ancient capital of the Persian Empire), they were able to turn their attention to the sciences in which the Iranians excelled, which in addition to astronomy and medicine, included gastronomy. The Iranians contributed much to the golden age of the Abbasids of the Caliphate of Baghdad. In doing so they yielded their claim to many of their finest culinary (and other) achievements, for all the new works were written in Arabic, the court language of the day.

Some of the most interesting and intricate Iranian recipes have come down to us only through the medieval Arabic cookbooks of the Caliphate of Baghdad. Many of the dishes are identifiable by etymology. But, it is probable that they differ in one singular ingredient from the original ancient Persian dishes: in the face of the Prophet's strictures on the evils of intoxication, the use of wine in their cooking would have had to be abandoned—a significant adaptation that was apparently made with some reluctance.

The demise of wine in Persian food was slow. As late as AD1100 (nearly 500 years after the introduction of Islam) "wine vinegar" was still in use in many dishes in the kitchens of the Caliphate of Baghdad, the very epicenter of Islam from the eighth to twelfth centuries. Even today, verjuice (see page 37), and light vinegar are added to many of the soups and stews to give an added piquancy, while cider or wine vinegar is recommended by some housewives for pickling.

Omar Khayyam, one of Persia's most famous mathematicians, astronomers, and poets (his *Rubâiyat* was fully translated into English by Edward Fitzgerald in the last century), was censured in twelfth-century Persia for his commendation of wine and women. His philosophical quatrains, written in a haze of alcohol, have long made him a favorite in the West.

In the twelfth and thirteenth centuries, the Crusades brought a further diffusion of Persia's culinary expertise across Europe. The princes and soldiers returning from the Crusades brought back new and exotic tastes from the world of Islam, and the subsequent demand for spices and herbs was one of the factors contributing to the European age of exploration.

In medieval England, much use was made of attar of roses; rose and orange blossom petals were made into jams and preserves in much the same way as they are in Iran today. The heavenly fragrance of Persian rosewater (*golâb*) that has long enhanced many a dish and an occasion was adopted in England as a base for a pleasant drink that became known as julep. Pomegranates, quinces, barberries, and mulberries, all common fruit in Persia, became popular.

The gardens of Jacobean England were filled with herbs from the Middle East for use by apothecaries as well as by the gentry for culinary embellishment and medical restoratives. Many of these are still familiar in modern Iran, though only recently becoming once more fashionable in the US and in England. A dish of mutton in an orange and cinnamon flavored sauce noted in Elinor Fettiplace's *Receipt Book from Medieval*

England (written in 1620) has a remarkable similarity to the duck and orange sauce of modern Iran.

While the Crusaders were attacking the western Caliphate of Damascus, the eastern Caliphate of Baghdad was under an even greater threat from the East. The Mongolian hordes poured into Iran, utterly destroying everything on their way. Whole towns and villages were laid waste, thousands of people were killed, and libraries and centers of learning razed to the ground. The Mongols established a new headquarters in Iran in preparation for continuing their westward invasion. The Il-Khans, a branch of the Mongol chieftain, ruled over Persia, but having little literary or cultural heritage of their own they quickly absorbed the Persian language, religion, and cuisine. Within two centuries Teimur (Tamerlane), a direct descendant of Genghis Khan, had become totally Iranianized. He branched off to India to establish one of the most sophisticated and extravagant regimes ever known in that ancient and sophisticated land. The court language of the Moghul (the Persian for Mongol) emperors of Delhi was Persian, their culture Iranian, and their religion Islam. Their food, of course, was wholly Persian.

The Moghuls took with them not only the traditions and language of the Persian court but also those of the Persian kitchen. The direct influence can be easily identified in many Indian dishes today: *biryani* is from the Persian word for baked (*beryân*), while *boorâni* is the Arabized Persian word for any yogurt dish mixed with vegetables.

The Persian bread (*nân*) made with yeast and baked in an oven (*tanoor*) took India by storm when it was first introduced there. It was a light yet substantial alternative to the unleavened and fried breads of the subcontinent. Today, the "Indian" tandoor-baked bread (*nân*) and chicken (*murgh*) are famous throughout the US and Europe via the popular and proliferating Indian restaurants. *Kofteh* (ground meat dumplings) and kebab, both Persian, are regular features on the menus of Indian restaurants from Singapore to San Francisco.

Certainly, the menu of an Indian restaurant is easily understood by an Iranian who speaks only Persian, though of course the dishes themselves, with added spices, may no longer be so familiar. Persian food is never hot and spicy. It has a delicacy in appearance and flavor that make it uniquely Persian.

To this day the two distinctive ingredients of the Persian cuisine remain the indigenous saffron and the Indian lemon that has been cultivated in Iran for at least 3,000 years. Both fragrant and richly beautiful, they have long endowed Persian food with piquancy and a rich elegance that are difficult to match. It is impossible to contemplate a classical Persian meal without either lemon or saffron—more often than not it will have both.

Another unusual element in Persian cooking is the blend of meats with fruits and nuts; and lastly, the method of cooking rice that is, without doubt, unequalled anywhere in the world.

A further important aspect of Persian cooking is its tradition. Not surprisingly, in a cuisine as long-lasting as this there are few dishes that do not have a story or a tale to go with them. The culture of the ancients comes down to us, from the legends of the mythical King Jamshid, the fabled triumphs of the ancient Persian conquerors, and the poetic glories of Omar Khayyam and Ferdowsi.

An Iranian kitchen is interlaced with proverbs, old wives' tales, miracle cures, and ancient wisdoms. It is filled with exotic aromas and crowded with cultural recollections of festivals and ceremonies. Its memory goes back more than 3,000 years. Its cures inspire a healing faith, its aromas excite a healthy appetite and its traditions arouse a national pride. It is, in short, the heart and soul of an ancient and remarkable nation.

IRAN'S DESTINY

Persia is the hinge between the Far East and the Middle East. Straddled between the Caspian Sea in the north and the Persian Gulf in the south, it forms a natural highway—and part of the ancient silk route—connecting Europe with Asia. It is a big country, its rhombus shape spanning more than 2,000 miles in each direction; and it is a high country, criss-crossed and encircled with immense mountain ranges. The central plateau has an average elevation of more than 3,000 feet and most of Persia's major cities, including the capital, Tehran, are between 4,000 and 5,000 feet above sea level; many of its smaller towns and villages are much higher.

The destiny of Persia has been shaped and controlled by its mountains. They dominate the landscape and have in turn both protected and confined the people. In ancient times, the mountains nurtured a disciplined and ambitious race that created the first world empire. The high terrain also served to discourage attack; only the most determined and fiercest of armies was able to penetrate the land of the Iranians. One of the most ferocious attacks was the devastating Mongol conquest in the thirteenth century, after which the Iranians withdrew behind their mountains, isolated and settled for the greater part of the next 700 years.

It is the mountains, too, that form a vast rain shadow, permitting few rainy days over much of the country for most of the year. Yet in the winter months, the rain-clouds fill those same mountains with snow and ice to form natural freezers and water reservoirs that provide a continuous source of ice and water throughout the long summer months. In the spring the snows melt to form tiny brooks and little rivers that run, not all to the sea, but to the central plateau where they quickly evaporate in the burning heat. To save the precious water, the Persians long ago developed an ingenious system of underground aqueducts (*qanât*) to carry the cool water directly from the foothills down to the villages scattered across the sunburned plain. Some of these tunnels extend from between 100 and 150 miles. The complex system of distribution and rationing of water still survives in Iran today despite the introduction of modern pumping systems.

While there are vast tracts of desert and semi-desert, the soil is generally good in Iran and once watered and cultivated it can produce surprisingly prolific crops. Western diplomats and adventurers who have traveled across the country over the past several centuries have been astonished by the abundance of fresh fruit, vegetables, and herbs to be found all over the high arid plateau of central Persia. It seemed impossible to them that the scattered sun-baked villages with no visible water supply could produce such a profusion of succulent fruit and vegetables.

The exceedingly dry air of the high plateau and mountains has meant that the safest and most effective way to preserve food is by dehydration. The Persians are masters at drying their fruits, vegetables, and herbs, and many of their finest recipes rely on the delectable dried grapes—golden raisins, raisins, and currants—as well as dried apricots, peaches, cherries, limes, berries, and orange peel. The cuisine would also be much the poorer without its dried peas and fava beans, legumes and nuts. Dried herbs make a frequent appearance too, particularly the flavoring herbs fenugreek, oregano, tarragon, dill, and mint.

Ancient Theory

While geography has shaped Iran's agricultural produce, religion has influenced its cuisine. When Zoroaster founded the ancient dualistic religion of Persia in about 600BC, his belief in the balance of life between the god of good and the god of evil influenced every aspect of life. His original concept of the God of Light and Goodness locked in constant battle with the God of Darkness and Evil could be seen to affect not just the external world but also the spiritual and physical well-being of each person. The struggle of the gods for supremacy over the earth manifested itself in the eternal cycle of day and night, summer and winter. An equally relentless conflict was reflected in the good and evil within each human. Everyone aspired to attain radiant good health and a sunny disposition over black despair and evil disease. Good health and godliness went hand in hand with good food. "You are what you eat" is a very ancient belief in Iran.

It was believed that the heat of temper or fever could be alleviated by the consumption of "cold" foods, while the coldness of melancholy or sickness could be eased by eating "hot" foods. Having defined the symptoms, it was simply a matter of prescribing the correct foods. To this end all food was classified as either "hot" or "cold," definitions that relate to the inherent properties of foods rather than to their temperature.

Over a hundred years after Zoroaster (about 500BC), Hippocrates, the Greek physician, elaborated on this concept when he stated that illness was caused by the upset of the natural balance of the humors of the body. To the categories "hot" and "cold" he added two more, "dry" and "moist." He maintained that all foods, like the humors of the body, could be divided into these four groups, the foods being defined of course by their inner qualities. The writings of Hippocrates survived to influence the medicine and eating habits of Western civilization as the Zoroastrian survived to influence the Persian. The theory of the humors of the Middle Ages had its roots deep in the ancient world.

Interestingly, a system similar to the ancient Iranian belief, Yin and Yang, had developed independently in China. The meeting of minds in AD200 or 300 simply served to reinforce the original concept both in China and in the Middle East. Thus the belief that diet can influence one's entire well-being was common everywhere. Indeed, Dr. Eugene Anderson, professor of anthropology at the University of California (speaking on the BBC in 1989), maintained that "at the beginning of the twentieth century, it was the most widely believed system in the world."

In Iran, even today, most people still adhere to the basic concept of "hot" and "cold." Every Iranian housewife knows which items of food are defined as "hot" and "cold" and she will ensure that her catering is properly balanced, particularly in times of sickness and in the care of her children. Hot-tempered or hyperactive children, for instance, are given "cold" foods to calm them, while docile and dull-witted children will be given "hot" foods to pep them up. Family ailments will all be treated first with a sensible diet, and only if the complaint persists will a visit be made to the doctor.

Before making any diagonosis, doctors will ask patients what they have eaten, as evidenced in the Persian joke below. Any cure will certainly include a simple diet based on the age-old "hot" and "cold" foods in addition to the requisite modern medicines.

> A man went to the doctor complaining of a weak stomach and a touch of indigestion. The doctor asked him what he had eaten that day. The man said, "Nothing much. I just had three kilograms of melons for breakfast and two kilograms of bread with three bowls of *harriseh* (a porridge of wheat and lamb) and a kilogram or two of pomegranates. And then I had several glasses of fruit syrup and two kilograms of sweetmeats to finish off. Otherwise, I've had nothing."

> The doctor wrote out a prescription, recommending the man take two kilograms of plums, two kilograms damsons, three glasses rosewater, two kilograms tamarinds and one kilogram *taranjabeen* (a medicinal seed). "It's the only thing that'll work for a 'weak' stomach like yours," said the doctor.

A list of definitions of "hot" and "cold" foods is given on page 287. The placement in one or the other category can at first seem quite arbitrary to the practical modern cook, but many doctors agree that most of the "hot" foods are rich in calories and carbohydrates, while the "cold" foods are generally light and insubstantial. It is a system that many modern doctors find difficult to reject out of hand. Dr. Vivian Nutten, a medical historian, said in 1989 that the medical profession is looking back to "the wisdom of the past" in attempting to prevent disease. Nobody denies that a healthy diet is vital to a healthy body. In any case faith and belief can work wonders—and, after all, if the patient shows little sign of improvement then it's always possible to fall back on the modern wonder of antibiotics.

The Influence of Islam

Of more recent and equally great importance to the cuisine of Persia has been the influence of the religion of Islam. Here we come across both the generous hospitality of the desert as well as Islam's strict prohibitions. The consumption of pig meat and unscaled fish is totally forbidden and they make no appearance in Persian cooking. The banning of unscaled fish can have made little difference to the majority of Persians on the high plateau. Far from any large expanse of water, they rarely tasted fresh fish of any sort, and this is still the case today.

Since the hot dry deserts do not suit cattle rearing, the Persians relied on sheep, goats, poultry, and game. As goat meat unfortunately tastes like strong sheep meat, their choice became very limited indeed. To compensate, they came up with a thousand and one different ways to prepare lamb and mutton.

For those of us familiar only with roast lamb, lamb chops, and lamb stew, the many inspired and exotic methods of preparing sheep meat come as a revelation. As well as grilling, stuffing, roasting, stewing, frying, and grinding, Persian recipes include poaching, dicing, shredding, pounding, and creaming, with a myriad of different contrasting or enhancing flavors. From wafer-like grilled kebabs and creamy meat-based porridges to stews, roasts, and dumplings, the range is as sweeping as it is sophisticated.

Meat, however, has never been plentiful in Persia and it will be seen that relatively little meat is used in many of the recipes, and for the vegetarian there are a gratifyingly large number of dishes that contain no meat at all.

The consumption of alcohol was also forbidden by Islam. Today the cuisine of Persia appears better suited to the ice-cold sherbets and yogurt drinks, but it was not always so and the banning of alcohol must have had a very profound effect on many dishes. Indeed it is thought that the distinctive sour flavor of many of Iran's dishes results from the adoption of lime juice and vinegar as a substitute for wine.

Persian Hospitality

The hospitality of the Persians is overwhelming. Their generosity and warmth toward their guests are shared with other Middle Eastern peoples and are a direct result of the religious tenets of Islam. Here, "A guest is a gift of God."

> Unlike the European, the Persian does not keep his doors shut at meal times. He would think himself deficient in his duty to God, did he not spread the table of his bounty for all; every one may share what he has, without his ever being displeased on account of the number of his guests.
>
> F. Shoberl, *Persia*, 1828

Nothing has changed. The Persians are still the most hospitable people in the world, and their cuisine is adapted to their generous cordiality. Formal entertaining in Persia, for instance, never calls for a table setting, because the number of people sitting down to a meal is never known. A dinner party for a dozen people will see enough food on the table for two or three dozen. It is always possible that several of the guests may bring along a friend or two and, in any event, a hostess must be sure that there is sufficient variety to meet everyone's taste, and enough of each dish should everyone decide to eat the same thing.

Such bounteous tables are not confined to the wealthy. The poorest families in the most remote villages will always extend a warm and generous welcome, and one that is quite frequently beyond their means. It is no exaggeration to say that a family will kill its last chicken in order to prepare a meal for unexpected or important visitors. The children and the neighbors will all rally to organize the preparation of the meal while the visitors are entertained in the parlor with tea or sherbet, sweetmeats, fruit, nuts, more tea, and fine conversation to while away the time until the feast is ready.

Such is the splendor and size of the meals offered to guests or served on special occasions that over the years the Persians have attained a reputation of having prodigious appetites. While they find the reputation quite gratifying and do little to refute it, the fact is that for the most part the Persians are moderate and discerning in their eating habits.

> My son, when you are invited to a dinner party, do not glance too often towards the kitchen, nor pay too close attention to the direction from which the food will appear; keep the reins of restraint in hand, be master of yourself. Never be the first to reach for the food, nor consider it proper to begin before others. Likewise, never be the last to withdraw your hand from the platter, lest the guests judge your soul to be gluttonous, or consider greed your master and appetite the measure of your personality. On such occasions, then avoid these faults which I have mentioned, and consider abstention the prerequisite of patience, firmness and deliberation.
>
> Ibn al-Moqaffa' (eighth-century Persian poet)

Bread, cheese, and herbs accompanied by a yogurt dish and rounded off with fresh fruit is the favorite meal among all classes throughout the summer months. The warming winter dishes of soups, meat dumplings, and omelets will all be accompanied by bread and herbs. Alcohol is rarely consumed, but the bubbling samovar will supply endless tiny glasses of light amber tea.

Rice is a festive dish and a great deal of it will be eaten whenever it is served—for, as the French visitor Sir John Chardin wrote in the seventeenth century, "One eats so much that one expects to expire; but at the end of half an hour you do not know what has become of it all."

Desserts are not eaten as a rule, though the Persians have a fondness for sweet pastries and confections as well as salted nuts mixed with dried fruits to eat with their tea after the meal.

> That which I have admir'd very much in the way of Living of the Persians, besides their Sobriety, is their Hospitality: When they eat, far from shutting the Door, they give to every one about them, who happens to come at that time, and oftentimes to the Servants who hold the Horse at the Gate. Let who will come at the Dinner or Supper-time, they are not in the least put out of their way.
>
> Sir John Chardin, *Travels in Persia 1673-1677*

FESTIVALS AND LEGENDS

The Iranian year begins on March 21 with the first six months having thirty-one days, the next five having thirty days and the last having twenty-nine (or thirty in a leap year). It corresponds, in fact, with the year of the Zodiac. Based on the calendar of pre-Zoroastrian Persia, it has survived with minor adjustments over the millennia. This ancient calendar was formalized under Zoroaster and the months were named after the guardian angels or chapters of the *Avestâ*, the holy book of Zoroastrianism. These names survive to this day in Iran.

The festivals based on the Old Persian calendar date back to the worship of Mithra and relate principally to the passing of the seasons, having no religious significance in Iran any more. While the longest night, *Shab-e Yaldâ* (Yuletide), is still celebrated by many in December, the festival of *Mehregân* in the autumn (coinciding with the harvest) is marked only by a few traditionalists. The festival of the new year (*No Rooz* or New Day) in March, however, is the most widely celebrated festival of the year in Iran today just as it has been for centuries. Actually, of course, until as recently as 1752, the New Year's Day in the US and in England also fell in the month of March.

Further adjustments were made to the Iranian calendar over the centuries, most radically in the eleventh century when Omar Khayyam made the careful calculations concerning the precise length of a year and introduced the concept of a leap year. But throughout the centuries the New Year celebration remained fixed at the vernal equinox, its traditions rooted in the myths and practice of the Medes and the Persians, its symbolism indebted to the ceremonial and social code of the Achemenians.

Before all these adjustments, the Zoroastrians had a simpler system, their calendar consisting of twelve months of thirty days each. The remaining five days of the year were looked upon as special days given by God, and it was during these God-given days that the ancestors visited their children on earth. Their visit extended over the turn of the year and into the first five days of the new year when they returned to the heavens in a cloud of glory.

One day of each month was also given the name of a guardian angel and when the name of the day coincided with the name of the month a holiday was taken. In addition, the 8th, 15th, and 23rd of each month were holidays, amounting to a total of about four rest-days a month. The anniversary of the birth of Zoroaster and the Festival of a Hundred (*Jashne Saddeh*), marking the start of the last fifty days and fifty nights to the end of the year, were both also celebrated.

No Rooz was always the most important festival of all, and the God-given days along with the first five days of the new year were set aside by the ancient Persians to entertain their heavenly guests. It was thought that the ancestors would wish to see their families prospering and in good health. Prosperity could best be demonstrated by clearing all debts, having a clean home, and a well-dressed and well-fed family who could generously entertain a great number of friends and neighbors. It was for this reason that the great Achemenian kings received the kings and rulers of all the subject nations of their empire each year at *No Rooz*. The extent of the empire and the value of the gifts brought to the Persian emperors is depicted on the walls of the Achemenian Palace of Persepolis in Iran.

Ensuring good health was more problematic, but they did break and replace all clay pots used for food storage (an extraordinarily advanced act of hygiene for the age). On the last Wednesday of the year, bonfires were lit on the flat mud roofs of the houses to guide the ancestors toward their homes, and food was laid out to welcome them. When all necessary preparations had been made and suitable precautions taken, the family could then give themselves up to entertaining and feasting for the ten days of the New Year festival. On the tenth day, the ancestors would once more return to Ahura Mazda, and all the family would leave their homes to witness the departure of the spirits up into the light of heaven.

More recently in Sassanian times (AD220-620), the *No Rooz* ceremony included the planting of seven edible seeds (wheat, barley, rice, lentils, beans, peas, and millet) atop seven columns. It was believed that the harvest of the coming year could be predicted by the growth of the seeds.

The next most important festival of the year was *Mehregân*, celebrated from the 16th to 21st of the seventh month (*Mehr*) of the year. From the 16th of this month the days became shorter and prayers were proffered for the sun's safe journey through the next six months when the hours of darkness were supreme. It was also believed that Adam and Eve were created on this day, and to mark this momentous occasion seven tables were laid, each piled high with fruit: oranges, apples, quinces, pomegranates, white grapes, black grapes, and lotus fruit. This latter was particularly revered for it grew with almost no water but only with God's care, and its perfectly formed flower was thought to symbolize the rising sun.

During the longest night of the year, *Shab-e Yaldâ* (eve of *Yaldâ* or Yuletide), everyone stayed up, keeping the fires burning and telling tales to pass the night, so that all would be awake to greet the birth of the new sun. This ancient festival in the month of *Dey* predates Zoroaster. *Dey* was the name given to the Creator or God (deity) by the ancient Persians, but in the Avesta, he was demoted to the guardian angel of creation and light. It is the root of our word "day," or the period of light in each 24 hours.

The festival of *Shab-e Yaldâ* is celebrated in Iran today virtually unchanged, with friends and neighbors calling on each other throughout the long night. A special mixture of seven dried fruits and nuts (salted and roasted pistachios, almonds, chickpeas, and watermelon or pumpkin seeds, mixed with dried figs, apricots, and raisins) is prepared. This mixture is called *âjeel* in Persian and the ceremony of seeing the night through is known as *shab-cherâ* or "night-grazing," which seems particularly apt. Other fruits are also brought in: huge melons cut up into bite-sized pieces, bowls of fruit (pomegranates, oranges, apples, and several varieties of grapes) are laid out along with platters of sweetmeats to be munched and yarned over through the night.

The New Year Today
The festival of the New Year (*No Rooz*) still follows the basic framework of celebration as in the days of ancient Iran, though many other traditions and myths have been built up over the centuries to merge into a spring holiday of ritual enchantment.

There are several splendid months of preparation and excited anticipation. In the home, a thorough spring-cleaning is imperative. This is followed by visits to the tailor, for every member of the family must have a new outfit for the holiday. The next priority is the baking of sweetmeats and pastries. Today, these are more often than not purchased, but fifty years ago, every home was a hive of industry and every kitchen filled with chatter and activity in the months leading up to March 21.

On March 11, trays of wheat seeds are planted and earthenware jars are filled with water and smothered in lentil seeds and carefully wrapped in gauze. They must be carefully tended over the next ten days and should sprout green and have grown to an even height by *No Rooz*.

In the seventeenth century, Sir John Chardin noted that the Persians:

> Make Green Flower-Pots in the Spring, which are very agreeable to the Eye; with these they adorn their Apartments, and their Gardens, by placing upon these Pots a Couch of sifted Earth, intermingled with the Seed of Cresses, and keeping it always cover'd with a wet Cloth. The Rays of the Sun, make the Seed sprout out, and you see the Pot all over Green, just like the Rind of a Tree over-run with Moss.

Shops are busy. The florists burst with forsythia, cyclamen, narcissi (from the Persian word *narges*), and hyacinths, the traditional *No Rooz* flower, for every home must be filled with spring flowers. Bakery shelves are stacked high with decorative boxes of nuts and dried fruits, sweetmeats, marzipan, fudge, pastries, petits fours, and chocolates.

The fruit markets are filled with fruit from all over the country: grapes, carefully kept through the winter, oranges from the Caspian, glistening black dates from the Persian Gulf, sweet oranges from Bam, the first tiny cucumbers that are delicate enough to be placed in the fruit bowl, persimmons, pomegranates, small medlars, and melons of great size.

The vegetable stalls are laden with the first herbs of spring and fresh fava beans for the traditional table, while the fish markets have an astonishing display of both fresh and dry or salted fish, for though the Iranians of the central plateau eat little fish as a rule, the New Year is a time for the expensive and the exotic.

Not that the familiar is forgotten: The aroma of roasting nuts hauls people into fruit and nut shops by their noses. No one can resist a handful of hot salted nuts. The pistachio nuts of Iran are unbelievably large and beautiful, their scarlet and green centers bursting forth from cream-colored shells. Freshly roasted and salted along with cashew nuts and almonds, they are mouth-watering and crunchily irresistible. A less expensive mixture will include hazelnuts and chickpeas, and the dried seeds of sunflowers, watermelons, and pumpkins.

Almost every fruit known to a Persian is dried: figs, peaches, pears, apples, cherries, mulberries, a huge variety of grapes, and—the finest of dried fruit—apricots. Some of the fruits with pits have the pit removed and a walnut or an almond embedded in its place. Turkish delight, flavored with rosewater and made into long rolls, is stuffed with almonds, cut into slices, and threaded up on a long cord to dry. Such shops are an Aladdin's cave of delights at all times of the year, but especially at *No Rooz*.

When camels and donkeys appear on the streets carrying huge bundles of thorn bush—though today, alas, the camels have been replaced by trucks—the first formal part of the *No Rooz* celebrations, bonfire night, is set to begin. Bonfire night is always held on the last Wednesday of the year, though in Iran, as in many parts of the Middle East, the "day" begins at sunset on the previous day. So on Tuesday evening, precisely when the sun sets and the sky glows red, small bonfires are made of the fast-burning thorn bush, no longer on the roofs to guide the ancestors but in streets and alleys to be jumped over by all who are capable (and by some who are not) while chanting the rhyme, "Give me your rosy glow and take away my sickly pallor."

Youngsters disguise themselves (often in Mother's *châdor*—the all-enveloping veil) and call on the neighbors, banging a spoon in an empty bowl. Traditionally, this was a reminder that the poor and hungry should not be forgotten during this season. The banging does not stop until the bowl is filled with rice, herbs, or fresh eggs, although today, sweets, chocolates, and coins are generally preferred. Teenagers make a wish, then stand on a street corner to hear the casual comment of the first passer-by to learn what their future will be. It is a wonderful night of excitement and anticipation.

The parents call on friends or neighbors and resolve their problems over a bowl of *âjeel*, composed of seven mixed dried fruits and nuts: raisins, walnuts, dried apricots, dried nectarines, dates, pistachio nuts, and hazelnuts; and seven varieties of fresh fruit:

pomegranates, quinces, apples, grapes, oranges, persimmons, and medlars. In the northern province of Mazandaran, *âsh-e ghazâneh* (nettle soup) is sometimes served to visitors on this occasion.

The New Year Table

To greet the arrival of the New Year (at the exact moment when the earth passes the vernal equinox), the *No Rooz* table (called *Haft Seen* or Seven S's) is laid. It is believed that each item symbolizes the seven guardian angels of birth, life, health, happiness, prosperity, beauty, and light, and they are symbolized by seven items beginning with the letter "S": *somâgh* (sumac), *serkeh* (vinegar), *samanou* (a sweetmeat made of germinated wheat), *sabzi* (herbs), *seeb* (apple), *seer* (garlic), and *senjed* (a dried lotus fruit) or *sonbol* (hyacinth). Also on the table is a bowl of boiled eggs representing the birth of the New Year, the clay pot or tray of herbs previously sown to signify growth, a goldfish in a bowl for freshness, a volume of poetry by the Persian poet Hafez, burning candles, and a mirror to reflect the light and joy of the New Year. Today a Koran completes the traditional *Haft Seen* table.

Some people light a candle for every child in the family, others insist on the inclusion of a vase of blossoms, a bowl of milk, a bowl of rice or a flask of rosewater. Some families float an orange in a bowl of water, others place an egg on a mirror, for there is a myth that the world is supported on the horn of a great bull who gets tired at the end of each year and carefully tosses the world on to his other horn. Children believe that there is a small jolt when this happens and that the orange will move in the water or the egg on the mirror at the precise moment of the New Year.

The most senior person present rises to greet the New Year, recites from the Koran, gives everyone a sweetmeat (to keep the mouth sweet for the whole year) and bestows gifts of gold and silver coins to the younger members of the family. The candles are kept burning throughout the ceremony. Some families light them on the eve of the New Year, while others insist on a pot of noodle soup simmering in the kitchen during the transition from the Old Year to the New Year to ensure that there will always be food in the kitchen throughout the coming year.

The *haft seen* is put away so that the first meal of the New Year may be laid. The traditional meal today consists of *sabzi polow* (saffron rice with herbs) accompanied by white fish and a herb omelet, and is a meal that symbolizes bounty (rice), growth (herbs), freshness (fish), and birth (eggs). Others also insist on the inclusion of *haft meem* (or Seven M's, i.e., seven foods beginning with the Persian letter "M"): *morgh* (chicken), *mâhi* (fish), *mâst* (yogurt), *meeveh* (fruit), *morrabbâ* (conserved fruit), *maveez* (raisins), and *mey* (rosewater or wine).

Rice has always been cherished as the most festive food and is eaten at *No Rooz* by even the very poorest. Indeed, it is often the only time of the year when the villagers of the high central plateau dine on rice.

Of course, varying levels of wealth and a wide range of climatic conditions within Iran led to a variety of foods traditionally being served at the New Year. Fish was unknown in the central deserts of Iran, and herbs are still hard to find in March in the mountainous regions where spring arrives late. On the other hand, those living along the mild shores of the Caspian in the north or along the warm southern Persian Gulf had abundant supplies of both herbs and fish. In the past, availability strongly influenced tradition. Today, habit and taste are the more likely arbiters of the New Year feast.

Noodles are thought to represent the threads of life, and since the start of a New Year is as good a time as any to take up the threads or the reins of one's life for a fresh start, *âsh-e reshteh* (Noodle Soup) is also served in many parts of the country. For others, the traditional meal for the first Friday of the year is *reshteh polow* (Rice with Noodles).

The New Year festival today lasts for twelve days, during which time a great deal of visiting goes on. There is a strict order in which the visiting must take place: younger family members call on the older ones first, as junior members of society call on senior members. Very large quantities of fruit, pastries, sweetmeats, tea, and sherbets will be consumed between meals.

On the thirteenth day of the New Year (*Seezdah Beedar*) it is considered bad luck to stay at home, so everyone goes out for a picnic. Many believe that the devil is attracted to the tray of herbs, which by now is beginning to turn yellow, and so must be taken far from home and ceremoniously cast along with the devil, into running water in the countryside. The passing of the old year is thus finally completed, and plans are made for the new year. Young girls tie blades of grass into knots and wish for marriage and a babe in their arms by the time the next New Year comes around.

Such an auspicious picnic requires the organization of all the creature comforts. Not for the Persians a sandwich and a thermos of tea. The complete *sofreh* including tablecloth, cutlery, crockery, glasses, condiments, bowls of *mast-o khiyâr* (yogurt with cucumber), fresh herbs, and pickles are all loaded up. A large saucepan of cooked *sabzi polow* (rice with herbs) is taken, along with a small portable kerosene or gas heater on which to heat it up. The hot *polow* must of course be served with fried fish, lemons, and wedges of herb omelet. In some regions, the new season's tiny fava beans are boiled whole in their pods, drained and sprinkled with crushed angelica seed or dried mint; in others, romaine lettuce leaves are dipped in a sweet minted vinegar syrup (*sekanjebeen*).

Freshly made yogurt and bread may be bought at a nearby village on the way. Baskets of fresh fruit and boxes of pastries, cake, and sweetmeats complete the meal. And last, but not least, Persian carpets, backgammon boards, and musical instruments are also added to the load, along with the samovar (for a constant supply of hot tea) and the ice box (for lots of cold drinks and cooled fruit). It is a most sumptuous feast and its only resemblance to a picnic is that it takes place out of doors.

This modern picnic to complete the New Year festivities is believed by many to relate to the habit of the ancient Persians who went out to bid farewell to their ancestors as they returned to the heavens.

Over the centuries, these enduring seasonal rituals, bound to the annual movement of the earth around the sun, have given an extraordinary sense of continuity and cohesion to a nation that is otherwise made up of a disparate people with a turbulent history.

The Influence of Islam

The religious festivals of the moving lunar Muslim calendar have slowly taken precedence over the festivals of the Iranian calendar (with the sole exception of the New Year). The generous hospitality of Islam found the bounteous tables of Persia much to its liking, and within a very short time culinary and religious traditions were generally well blended.

It is not unusual in Iran for prayer meetings to have an interval for a substantial and tasty meal or for memorial services and passion plays to be peppered with sustaining refreshments. The kitchen plays a busy and important part in the life of the mosque.

Interestingly, some of the dishes have come down directly from Zoroastrian Persia to Muslim Iran. For instance, the ancient Persians prepared a dish of *halvâ* (an ancient and simpler version of the halvah on sale in the West today) during the New Year festival for the departing ancestors on their long journey back to the heavens. Today, this dish is prepared only on the death of a relative and is offered to mourners at the cemetery. A dish of celebration has evolved into a dish of bereavement. While *halvâ* is Arabic for sweet, the recipe for *halvâ* given in this book is a version from ancient Persia. The more festive variations of *halvâ* with pistachios made in Iran today are similar to those found all over the Middle East and in more recent years in the West.

Generally, however, the Muslim influence on the food of Persia was negligible because few traditions of special dishes for religious festivals could be established within the framework of a shifting calendar. The holy days of Islam are celebrated ten or eleven days earlier each year, moving backward through the seasons, thus making it impossible for any seasonal dishes to acquire permanence.

Those few dishes that relate to certain festivals tend to be all-season foods, such as *gheimeh* (split peas and lamb), which is as easily made in the winter as in the summer. The food of the people, the thick soups and potages, probably survived unchanged into the Islamic era, though many became attached to the festivals of the new religion, or are made on special occasions, such as the departure of a loved one on the pilgrimage to Mecca.

In recent years, certain splendid dishes are served at almost every festive occasion. The celebration of a wedding usually features *shireen polow* (a rich sweet-savory rice). But since the entertainment of guests is by definition a festive occasion, many of Persia's finest dishes are frequently prepared for visitors. It means that visitors to Iran are often under the impression that the country's cuisine is confined to these few festive and rich rice dishes. As will be seen from the selection of recipes in this book, limited as it necessarily is, nothing could be further from the truth.

IN A PERSIAN KITCHEN

Iran or Persia

Iran has always been known as Persia in the West. The Iranians, on the other hand, have always known their own country as Iran ever since the Medes and the Persians united to form Iran more than 3,000 years ago. The reason for this disparity is that much of early Western knowledge of the Iranians and their empire was gleaned from the contemporary writings of the ancient Greeks, who knew the original Persians when they were expanding the frontiers of their empire.

The heartland of the Persian Empire was Parsis (or Persia) and its capital was known by the Greeks as Persepolis (Persian city). But ever since the days of the empire many countries and peoples have continued to exist within Iran; the names of the modern Iranian provinces reflect that history. Azerbaijan (formerly part of the Soviet Union), Kurdistan (partly in Turkey and Iraq), and Baluchistan (partly in Pakistan) have been for centuries part of greater Iran, though to this day each has retained its own language, customs, and traditions.

Parsis, however, still survives in its entirety in the southern province of Fars. Of more significance, it was the language of Fars that came down to modern Iran. Persian (known as *Farsi* in Persian) is the official, though certainly not the only, language of Iran today.

A similar political structure and history can be seen in Great Britain today with the English, Scots, Welsh, and Irish together forming Britain. Mindful of the desire of the Irish, Welsh, and Scots to retain their own national identity (despite the dominant role of the English, and especially of their language), I have tried to be sensitive to the identical feelings of the peoples and countries within Iran. I confess, though, to succumbing sometimes to the Western habit of referring to Iran as Persia. This is in no way intended to deny the dominion of the many peoples of Iran over the sophisticated diversity of the Persian (Iranian) cuisine.

Availability of Ingredients

The largely unrecognized but nevertheless extensive influence of Iranian cooking over the centuries on the cuisines of the West means that many of the methods and ingredients in this book will be familiar to Western readers. Nevertheless, a brief glossary of commonly used herbs and spices appears is included to assist in the purchase of those herbs and spices necessary to produce an authentic Iranian meal (see pages 25-46). Throughout the book, I have also suggested substitutes for those few ingredients not easily available in the West.

Layout of the Book

Formal dinners in Iran are more flexible affairs than those in the West.

At a dinner party the table will be spread with a wide variety of dishes, from soups and snacks to main meals. Courses that follow one after another are not part of an Iranian meal, nor are serried ranks of cutlery. Everything is displayed on the table in wondrous profusion, a wide variety of dazzling delights arranged around a glistening centerpiece, usually a dish of garnished rice. Each person can make an individual choice and come back for more as often as desired. It is the gourmet's (and gourmand's) delight—the ultimate buffet dinner.

For this reason, you will not find the recipes in this book arranged in the usual "course" order. It would be alien to attempt to confine them in the straitjacket of classic Western order. They appear largely according to their importance on the buffet table.

Weights and Measures

Of all the problems that beset the writer of a cookbook, none is more weighty than coming to terms with the variety of scales and measures in different parts of the world. It is true that the metric system is acknowledged as standard in most countries today, but not, unfortunately, in most kitchens, where the pint, the cup, and the spoon still reign in supreme confusion. The fact that the imperial pint of Britain is larger than the American standard pint seems irrelevant in many recipes but probably explains the failure of many others. Cups and spoons vary in size too, a Persian teaspoon being the size of a Western coffee spoon. Persian cookbooks often call for soupspoons, which is odd since soupspoons are unknown there; even more confusing is the Persian *paymâneh*, which is assumed to be a "cup" but which actually means a "measure."

In addition, a wide variety of weights and measures were in concurrent use within Iran until as recently as the last century. Different names were used in different provinces for the same weights, and—rather more of a problem—the same names were given for different weights. A Tabriz *man*, for instance, was heavier than a Shiraz *man* while a *sang* (stone) was the weight of a large stone that varied from district to district and in any case was used only to weigh water. In early recipe books, quantities of water were always given by weight rather than volume.

The early twentieth century saw the standardization of weights and measures, and the adoption of the metric system throughout Iran. Such was the variety among the old weights, many of them were able to be incorporated into the new system. One *man*, for instance, is now taken to mean three kilograms (about 7³/₄ pounds) all over the country, while one *chârak*, which was a quarter of a *man*, was fixed at 750 grams (about 27 ounces), and one *seer* (or one tenth of a *chârak*) at 75 grams (about 2¹/₂ ounces). Modern Iranian recipe books still refer to *chârak* and *seer*. Another weight in common use is the *mesqâl*, which is equal to five grams (about ¹/₆ ounce), and is used to weigh gems and saffron.

In earlier days, the handiest measuring cup was the hand itself. A cupped hand or the back of the hand for dry goods was used to measure smaller quantities in the kitchens of the Safavid court, according to a sixteenth-century Persian cookbook. Since the quantities of food being prepared were so vast for the king and his host of attendants, anything less than a handful was rarely called for.

Given this background, it was especially difficult to pin down a capable and successful cook who had never weighed or measured anything in her life, except by experience, to be specific about the weights of ingredients in her dishes. I am not talking about minor decisions regarding the size of a "pinch" or the extent of a "hint" (although one cook's pinch may be another cook's handful), but quite major decisions about the dimensions of "a large saucepan" or the amount contained in "half a bowl." And how much does an empty tin of fifty Players cigarettes hold, or the plastic scoop from an extra large box of detergent? Such puzzles have exercized my imagination and my family's patience over the past several years.

Again, no Iranian housewife ever appears to cook for less than a dozen people at a time. I have been given recipes for dishes large enough to feed a small army and have found that it is not always as straightforward as it would at first seem to reduce the ingredients in proportion.

Fortunately, for most of the dishes included in this book, it is rarely necessary to be minutely precise in one's measurements (except in the case of cakes and pastries). I have confined myself to trying to capture the essence of the dish without restricting the freedom of individual taste. Each dish, of course, has its basic and unique flavor, but at the same time, each family from each town from each region will have its own version. There is no definitive version, but there are a number of very good ones, and in each case I have tried to give one of the better ones.

In any event, all recipes are given in the American volume system of cups and spoons. For simplicity's sake, I have taken one ounce to be equal to thirty grams, except in the cake and pastry recipes where it is necessary to be more precise. For most of the recipes in this book, exact measurements are not called for: the amounts given in the recipes are an intimation rather than a regulation.

Specialized Equipment

The average modern kitchen in the West is very well equipped to cope with the preparation of most Persian dishes. There are only one or two items that may not be on hand and can make life a lot easier if it is intended to prepare Persian food with any frequency.

The single most important item is a large saucepan in which to cook rice. Rice expands quite a lot when it is soaked, even more when it is boiled and steamed. If the rice is steamed with other ingredients the total volume becomes even greater. A table is given on page 61 indicating the minimum sizes of saucepan required for varying amounts of rice. The best saucepans for cooking rice are the two-handled heavy-weight aluminum boiling pots (they should not be too tall) available at shops specializing in kitchen equipment. In any event, it is no bad thing to have a large saucepan in the kitchen for pasta and party dishes.

Another necessity, and something unlikely to be found in every Western kitchen, is a rice colander and a sturdy skimmer for dishing up the rice and removing the *tahdeeg* (the crispy bottom of the rice) from the saucepan. The skimmer should be manufactured in one piece, not two pieces riveted or screwed together as most egg slicers are, because it is likely to bend and snap under the pressure of removing the crunchy bottom.

A small pestle and mortar is useful for grinding saffron. Best made of stone, marble, or clay (but not wood, which is too soft) it should be small enough to hold in the palm of one hand because the amount of saffron required is very tiny. A larger mortar means that a larger amount of saffron must be stored and, if stored for more than a month or so, it will lose much of its strength and delicate aroma. Saffron is far too expensive to risk that.

Some items of specialized equipment that are standard in a traditional Persian kitchen can easily be replaced. The *damkoni* (a steam lid) is a loosely woven 3-inch-thick wicker lid wrapped in a clean cloth and used in place of the saucepan lid while the rice is steaming. Wrapping the saucepan lid in one or two clean kitchen towels is equally effective.

As for the large pestle and mortar that always stood so ponderously in the corner of every large kitchen in Iran, it can, thankfully, be replaced for most operations by the quick and painless electric food processor, although there are those who maintain that the processor does not create the same authentic texture and flavor as a pair of strong arms and a sharp knife or sensitive hands. A grinding machine is also very handy for the preparation of many dishes.

Other useful items are: a waffle iron for making *nân-e panjere'i* (a kind of Persian waffle); a long, thin rolling pin for making very thin filo pastry; a candy thermometer; a wicker fan (or an electric hand hair-dryer) to fan the charcoal; and several sets of skewers for making kebabs.

From the earliest times in Iran, the summer glut of herbs, fruits, peas, and beans has been preserved (by drying, salting, pickling, or reducing) for use in the winter months. Today, many of these ingredients are well known to us in the West and easily available in the shops here.

Black-eyed peas, red kidney beans, mung beans, chickpeas, and lentils, as well as dried apricots, prunes, currants, and golden raisins have been familiar standbys in our kitchens for years. It is quite unnecessary in this book to introduce such familiar items to the cosmopolitan cooks of today. Only those items that may be less well known or prepared in a different way, but which are frequently found in a Persian pantry, are given below.

Almonds *Bâdâm*

Almonds have been known in Europe for hundreds of years and grown in Persia for thousands of years. Even to this day Iran is one of the world's leading exporters of almonds. They are a popular ingredient in a variety of Persian dishes, from *shireen polow* (a festive rice dish) to sweetmeats and pastries and a garnish in a great number of dishes, both sweet and savory. In Iran they are sold in all forms: in the shell, shelled, peeled, split, salted, slivered, and ground.

To prepare slivered almonds, buy whole, shelled almonds, pour boiling water over them and soak until soft, then peel, split, and slice them lengthwise into matchsticks. They can then be dried and stored in a jar, or better still in the freezer. Persian housewives store them along with a handful of orange blossoms to give them an even lovelier fragrance. The almond flakes on sale in supermarkets are not suitable for Iranian dishes as they are too thin and tasteless.

Angelica Seed *Golpar*

A member of the parsley family, angelica has grown wild in Europe since it was first introduced in the sixteenth century. It was initially cultivated for its root, which was thought to be a powerful antidote to the plague; within a century its leaves, stems, and seeds were also in popular demand. Today its use in the West is largely confined to the stem, which is candied to decorate cakes and trifles, though the seeds are also used to flavor some liqueurs, Chartreuse in particular, or sometimes to replace juniper seeds in gin.

In Iran, the seeds are thought to aid digestion, and to this end they are ground to a powder and sprinkled over cooked fava beans and other dishes containing legumes, to relieve flatulence. In the northern provinces, where the plant grows readily, the seeds are also added to soups and some pickles.

Angelica is easy to grow, provided the seeds are planted within days of their ripening, as they quickly lose their germinating power. The plants flourish best in dappled shade.

Barberries *Zereshk*

The barberry has gone out of fashion in the US and in England, though it always figured large in cookbooks from medieval times up to the last century. Too sour to eat, *Berberis vulgaris* is a valuable source of malic acid and was used to add interest to quinces and other bland fruit in earlier times. As recently as 1913, May Byron recommended barberries as "peculiarly valuable" in preserved form; she gave three recipes for jams and jellies in her *Jam Book*.

But the barberry bush was doomed in the West once it was discovered to harbor wheat-mildew parasites. Its extermination was completed with such enthusiasm that it disappeared completely from the countryside, though it can still occasionally be seen making a brave appearance in town gardens where it poses no threat to the wheat crop.

In Iran, the barberry is still popular. The berries are dried and stored, and throughout the year they add brilliance and a refreshing tartness to a number of dishes. They are sprinkled over some rice dishes, used in stuffings, and added to *kookoo-ye sabzi* (herb omelet) to give extra zest. They are the principal ingredient in the stunning *zereshk polow*.

If you are unable to find a sturdy *Berberis vulgaris* growing nearby (or even if you do but are uncertain of its authenticity), then do not despair. Dried barberries (*zereshk*) are available from any number of Iranian supermarkets in the West. They will need picking over, de-stemming, and washing, but will come back to life once again when briefly sautéed in butter.

Crystallized Sugar *Nabât*

Lumps of crystallized sugar or rock sugar are always to be found in both medicine and kitchen cupboards in Persia. They are highly recommended to settle stomach upsets, cool burning fevers, and ease aching throats.

On special occasions, small pieces are served with tea in place of the usual lump sugar (both sorts in any case being harder and therefore preferable to the modern quick-dissolving lump sugar in the West). The sugar is also crushed into tiny pieces, lightly mixed with a little water, and poured over *morasa' polow* (Jeweled Rice), a festive rice dish: the result is a sparkling dish of remarkable beauty. Crystallized sugar is available at Iranian stores and at stores specializing in baking supplies.

Dried Buttermilk *Kashk*

In Iran buttermilk is allowed to dry in the sun. As it begins to firm up, it is rolled into balls and dried hard. It can be stored either in balls or crushed into a powder. The balls are used to thicken and enrich hot soups or stews just before serving, or the powder can be mixed with water to make a thick sour white sauce. A most famous and popular dish called *kashk-e bâdenjân* (Eggplant with Dried Buttermilk) is impossible to make without this creamy sour sauce. Powdered *kashk* is available in Iranian stores in the West but unfortunately is not always fresh.

Dried Limes *Limoo Amâni*

Dried limes come originally from Oman hence their Persian name: *limoo* (lime) *amâni* (Omani) and are one of the few fruits, other than dates, grown commercially in the Arabian desert. Limes have also been cultivated in Iran for centuries and are highly prized by the Persians, who like their food to have a sour flavor. The limes are left to dry in the sun, and are by far the most popular souring agent of all, being available the year-round.

There are two sorts of dried limes: almost black and cream-colored. The lighter ones are reputed to have a more delicate flavor and it is these that are preferred in Iran. In the West, however, both sorts can be found in Iranian and Middle Eastern stores. The black limes tend to darken the color of the sauces, which in the case of *ghormeh sabzi* and other herb stews scarcely matters. But for the lighter-hued stews such as *gheimeh*, the paler ones, which are slightly more expensive, are preferred.

If it is impossible to find dried limes, then simply buy some fresh limes when in season, boil them in lightly salted water for five minutes, strain, then spread on a wire rack, and place to dry in the sun (or in a boiler room). They will change color and darken as they dry and the whole process may take a week or more. They should be thoroughly dry right through (sounding hollow when tapped) before being stored in a jar in a warm dry cupboard.

Whole dried limes and powdered dried limes (*gard-e limoo*) are both used in various Persian stews, and sometimes both in the same stew. When using whole ones, they should be quickly washed in water, then pierced in several places with a sharp pointed knife to allow the full flavor of the limes to diffuse throughout the stew. Although limes are added to the stew for flavor only, many people delight in squeezing the cooked and softened limes between their spoon and fork to extract the last drop of juice. Others, with an even greater penchant for sourness, cut them into small pieces to eat with their meal.

Powdered dried lime is imported in small packages from Iran and stocked in Middle Eastern stores. It is also possible to make your own powder: wash the limes, then break them open with a sharp knife, and remove the seeds. This is important if the powder is not to have a bitter flavor. Let dry thoroughly again before grinding them finely in a pestle and mortar or an electric coffee grinder.

Fats and Oils *Roghan*
The earthenware jars of oil so popular in the fables of the Middle East were certainly common enough in the kitchens of Persia well into the last century. They would not, however, have contained the purified liquid vegetable oils of modern times, but rather some rendered sheep-tail fat (*roghan-e donbeh*) for use in meat and savory dishes or a soft thick clarified butter (*roghan-e karreh*) for use in rice dishes, sweetmeats, and confections.

Clarified Butter *Roghan-e Karreh*
Clarified unsalted butter is preferred when making sweetmeats and desserts, and also in the preparation of plain white rice and the more delicate mixed rice dishes. Quite often, vegetable oil is used for making *tahdeeg*, the crusty bottom of the rice, while clarified butter is poured over the rice just before serving. Clarified unsalted butter is invariably used to make sweetmeats, desserts, and confections: it has a

more delicate flavor and the pastries may be kept for months without turning rancid.

To clarify butter, melt it in a pan until it froths, strain throught a fine cheesecloth to remove all the impurities and keep it in a covered container in a cool place. If you need a little for the rice only, then melt it and pour over the dished-up rice directly through a sieve just before serving.

Fat-Tailed Sheep-Tail Fat *Roghan-e Donbeh*

Most visitors to Iran are intrigued by the sight of the Persian sheep grazing on the central plateau, because they appear to have so little grass to eat and yet have such enormous fat tails. It was noted by M.L. Ryder in *Sheep and Man* in 1983 that such sheep existed in ancient Iran as long ago as 300BC. Marco Polo was one of the earliest Europeans to give a contemporary report on them when he traveled through Persia in the thirteenth century:

> We find here also sheep that are equal to the ass in size, with
> long thick tails, weighing thirty pounds and upwards, which are
> fat and excellent to eat.

Sir John Chardin also noted in his *Travels in Persia* in the seventeenth century that "there are some of those Sheep which we call Barbary Sheep with great Tails, one whereof weighs about Thirty Pounds."

Like the hump of the camel, the fat tails of the sheep serve as an emergency supply of sustenance for an "arid" day. Since the sheep in Iran have little need for fat to be distributed throughout their bodies to keep out the damp, the meat remains lean, all the fat being stored in the tail to be called upon during periods of drought.

The tail fat unfortunately smells unpleasant while being rendered but, once rendered, it is infinitely more delicate in flavor than body fat, and gives a pleasing fragrance and richness to many Persian dishes that is difficult to emulate. As recently as forty years ago, housewives in Iran would always ask the butcher to add a piece of *donbeh* to their purchase of lamb, and many Iranians recall how, as a child, they relished a sandwich of the crispy remnants of the tail after rendering.

Donbeh has gone out of fashion in recent years, largely because of a shortage of local meat supplies in Iran and also because of the cholesterol threat. It is interesting, however, that recent research has shown that tail fat appears to be far less likely to clog arteries than body fat.

Since sheep-tail fat is unavailable in the West, the choice of cooking fat in meat dishes is optional. In Iran, *roghan-e nabâti* (vegetable oil) has largely replaced the tail fat. In Europe, many

Iranians prefer the solid vegetable oil as being the least offensive, since it has virtually no flavor or odor of its own. But polyunsaturated oil is also popular for everyday use because it is perceived as being more healthy in the long term. In the recipes in this book, I have included oil in the list of ingredients only when a specific amount is required. For simple frying, the fat or oil you normally use is perfectly satisfactory unless otherwise stated.

Mixed Spice *Advieh*

Long before the word "additive" acquired such alarming connotations, it was common practice for cooks in many parts of the world to have on hand a homemade mixture of herbs and spices to add to food to heighten the flavor and fragrance of their dishes. Probably the most famous of these mixtures is the French *bouquet garni*, hotly followed by the Indian *garam masala* or the ubiquitous curry powder. (*Garam masala* is derived from the Persian *garm* meaning hot and *masaleh* meaning ingredients or materials.)

Until fairly recently, such mixtures and blends were entirely a matter of individual taste and inclination, varying from one household to another so that, although the intrinsic flavor of the dish would be retained, each would at the same time acquire a subtle distinction. The commercial marketing of curry powder and even of *bouquet garni* has contributed to the standardization of flavorings, so that in the West today even when cooks mix their own spices and herbs, they tend to follow a standard, well-tried blend, the aim being the attainment of freshness and pungency rather than individual flavor.

Such modern standardization has barely scratched the surface in the kitchens of Iran. The Persian blend of spices is known as *advieh*, which is the plural for medicine in Arabic and presumably a mixture that was intended to improve the medicinal qualities of the food as well as its flavor. In the 1970s several commercial brands of *advieh* appeared on the market in Iran, but none made any great impact on the Persian housewife who was very well used to preparing her own, and who had in any event a healthy suspicion of any commercial and anonymous powdered mixture.

But, since many rice, meat, and vegetable recipes, both printed and oral, specify the inclusion of varying amounts of *advieh*, it was important that I determine its composition even though not every Persian housewife uses it every time. This was not an easy quest: some cooks only sprinkle a little turmeric or cinnamon, or perhaps a little powdered coriander seed for fragrance or a bay leaf to "cut" the muttony flavor of the meat, while others make up a blend or several different blends: one for delicate and fragrant dishes, another for hearty everyday meals, and a third for an aromatic sprinkling when serving festive dishes. The individual sprinklings of the blends are all known collectively as *advieh*.

There is nothing new in this habit. In the sixteenth century "hot *advieh*" (pepper, cloves, ginger, and cinnamon among others) was featured among the ingredients in some of the recipes in the cookbook of the court of the Safavid kings. Not only do the preferred spices differ from cook to cook and region to region, but also from occasion to occasion. Depending on the food and the mood of the party, certain spices are also added to balance the "hot" and "cold" properties of the dish (see page 287).

In the Persian Gulf, the spices used are very similar to those in a mild *garam masala*, reflecting the local trade between the ports of the Persian Gulf and the Indian subcontinent. A popular *advieh* blend from the south of Iran includes coriander seed, turmeric, cinnamon, cumin, cardamom, and black pepper and is reminiscent of a curry powder, though it is more delicate, for hot chilis, red peppers, ginger, and garlic never appear in any Persian *advieh* recipe. Some mixtures will, though, include nutmeg or cloves. This explains why some Iranians recommend the addition of a mild curry powder in place of *advieh* while others fiercely reject it as an alien intrusion.

Advieh from the sunny uplands of the Persian plateau and from the northwestern region contains dried rose petals that give a rare and heady fragrance when sprinkled over delicate rice dishes during the steaming process. The following recipes are suggestions for *advieh* mixtures for different tastes and occasions. They are recommendations only and are given to indicate what a Persian housewife might include in her own *advieh*. But it must be stressed that such preparations need be made only by those who cook Persian food often, since the effectiveness of all spices deteriorates more quickly when they are ground. Once mixed, the *advieh* is best kept in a dark-glass screw-top jar in a cupboard away from the light and for no longer than three months. In most of the recipes in this book, I have listed each of the spices necessary to produce an authentic meal without the need to resort to the preparation of a special *advieh* mixture.

Advieh No. 1

from the Persian Gulf, for hearty, everyday dishes

4 tablespoons cumin seed

2 tablespoons caraway seed

4 teaspoons each cardamom seed, whole black pepper, and cloves

10 tablespoons each ground coriander and cinnamon

5 tablespoons turmeric powder

Advieh No. 2

from the Central Provinces, for use in delicate recipes

6 tablespoons each ground coriander and cinnamon

3 tablespoons cardamom seed
4 teaspoons each whole black pepper and cumin seed
2 tablespoons nutmeg

Advieh No. 3
to give a heavenly fragrance to special rice dishes
½ cup plain shelled pistachio nuts
4 tablespoons cinnamon
4 teaspoons cardamom seed
6 tablespoons dried rose petals
20 threads saffron
¼ cup sugar (if using with a sweet rice)

Nigella Seeds *Siâhdâneh*

The Persian word *siâh* (black) *dâneh* (seed) means much the same as the English, nigella being derived of course from the Latin *niger* meaning black. These tiny black seeds are from the plant *Nigella sativa* (which is first cousin to Love-in-a-mist, *Nigella damascena*) and can easily be obtained at specialty or Middle Eastern stores. In India they are in the spicy mixture handed out after meals and are often sprinkled over vegetarian dishes, but in Iran they are used solely in the preparation of pickles and preserves, to which they impart a distinctive flavor.

Orange Peel *Khalâl-e Nâranj*

While the Europeans have long sugared and preserved orange peel, the Persians have always dried it. It is an indispensable ingredient in many Persian dishes, from the Safavid *motanjan polow* to the Mazandarani orange stew. The northern *nâranj* (sour orange) grown in the orange groves of the lush Caspian littoral is traditionally used for peeling and drying. But such oranges are hard to find in the West, except occasionally when they appear under the name of Sevilles. Fortunately, the peel from ordinary sweet oranges works almost as well.

The oranges should be peeled as thinly as possible—best done with a potato peeler, so that only the zest is removed, leaving the white pith behind. Then cut the peel into thin slivers and spread on a tray to dry. Alternatively, they can be placed between folded layers of paper towel and microwaved for two minutes on high, left for two minutes, then turned and microwaved for another two minutes on high.

However, with the year-round availability of oranges nowadays it is hardly necessary to dry them, except to have a small store ready for a quick meal. Fresh orange peel works just as well in all the dishes, but whether it is freshly sliced or dried, it must first be covered with cold water, brought to a boil and drained three times to remove the bitterness and reduce its hardness before being added to any of the dishes.

Pistachios *Pesteh*

The name pistachio is derived from the Persian word *pesteh*, pistachios being indigenous to Iran. Of all the nuts in the world, pistachios are quite the most beautiful. In their native soil they attain an exquisite flavor and grow to a great size. The Persians make much of them: whole shops are devoted to the preparation and sale of nuts and dried fruits, and the pistachio transcends them all.

They are carefully arranged in whirling circles of great complexity in elegant cellophane boxes tied with ribbons just as the cream-colored smooth shells are forced open by the red-skinned nuts beneath. *Pesteh khâm* (plain pistachio) are the most beautiful but *pesteh shoor* (salted pistachios) are much tastier. The bowls of mixed nuts and dried fruit to be found in every Persian home would be incomplete without a sprinkling of pistachios. In wealthier homes, salted pistachios are served alone and always prove the most popular.

But pistachios are not just for nibbling with drinks. Their fine flavor contributes to many a sweet and savory dish in the cuisine of Persia. For cooking, it is necessary to buy *pesteh khâm*, the smaller raw, unroasted pistachios (which are thankfully slightly less expensive). They can be purchased without their shells, when they appear rough-skinned and dark red, at Middle Eastern and Iranian stores as well as at good grocers. The darker and shabbier looking they are, the older they will be and they will need longer soaking—at last ten minutes, possibly more. But the rough dark skins will come away easily when soaked well, revealing the pale green nut in all its simple glory beneath.

For many dishes, it is necessary to cut the pistachios into slivers, and as with almonds, soaking will make them more pliable. They can be dried again and stored, in a jar or in the freezer. The pretty pale green slivers can be found ready prepared in Iranian stores. They are an important ingredient in a number of *polow* and are sprinkled as a garnish over both savory and sweet dishes. Ground up, they are added to the more exotic *advieh* (see page 31) and also mixed with almonds to make a delectable Persian *bâglavâ* (baklava).

Robs or Syrup *Robb*

Robs were common enough in medieval times, and in the eighteenth century Samuel Johnson defined them in his dictionary as "inspissated juices" or fruit juice extracts commonly considered to be medically beneficial.

Two hundred years later, Mrs. C.F. Leyel, in her fascinating book *Herbal Delights* published in London in 1937, said that "a rob is the juice of a fruit made so thick by the heat either of the sun or the fire that it is capable of being kept safe from putrefaction." She went on to say that the juleps, robs, and electuaries that came to Europe with the Arabs in the seventh century were still "a vital part of all European Pharmacopoeias." The rise of modern medicines over the past fifty years, however, has meant the loss of many herbal cures, such as the "rob of elderberries to prevent a chill after bathing" that Mrs. Leyel recommended.

In Iran, too, the *robb* no longer plays any significant role in medical treatment and even in the kitchen it is much less important than it used to be. In the sixteenth-century cookbook from the Safavid court, no less than eight different *robb* were used in a variety of stews, including apples, quince, barberry, and sour grape. Fifteen years ago, Mrs. Montazami, in her book *The Art of Cookery* published in Tehran, gave instructions on how to make only three: pomegranate, tomato, and Seville orange, though this last is rarely found outside the kitchens of the Caspian region, where it is used in many poultry dishes. The first two, however, are frequently used in soups and stews all over Iran.

Pomegranate Paste *Robb-e Anâr*

The thick dark tartness of Persian pomegranate syrup enriches many a soup and stew. But it is in that most aristocratic of all Persia's stews, *fesenjân*, that the true purpose of its existence is made clear. Its rich sharpness combines with the ground walnuts to produce a sauce of truly magnificent flavor and texture.

There are several types of pomegranate syrup on sale in Middle Eastern and Iranian stores, not all of them entirely suitable for Persian dishes. Those imported from the Lebanon, although thick, are too bitter; those from the US are too thin. For Persian dishes, and for *fesenjân* in particular, the syrup imported from Iran produces a truly authentic flavor. Grenadine syrup, sometimes sold in place of pomegranate syrup, is not suitable for savory cooked dishes, though it makes a pleasing drink.

It is not easy to prepare *robb-e anâr* in the West because the pomegranates available are usually very pale, sweet, and watery compared with the tart ruby-red richness of those available in the Middle East. The juice (even when reduced) from these sweet pomegranates has no real bite and little in common with the tangy black *robb-e anâr* of Persia. The only way around it is to use more of this pale sweet juice than is called for in the recipe and to add lemon juice for tartness. While this results in a pleasant enough stew, it will not have the authentic flavor of a true *fesenjân*. Fortunately, Persian *robb-e anâr* is always available in Iranian and Middle Eastern stores, and it keeps well for months on end.

Tomato Paste *Robb-e Gojeh Farangi*

Throughout the late summer months and on into autumn, the flat roofs of rural dwellings all over Iran are spread with trays of tomatoes thickening in the hot Persian sun. When they have been sufficiently reduced, the resulting pulp is strained to produce a smooth thick sour tomato paste that is stored for use in the winter months to give color and flavor to numerous savory dishes.

The Persian for tomatoes, *gojeh* (plum) *farangi* (foreign), reveals their alien background, but, as in so many other countries, they have become an almost indispensable ingredient in the cuisine. The tomato rob particularly has great appeal: its strong color and fermented sourness enhance many stews, particularly those (such as *gheimeh*) that had previously relied on the golden hue of well-fried onions, split peas, and turmeric for their color.

The Persian *robb* is easily replaced by tomato paste on sale everywhere in the West in jars and tubes. Its lack of sour flavor can be compensated with other souring agents such as lime or lemon juice.

Rose Petals *Barg-e Gol*

Just as the rose is as much a part of Persian literature as the nightingale, so is its delectable fragrance as much a part of the Persian cuisine as the lemon and saffron. In pre-Islamic days, rose petal wine was exported by the Persians to China. Today the finest rosewater extract is still a major Iranian export.

The central desert city of Kashan is famous for its intensive production of *atr* (extract) of roses and *golâb* (rosewater). The hot, dry desert air intensifies the heady fragrance of the roses, which bloom and die in the burning sun of a single day:

> Each Morn a thousand Roses bloom you say;
> Yes, but where is the Rose of Yesterday?

Omar Khayyam

The province of Azerbaijan in northwest Iran is also renowned for its beautiful roses, the petals of which are preserved in jams or dried to adorn and enhance many dishes, both sweet and savory. Every Persian kitchen in the northern provinces will have a supply of powdered dried rose petals: they can be added to one of the exotic sweet *polow* during steaming to impart a fabulous fragrance, or a little sprinkled on to a cooked chicken gives a specially delicate flavor. They can be one of the ingredients of *advieh* (see page 31), and they feature frequently in desserts and sweetmeats. Dried rose petals are of course also made into conserves and jams. Whatever the purpose, they are only ever used in very modest amounts, sprinkled with a light hand to give a mysteriously eastern air to a dish. A heavy hand can dominate with a too sweet aroma.

> Alas that Spring should vanish with the Rose,
> That Youth's sweet-scented Manuscript should close.

Omar Khayyam

Rosewater *Golâb*

Rosewater is another indispensable item in the Persian cuisine. A few drops are added to desserts and sweet confections and even occasionally to an exotic savory rice dish, but as with rose petals, moderation is the order of the day. Rice puddings and Persian ice cream benefit greatly from the addition of a little rosewater.

The rosewater available from all Middle Eastern stores is much better for Persian dishes than that sold in chemists or the rosewater extract sold in small bottles at supermarkets that tends to be too concentrated and sweet.

Saffron *Za'farân*

Saffron is the golden spice—in value and in color. It is the most expensive spice in the world, costing almost as much as gold, and is therefore sold not by the gram or the ounce but by the carat. In the days when it used to be sold loose in Iran, the neighborhood grocer (who rarely possessed a set of gem weights) would sell it against the weight of a rial coin (about the same size and weight as a dime). This practice died out with the introduction of pre-packed saffron in the 1970s.

Saffron consists of the dried stigmas of the crocus flower (*Crocus sativus*). Each bulb produces one or two blossoms, and each blossom only three stigmas, which must be carefully gathered by hand and dried. As it requires about 80,000 blossoms to produce a pound of dried saffron, it can be seen that the production is a labor-intensive and costly activity.

Because of its expense, saffron has always been a symbol of wealth and elegance. The ruling classes of ancient empires used it to enhance their food, dye their robes, and perfume their banqueting halls. By at least 500BC, saffron had spread from Persia to India in the east and Egypt in the west, where it was equally esteemed. In India, following the death of the Buddha, it was ordained that the robes of the elite class of Buddhist priests would forever be dyed with saffron; in Egypt, Cleopatra is said to have used it for her complexion, while the Greeks strewed their courts with it on festive occasions. Nero ordered the Romans to sprinkle the streets of the city with saffron water to honor his return to Rome. Conspicuous consumption was the order of the day.

The aristocrats of ancient Persia not only dyed their robes and perfumed their halls with saffron, they also benefited from its medicinal properties. It was considered a splendid tonic for the heart and for the relief of melancholy, though its effects could be reversed if used to excess. Too much saffron could produce a state of alarming euphoria and even death from compulsive laughter. A hint of its fragrance, on the other hand, induced sleep, so the bedding of the wealthy was frequently dyed in saffron to give off a soporific ambience.

But it was in gastronomy that saffron made the most lasting impression in Persia. It was used in the preparation of food to enhance the flavor, the fragrance, and the beauty of the dishes set before the royal court and for all festive occasions.

Saffron was first brought to Europe by the Romans but its use diminished with the decline of the Roman Empire. The lack of a large ruling class of wealthy and refined aristocrats during the Dark Ages no doubt depressed the market, and it wasn't until more than 500 years later, when it was reintroduced by the Arabs, that its cultivation began to blossom again in Europe. Saffron came into favor once more with the Renaissance and its arrival on the shelves of the kitchens and pharmacists was greeted with enthusiasm.

It was even grown with considerable success in England despite the chill, damp climate. Culpeper noted in his *Complete Herbal* in the seventeenth century that saffron "grows in various parts of the world, but it is no better than that which grows in England." The leading center of saffron production in England was at Saffron Walden in Essex, and Mrs. Leyel noted in her *Herbal Delights* that saffron crocuses could still be found growing wild near Derby and Halifax in the 1930s.

Today, Europe's crop is mostly grown in Spain and southern France, though the world's leading exporters of saffron are still Iran and Kashmir. The Iranians believe that the most aromatic saffron comes from the sunny plateau of central Iran, and certainly the deep golden color and concentrated rich fragrance of Persian saffron are hard to beat.

> There is Saffron and it is the best in Nature; it grows in
> several parts of Persia, but they esteem that above the rest
> which grows by the side of the Caspian Sea, and next to it is
> that of Hamadan.
>
> Sir John Chardin, *Travels in Persia 1673-1677*

Saffron's costly rarity has often led to imitation and adulteration over the centuries. So widespread and lucrative was the practice in fifteenth-century Germany that offenders were burned and buried alive. Even today, the practice (though not the punishment) continues, and it is still unwise to buy powdered saffron, which is susceptible to dilution.

In view of the expense, it is as well that only very little is required in any single dish. As rice with a rich golden color is thought desirable, safflower (an inexpensive substitute) is sometimes used in restaurants, but it lacks the delicate fragrance and flavor of true saffron, and is not recommended.

Liquid Saffron

The Iranians usually grind the saffron threads to a fine powder and mix with warm water before adding it to their dishes. For easy reference, I refer to this blend as liquid saffron in the recipes in this book.

To make liquid saffron, ensure that the saffron is completely dry. If you suspect it may not be, then put 20 to 30 threads in a tiny mortar and place in a warm oven for a few minutes. Add half a dozen grains of sugar and with the pestle (or the back of a teaspoon) crush the saffron and sugar to a fine powder. If using within an hour or two, mix with four or five teaspoons tepid water and leave to infuse to a deep orange color. If the ground saffron is mixed with boiling water it can be kept in a jar for several weeks. In the recipes in this book, all reference to "liquid" saffron means saffron ground and dissolved in water in this manner.

Salep *Sa'lab*
The roots of the orchid (particulaly *Orchis mascularis*) are dried and crushed into a fine white powder to produce this thickening agent. Once common in medieval Europe, it is still used in some parts of the Middle East as the basis of a cooling summer drink. In Iran, it gives a unique and pleasing elasticity to the delectable ice cream of Persia. Only a little is required, but it is a vital ingredient if you want to make an authentic Persian ice cream. Salep can be bought in some Iranian and Middle Eastern stores.

Sesame Seeds *Konjed*
Sesame seeds were once considered a precious commodity in ancient Persia, and both the seed and the oil of the sesame plant were valued ingredients in many dishes. So revered was it that when Ali Baba attempted to enter the thieves' treasure cave, he invoked the sesame seed to open the way.

Its use today, however, has been greatly reduced. The seeds are still used to garnish some Persian breads, specially *Nân-e Barbari* (see page 48), a practice adopted by both the Greeks and the Romans. The seeds are also ground to a fine powder for the preparation of halva. Sesame seed oil is little used in modern Iran.

Sour Grapes *Ghooreh* and Verjuice *Âbghooreh*
In Persia, verjuice is made only from sour grapes (and not, as in the West from crab apples as well). In early summer, when the first bunches of small green grapes form, the crop is thinned to encourage the sturdier growth of the remaining bunches of grapes. In earlier times, they used to be left to thicken in the sun like a *robb*.

These tiny sour grapes are in great demand to give a tart flavor to summer stews and soups. They are particularly delicious in eggplant stew (see page 103). The Persians consider both the grapes and the juice invaluable in bringing down fevers. Verjuice is bottled for use throughout the year and is available from Iranian stores, but once opened it is best frozen in small portions, since it has no preservatives in it.

Sour grapes can be found on sale at Middle Eastern stores for a brief period in the summer. They can be cleaned, washed, and put in a plastic bag for freezing, or pressed and frozen in cubes. In these days of imported summer fruits and vegetables from all over the world in all seasons, it is as well to have a supply at hand to add an authentic flavor to "summer stews" in the winter. Dried and powdered sour grapes are also available from Iranian stores in small packs and are very useful to keep on hand in the kitchen.

For anyone who cooks Persian food with any frequency, it is not a bad idea, if at all possible, to cultivate one's own grapevine, or at the very least to cultivate the friendship of someone who has one. The tiny sour grapes and the young fresh leaves alone make the possession of a grapevine very worthwhile for any Persian cook.

Starch *Neshâsteh*
Cooking starch is usually derived from wheat in Iran, but the cornstarch available in the West will serve the same purpose in the recipes in this book.

Sumac *Somâgh*
Another popular souring agent, sumac is used as a condiment in Persian cuisine. Sumac is a coarse, red-brown powder with an astringent sour taste made from the dried, ground drupes of the sumac shrub that grows all over Iran. In the past, the powder was also mixed with water to make a sour juice for use in cooking and in medication (to prevent diarrhea and aid digestion). Stews and mixed rice dishes were made with sumac as the chief flavoring ingredient, but nowadays it is used principally to sprinkle over kebabs. All Iranian restaurants serving grilled meats have sumac among the condiments on the table. It is available in Middle East stores.

Syrup of Grapes *Sheereh Angoor*
This can occasionally be found in Iranian stores in the West. It is made by reducing grape juice to a thick substance. If it is not available, then cane syrup may be used in its place. It is a little too sweet, so it is important to exclude any sugar that might be included in the recipe, or to add the juice of an extra lemon.

Tamarind *Tambrehind*
The sour fruits of the tamarind tree in India look so much like dates that the Arabs called them exactly that: *tamr* (date) *hind* (Indian). It was the Arabs who introduced the tamarind to Iran as well as to North Africa, Spain and thence to Western Europe in the seventh and eighth centuries. Its salty sourness was a very real temptation to the Persians, especially in the regions of the south and east.

Compressed and dried tamarinds are sold in packs at most Indian stores, but for Persian recipes the packs of dark brown tamarind pulp on sale in Middle Eastern stores are preferable. Whichever is used, it must first be soaked in boiling water, cooled, squeezed by hand, and strained through cheesecloth or a fine mesh sieve to ensure the removal of all the sharp, pointed thorns and seeds.

Turmeric *Zardchoobeh*
Known in the West for centuries as "Indian saffron," turmeric is called

"yellow twig" in Persian, though in truth it should be called "yellow sawdust," not because it tastes like sawdust, but because it is mostly sold in powdered form. Unlike saffron, it is not expensive and there is no incentive to adulterate the powder.

Indigenous to India, turmeric is an important ingredient in curry powder and its strong yellow color is often used to color rice, particularly in India and the Far East to emulate the golden color of saffron. In the US, it gives mustard pickles their distinctive yellow color.

In Iran turmeric is used in meat stews to "cut" the muttony flavor of the meat but only rarely to color rice. It is never used in place of saffron, though it is included in one or two rice dishes in its own right.

Walnut *Gerdoo*

A familiar sight on the streets of Tehran in the winter months is the walnut seller. Wrapped up well against the bitter cold, he presents an artistic display of fresh walnuts, carefully arranged in little heaps of four (known as *fâl*). Gleaming white, shelled only moments before, they are kept glisteningly fresh by continual bathing with water. The bright glow of the hissing kerosene lamps heightens their enticing sheen.

Such walnuts are 3,000 miles away from the dark-skinned, shriveled nuts frequently found on sale in the stores here. And yet fine walnut trees are common enough in the US. What happens to the pale-skinned walnuts? Where do all the whole walnuts go between one Christmas and another? And why do shelled walnuts always appear to be born with a dark brown skin? If the skins are very dark and coarse, it is no bad thing to soak them briefly in boiling water to remove the thickest skins, but it is a fiddling job and not necessary for most dishes.

The walnut tree was known as "the Persian tree" by the ancient Greeks who believed that, while men lived on acorns, the gods feasted on walnuts. In modern Persia, walnuts are a vital ingredient in the classic *fesenjân* (duck in walnut and pomegranate sauce), but they add crunch and flavor as an ingredient to many dishes, from soups and stews to omelets and desserts. Unripe green walnuts are preserved in the early summer and are considered a great delicacy. A choice stew of green walnuts and lamb is an unforgettable treat.

Yogurt *Mâst*

Yogurt has always been widely used in Persia both as a food and as a medicine. It was known in many countries as "Persian milk" and is thought to have been made ever since the goat was domesticated in Persia in about 8,000BC. Yogurt has a longer life than milk and is one of the most easily assimilated of protein foods, containing significant amounts of calcium.

Today, yogurt is a familiar enough product in the West, but the low-fat, fruit-flavored yogurts of the Western supermarket are a far cry from the tart, creamy yogurts of Persia. Most Persian housewives make their own yogurt each day, for the uses are many and consumption is high.

In the past, yogurt-sellers would come around to the doors of the houses, but today turquoise-blue bowls of fresh yogurt topped with a buttery skin fill the glass-fronted refrigerators of the grocer's shop on every street corner in every city and town in the country—just in case supplies run out at home.

In the kitchen, yogurt is used as a tenderizing marinade for meat that is suspected of being tough, or mixed with an egg yolk and saffron to make a crunchy crust in the bottom of the pan in rice dishes. It is the principal ingredient in a refreshing summer soup, or added as a tart cream to hot soups in the winter. Mixed with rice and meat, it produces a stunning baked rice dish. It is frequently served plain as a side dish, or it can be mixed with other ingredients into lunchtime snacks of endless variety. It can be mixed with fresh spring water, chopped mint, and salt to make a cooling summer drink. It is, however, never mixed with summer fruits as it is in the West, for such mixing would result in a clash of the humors, since most soft fruits are "hot" while yogurt is "cold."

In the medicine cupboard, yogurt blended with finely chopped fresh garlic is recommended as a cure for malaria and as an antidote for many other complaints. Plain live yogurt is prescribed for dysentery and stomach upsets. It is also thought to slow the metabolism, to have a calming influence on those who are tense and highly-strung, and to induce sleep.

Yogurt is also found in the beauty salon where it is highly recommended as a restorative cream for the skin and as a soothing cream for sunburn. It is a cheap and effective facial cream. Its applications are endless and its efficacy unquestioned. It is the ultimate health food, and the cuisine of Persia would be the poorer without it.

A great variety of yogurt can be found everywhere now. The type of yogurt that most closely resembles the taste of Iranian yogurt is the live natural variety found in health food stores, although too often it is made with skim milk and is thus less creamy than a typical Persian yogurt. For some dishes, the yogurt is strained through cheesecloth until it becomes thick. The liquid is added to stews and soups. The strained Greek yogurt is excellent for many dishes and its bland flavor can easily be adjusted with lemon juice.

HEAVENLY HERBS

It is believed in Iran that if a woman eats bread and cheese with herbs at the end of her meal, her husband will never look at another woman.

Herbs have a significance in Persian cooking quite unknown in the West. They are not eaten sparingly or only occasionally to complement a simple meal or to garnish an elegant dish, but are lavishly used in stunning and subtle combinations. And they are, rather naturally, sold not by the sprig but by their weight, in great fragrant bunches. Cilantro, dill, mint, marjoram, tarragon, and fenugreek, Persian chives, sweet basil, and French parsley, each bound in large bundles, are stacked against the wall in every supermarket throughout the country, next to heaps of green and white scallions and scarlet button radishes. All are liberally and frequently sprinkled with water to keep the green brocade wall fresh in the cool shade of the shop on a hot summer's morning.

Each day, from early spring to late autumn, the herbs are picked and sent from the market gardens surrounding the city. Truckfuls come overnight from the northern provinces, winding their way from the lush green valleys of the Caspian region over the high mountain passes to the dusty city in the central plateau. In winter, early crops come from more distant provinces: Khuzistan in the southwest or Fars and Kerman in the south, so that most cities have a constant supply for at least eleven months of the year.

PERSIAN HERB BOWL *SABZI KHORDAN*

The simple herb bowl of Persia requires no dressing. It stands or falls on the freshness of its contents and the balance of its flavors and colors. Traditionally, the summer herb bowl will contain mint, tarragon, marjoram, Persian basil, garlic chives, radishes, scallions, and a delicate herb with a slightly spicy flavor called costmary (or sometimes cost or alecost).

Freshly picked and washed, shaken free of excess moisture, the herbs are tossed together and served overflowing in a shallow bowl to accompany every meal throughout spring, summer, and autumn. Eaten with feta cheese and the soft, thin flaps of Persian bread, they form the ideal appetizer, cleansing the palate and sharpening the appetite. It is all too easy to make an entire meal of this clean and refreshing dish, and indeed it is often more than adequate during the intense heat of a summer's day in Iran.

There is nothing new in this habit. Cicero noted in about AD50 that the Persians were in the habit of eating herbs with bread. "They made," he said, "so delicious a meal, that the splendor of a Syracuse table would not have tempted them."

Mint *Na'nâ*

A prolific plant that grows well in any garden or window box. The fresh young leaves are preferred for the salad bowl and constant cropping is advisable. Mint on its own with feta cheese and fresh Persian bread (which is entirely free of salt or sugar) is a delightful snack, while in the winter months, when fresh mint cannot be found, onions or peeled walnuts are a satisfying substitute.

Fresh mint is used to great effect in a number of mint and parsley stews from the province of Mazandaran, while the combination of chopped mint, cucumber, and creamy yogurt is a favorite summer soup for Iranians from all walks of life. It is often made more exotic with the addition of a few chopped chives, walnuts, and raisins, and garnished with rose petals. Dried mint and hot oil are poured over a number of winter soups to give a musky hint of summer fragrance. Called *na'nâ dâgh*, a teaspoon of dried, finely crushed mint is fried in two tablespoons of oil or clarified unsalted butter.

Persian Basil *Rayhân*
A relative of the basil family, Persian basil is an important ingredient in the herb bowl, and is specially delicious with kebabs. Like its European counterpart, *rayhân* is easy to grow in the garden during summer. Here, even in a mild summer (or in the greenhouse), it is best to pick the leaves while still young and quite small as they can quickly become coarse. The season at best is depressingly short, but *rayhân* can be found in Iranian shops throughout the summer months. The purple basil available in the West has a very similar flavor to Persian basil.

Garlic Chives *Tarreh*
Larger and flatter than European chives, but more delicate in both flavor and texture, *tarreh* can also be found at Iranian stores during the summer. In the West, the plants grow very well from seed but in Iran they need to be well watered, which is no doubt why they are called *tarreh* (wet) in Persian.

While chives have long been known in Iran, their bigger brother, leeks (*Allium porum*) are relative newcomers as is clear from their Persian name *tarreh farangi* (foreign chives). Leeks are little used in Persian cooking in Iran, though they are useful in the West as they most nearly replace the flavor of *tarreh* in the cooked dishes during the winter months. If you cannot find *tarreh* for the herb bowl, then replace them with chives, or with the fine green leaves of scallions. Cut off the white bulbs of the scallion (and add to the herb bowl), then trim the green leaves, discarding coarse or discolored ones, and cut into 2-inch lengths.

Costmary *Shâhi* or *Tahteezak*
This is easy to grow from seed in the West, which is no surprise for it was "so frequently known to be an inhabitant in almost every garden" in early seventeenth-century England that Nicholas Culpeper thought it needless to describe its appearance in his *Complete Herbal*. He recommended it for many kinds of agues and headaches and specially for women's complaints, hence its name. Its other local English names point to its various uses in medieval times: alecost because it was used to flavor ale, and biblecost because its aromatic leaves were placed as bookmarks in the bible.

In 1747, Mrs. Hannah Glasse gave instructions in *The Art of Cookery made Plain and Easy*, for a conserve of costmary flower petals, which entailed much pounding of the tiny petals with sugar, but which, she asserted, would keep seven years if properly sealed.

The leaves, which attain a great size—up to 8 inches long if not picked—have a flavor reminiscent of mint, lemon, and balsam, and can be added to a green salad with great effect. For the Iranian herb bowl, they are best picked when not much more than 2 inches long. If possible, all herbs should be picked just before using, and this is specially true of costmary leaves, which have a tendency to wilt if kept long without water. Costmary is rarely used in cooking in Iran.

Tarragon *Tarkhoon*

Indigenous to Persia, both the herb and its name arrived in Europe in the eighth century via the Arabs. *Tarkhoon* is an important part of the herb bowl, its delicate anise flavor enhancing many a sandwich of cheese or kebab. It is also used to flavor most Persian pickles, and is dried and crushed into many soups and stews. It is considered especially beneficial in preventing flatulence and aiding poor digestion.

Marjoram *Marzeh*

Common enough in the West, marjoram can be found on sale at farm stands and better supermarkets. Only a few leaves of marjoram are called for in a bowl of *sabzi khordan*.

Radish *Torobcheh*

No herb bowl would be complete without a sprinkling of small scarlet *torobcheh* (radishes), sliced across the top to give a glimpse of a crisp white center. When young and tender, the leaves are also sometimes added to the herb bowl. In Iran radishes are generally considered beneficial: they are believed to cleanse the blood and to dissolve gravel and stones. They are available all the year-round, so that in winter when the herb bowl can be somewhat sparse, radishes will always make a bright appearance. Freshly baked bread and crisp radishes (along with any of the salad herbs) are placed on the table before all else in a Persian restaurant.

Watercress *Bâlâghoti*

Watercress has a similar flavor to costmary and is often used by Iranian housewives in the West, along with mint, tarragon, scallions, radishes, and a sprinkling of marjoram and oregano to form the basis of a very satisfactory herb bowl.

HERBS FOR COOKING

Some herbs (chives, for instance) are used both in cooking and in the salad bowl. But the main cooking herbs are rarely eaten raw. These are usually sold in 6-ounce bundles, but you will find they weigh progressively less as they lose their freshness. Quantities of herbs given in recipes are thus only intended as a guide.

Coriander *Geshneez*

Together with parsley and chives, coriander (the leaves of which are called cilantro) forms the basis of many of the cooked herb dishes so popular in Iran, and can now be easily found in the West. If cilantro is unavailable, it can in part be replaced with parsley, while dried herbs (see page 46) are frequently used to augment fresh herbs.

Coriander is native to the lands of ancient Persia and India. Both its leaves and its seeds are used extensively in cooking. The Romans brought coriander to Europe, though they appear to have used the seeds only. The English followed their practice and flavored bread and biscuits with ground coriander seed until as recently as the last century. Whole coriander seeds are still much used to flavor pickles. In India, ground coriander seed forms the basis of *garam masala*, but its leaves are also used in many curries and savory dishes.

In Iran the leaves are more often used than the seeds, and any use of the leaves in these recipes is referred to as cilantro. As already noted, whole coriander seeds are sometimes used in pickling, while ground coriander is occasionally found in the *advieh* (mixed spices) or perhaps sprinkled on meat and poultry to reduce the fatty flavor.

Parsley *Ja'fari*

This is the flat-leafed variety of parsley, vital in Persian cooking. It has always been considered a beneficial herb in Iran, and it forms the basis of several herb dishes. Fortunately, the curly-leafed parsley, so easily available in the West, can be substituted in most dishes calling for *ja'fari*.

Dill *Sheveed*

Dill is indigenous to Iran, western India, and the Far East. It should not be confused with fennel, which looks very similar but has a quite different flavor and fragrance. Dill has been common all over the Middle East from very ancient times, and it had already spread to Mediterranean Europe by the third century. Charlemagne is credited with bringing it to northern Europe in about AD800. The Scandinavians were most appreciative and they use it in many of their dishes, particularly with salmon and cucumber.

In sixteenth-century England, a famous gourmet and a contemporary of St. Anthony Sherley, the first British ambassador to Iran in 1599, suggested adding a good handful of chopped dill and several chopped shallots (including the green tops) to spinach, to be served with a little butter and lemon juice. This is exactly how a Persian housewife might prepare spinach today.

Dill is recommended in Iran for lowering cholesterol levels, and its lacy aromatic fronds are used in many dishes, from soups and omelets to rice dishes and stews in a variety of unusual combinations. Fava beans and dill make a happy partnership in several dishes, the aromatic strength of the dill enhancing the delicate flavor of fresh new fava beans. In preserves, both dill leaves and dill seeds are used with green peppers and garlic to give a deliciously spicy flavor to *kheeyâr shoor* (gherkins in brine). A simple *polow* of rice with fava beans is made into a fragrant dish fit for a king with the simple addition of a couple of handfuls of fresh chopped dill.

Fenugreek *Shambaleeleh*

The slightly bitter taste of fenugreek gives the most noble of Iran's herb stews, *ghormeh sabzi*, its distinctive flavor. A few sprigs can also add pungency to a number of other dishes, particularly the Persian herb omelet. As long ago as the eleventh century, one of Persia's most famous physicians, Ibn Sina (better known in the West as the "Arab" Avicenna) recommended fenugreek for diabetes. Today it is still used in medicines for diabetics as well as for sufferers from high blood pressure. It can be dried very effectively for use during the winter months.

Other herbs used in Persian cuisine include:

Bayleaf *Barg-e Boo*

The dried leaves of the bay tree are sometimes crushed and fried with the meat in those stews made with mutton to offset the strong muttony odor. Its Persian name simply means "leaf of fragrance."

Oregano *Âbishen*

Both oregano and marjoram are considered effective in the prevention of flatulence and frequently, but sparingly, used in the substantial soup dishes that contain legumes, especially beans.

Water Mint *Pooneh*

A member of the mint family, water mint can be seen growing wild in ponds and marshes. In Iran, it is often used to flavor pickles and preserves, particularly in the Caspian region in the north where it grows prolifically.

Spinach *Esfenâj*

Indigenous to Persia and not strictly a herb, it is often used as one in Persian cooking. It makes a tasty stew with lamb and prunes, and is the basis of a rich soup. It often makes up for a shortfall in the weight of herbs. Too much spinach will of course alter the flavor of a dish, but it is handy (especially in the form of commercially frozen packages) when herbs are scarce and expensive. It is also mixed with yogurt or served with eggs.

DRIED AND PRESERVED HERBS

The dry climate of Iran means that much use is made of dried herbs. In the hot, dry summer months every village household is engaged in drying herbs, and no Iranian housewife would be able to imagine preparing a meal in winter without a large stock of dried herbs from which to choose. They are not simply a wonderful reminder of summer during the bleak days of winter, but they also serve to enliven and enrich meals during times of scarcity. Although winters are relatively short in Iran, they are very harsh on the high plateau and in the mountain regions, and whole villages can be cut off for weeks on end by deep snowdrifts and, later, floods and mud.

Just as cilantro, parsley, and dill are never found in the salad bowl, some salad herbs are never used in the cooking pot. Costmary, for instance, never features in cooked dishes, and marjoram and basil only very rarely. These herbs are therefore never dried.

All other herbs, if carefully cleaned and dried very quickly, are remarkably successful in cooked dishes. Herb rice (*sabzi polow*), for example, is excellent made with dried herbs, as is fava bean rice made with dried dill.

Soaking the dried herbs in warm water for at least twelve hours will help to restore their moisture and lively texture, so that they can be used, for example, in a herb omelet. Dried mint, while losing its fragrance when dried, retains much of its strong flavor and is recommended for use in some stews and as a garnish for many winter soups and even some summer yogurt dishes.

In the West, there are two ways to carry the summer joys of herbs over into winter: drying and freezing. Drying herbs without the help of the Iranian summer heat can be a daunting task, but the best way is to chop and spread them on a tray and place on a sunny windowsill for a day or so, stirring them around from time to time. Microwave drying is much quicker for small amounts.

The easiest way, especially for those new to Persian cooking, is to purchase herbs already dried (there are a number of Iranian super-markets in the West that now sell packages in the correct proportions) and, in any case, it is not a bad thing to have a couple of packs of dried herbs ready for unexpected visitors. Once dried, herbs must be kept away from the daylight and are best stored in airtight containers in a dry atmosphere. Instructions on reconstitution are given in the recipes.

Another good way to keep herbs is to freeze them. They keep very nicely for up to three months, which is more than enough to cover the season of dearth and to have some on hand for emergency meals. When preparing herbs for freezing, it is important to ensure they are not chopped or frozen while dripping wet. After washing the herbs, shake them well (or put them in a salad spinner), then spread on a rack to dry off for an hour or so, turning them over from time to time, before chopping and freezing. This holds true in preparing herbs for any dish. Once washed, they must be left to drain and dry, for if chopped when dripping wet, they can become a mush.

BREAD
First Things First

Such is the importance of bread (*nân*) in the cuisine of Persia that the first chapter of a seventeenth-century book written by the chef of the royal kitchens of the Safavid court was given over to bread alone. As the author pointed out, "bread precedes all other food." There seems little reason to break with tradition here. Bread is the staple food of the Iranians in all regions, except for the narrow Caspian littoral in the north where rice supplants it. It makes an appearance at every meal, be it the most splendid banquet or the humblest repast.

And the same mystique that attaches itself to bread in the West is also found in Iran. Persian poetry has many references to the staff of life, and it is always treated with the greatest respect. Even today it is a sin to allow bread to fall to the ground or to drop "beneath the feet." Bread is never thrown away. A sufficient quantity is bought fresh every day and consumed immediately, or if not, then certainly it will be eaten up at the next meal. Some of the breads store very well; others do not, but they will not be wasted. Dried bread is broken into pieces and added to soups and stews (like croutons), dunked in tea, or ground into breadcrumbs.

> Here, with a loaf of Bread beneath the Bough,
> A flask of Wine, a Book of Verse—and Thou
> Beside me singing in the Wilderness—
> And Wilderness is Paradise enow.

In many regions, bread is used in place of cutlery and is thus vital in the eating process. Most modern Iranians cannot contemplate a meal without bread on the table and there are dozens of different types to satisfy all tastes: soft thin breads to accompany kebabs, whole wheat breads to eat with savory dishes, thicker breads to eat with cheese and herbs, soft sweet breads or crispy breads to eat with tea. They are unlike the loaves of the West in that they are "flat" breads, but they are all, without exception, well leavened and light. At least four of them are nationally popular.

Bread is rarely made in urban homes in Iran today. Every city block has two or three specialty bakers who prepare one type of bread three times a day: in the morning for breakfast, at noon for lunch, and in the evening for dinner. Each bread serves a specific purpose and will be bought to suit the meal that is being prepared in the home.

BREAKFAST BREAD
Nân-e Barbari

This thick, golden, crusty bread is the nation's favorite breakfast bread. Leavened and puffed up to 1-inch thickness, it is delicious with fried eggs or sweet omelet (*khâgineh*), conserves, cheese, or clotted cream sprinkled with sugar (all favorite breakfast dishes). In winter it also serves as an accompaniment to the thick wheat porridge (*haleem*) or hot liver kebabs (*jigarak*) that are so popular in the cold mountainous regions.

This bread is usually baked in long 24-inch oval flaps, though it also comes in large rounds in some regions. My sister-in-law, Batul, who gave me this splendid recipe, makes bread for all the family, but because, like most of us, she has only a standard oven, she makes two small loaves, about 12 inches long, at a time. The recipe below will make four of these small flaps.

---

1 level teaspoon dry yeast
½ cup tepid water
4 cups bread flour
1 heaping teaspoon salt
¼-½ cup cold water

Glaze
1 tablespoon tepid water
½ level teaspoon flour
½ level teaspoon baking soda

Garnish
Sesame seed (optional)

Sprinkle the yeast on the tepid water and leave for 10-15 minutes.

Mix the salt in with the flour, then slowly mix and knead in yeast water. Slowly add the cold water, mixing and kneading until the mixture holds together but is not sticky. Continue to knead until the dough comes away from the sides of the bowl and the dough bounces back from poking it with your finger (about 10-15 minutes kneading in total but longer if making a larger amount).

Cover with a slightly damp cloth, then put a sheet of plastic over that, and leave in a warm room for 3 hours or in the kitchen overnight.

With lightly floured hands, punch and pummel the dough and knead it for a few minutes, then let rise again for another hour or so.

Preheat the oven (and flat baking sheet) to 475°F.

Prepare the glaze by mixing the tepid water with the flour until smooth, then stir in the baking soda. Mix to a smooth thick liquid.

Sprinkle a pastry board lightly with flour, and with lightly floured hands pummel and knead the dough for a few minutes, then divide into four equal-sized balls. Working on one ball at a time, pull the fourth into an oval shape, spread over some of the glaze, then with the fingers stretch and pull to a length of about 12 inches, working the glaze over the dough evenly. Make two lines of indentations down the length of the dough and sprinkle a half teaspoon of sesame seeds over the bread, if desired.

Prepare another "loaf," then place them side by side on the baking sheet. Bake for 7 minutes until slightly risen and a light golden color. (Lift one of the loaves to ensure that it is well cooked and golden underneath.)

Place on a wire rack to cool.

Repeat the process with the other two balls of dough.

Cold barbari bread may be restored to its original tasty freshness by being placed in a warm oven. Wrapped, it freezes well for 3-6 months. Allow to thaw at room temperature and heat through in a warm oven.

MILK BREAD
Sheermâl

Very popular with children and a delicious teatime snack: Make as for Breakfast Bread (*nân-e barbari*) but mix the dough with milk and add 1 level teaspoon superfine sugar to the glaze.

STONE-BAKED BREAD
Nân-e Sangak

This whole wheat bread is a particularly delicious "sandwich" bread to eat with kebabs and herbs. Indeed, the specialty baker making this bread frequently has a shop not too far away from the takeout kebab seller: the kebabs (usually ground meat kebabs) are rolled in a flap of this bread. Made in part with whole wheat flour, it is more chewy than other Persian breads, and is best when freshly baked.

The leavened dough is pulled out in a long oval shape (which is wide at one end, more narrow and pointed at the other) and flipped on to a bed of scorching hot pebbles (*sang*) where it quickly puffs and bakes. (In the recipe I suggest pulling the loaves into a square shape more in keeping with the shape of domestic ovens.) As the bread cooks, it lifts easily from the stones.

The main difficulties in making this bread are finding the right-sized pebbles in the necessary quantity and, having found them and placed them in an oven tray, lifting the resulting very heavy tray in and out of the oven. However, the delicious result is well worth the effort.

Gather rounded pebbles, about 1 inch in diameter, to cover your oven tray, thoroughly wash and dry them, and leave them to soak in a bowl of oil for 24 hours. Then drain and spread them across the oven tray. During the first sessions of baking, some pebbles may stick to the bread, but simply brush them off back into the tray. The stones will need an occasional cleaning and oiling.

....

1 level teaspoon yeast
½ cup tepid water
1 level teaspoon salt
1 cup whole wheat flour
3 cups bread flour
⅓ cup cold water

....

Sprinkle yeast on the warm water and leave for 10-15 minutes.

Mix salt with flour, then slowly add the yeast water, mixing and kneading it in. Then add the cold water slowly, kneading the mixture until it holds together. Continue to knead until the dough comes away from the side of the bowl and your fingers bounce back from it (about 10 minutes of kneading in total).

Cover with a slightly damp cloth, then put a sheet of plastic over that and leave in a warm room for 3 hours, or in the kitchen overnight.

Break down the dough by punching it and kneading for 5 minutes, then let rise for another hour.

Preheat the oven (and tray of stones) to 475°F.

Punch the dough and knead it with lightly floured hands. Divide into two. With slightly wet hands, pull one half out into as large a square shape as possible.

Lay on top of the piping hot stones and bake for 7 minutes until well cooked and dark golden in color. When it is properly cooked, it should lift away from the stones fairly easily. Place on a wire rack to cool.

Repeat the process with the second half of the dough. This bread is best eaten while still warm.

THIN FLAT BREAD
Nân-e Taftoon

This bread is found all over Iran, in every home, in every restaurant and in every caravanserai, hotel, and coffee house on the highways and byways of Persia. It comes in large thin flaps and is a light and most useful bread that can be stored for weeks on end. The thin flaps can be stacked and wrapped in cloths and stored in a cool place. When required, a flap or two is sprinkled with water and briefly heated (in an oven or on top of a cooking pot): they quickly become pliable and tasty.

This bread accompanies all savory dishes and is also frequently used in place of a fork. Rolled up with a number of other ingredients (most frequently with feta cheese and herbs) it makes a tasty sandwich.

There are a couple of restaurants in the West that now bake this bread for their own use but who will make extra on request to sell to the general public. I cut the flaps into quarters, wrap and store them in the freezer. They thaw quickly when needed and are delicious with most Persian dishes. Make each flap to fit the largest baking sheet for your oven.

---

1 level teaspoon yeast
4 cups bread flour
½ cup tepid water
1 level teaspoon salt
⅓ cup cold water

Sprinkle yeast on the warm water and leave for 10-15 minutes.

Mix salt with flour, slowly add the yeast water, mixing and kneading it in. Add cold water slowly, kneading the mixture until it holds together. Continue to knead until the dough comes away from the side of the bowl and your fingers bounce back from it (about 10-15 minutes kneading).

Cover the bowl with a slightly damp cloth, then put a sheet of plastic over that, and leave in a warm room for 3 hours or in the kitchen overnight.

With lightly floured hands, punch the dough and knead it for a few minutes. Let rise for another hour.

Preheat the oven and a large flat baking sheet to 475°F.

With lightly floured hands, pummel the dough and knead until it is pliable. Divide into six equal-sized balls. Cover with a cloth while you roll out one thinly on a floured board into a square to fit the baking sheet.

Lay carefully on the hot baking sheet and bake for 2-4 minutes until pale golden and cooked. Place on a wire rack to cool. Repeat the process until the dough is finished.

RICE
Sumptuous Dishes

There is an ancient Persian legend that claims that it was the mythical King Tahmures who brought rice to Persia from China in about 835BC. In fact, rice was almost certainly brought into Iran by Turkic tribes via northern India some 2,000 years ago. The Old Persian word for rice, *araz*, is the root of the Arabic *arozz* and the Greek *oryzob* from which our own word rice is derived.

Rice has long been held in the greatest esteem by the Persians. The reverence shown toward it has led to a much more recent legend about its origins. Sir Thomas Herbert, a seventeenth-century traveler to Persia, related the following tale in his description of the *Famous Empires of Persia and Indusant*:

> On a time, Mahomet being earnest in his prayers was
> accidentally conveighed into Paradize, where being very earnest
> in beholding its rare varieties, at length hee cast his eyes upon
> the glorious Throne of the Almighty; and (perceiving the Lord
> to turne about) fearing he should be severely whipt for such
> presumption, blushes for shame, and sweats with terror; but
> loth to have it seene, wipes off his brow the pretious sweat with
> his first finger, and threw it out of Paradize: it was not lost, for,
> forthwith dividing it selfe into six drops, all of them became
> miraculous creatures: the first drop became a fragrant Rose
> (therefore is rose-water much used there), the second, a grain of
> Ryce, (a holy graine)…

But, despite (or perhaps because of) this great love the Persians have for rice, it is not in fact the food of the common people, except in the northern provinces of Gilan and Mazandaran where it is grown. For most Iranians it is the food only of high-days and holidays. Here it is not the starchy filler of the laboring classes, but a prized delicacy of festivity and celebration.

Beautifully cooked, served quite simply with butter and saffron and perhaps accompanied by a little grilled meat or chicken, it is rice at its most refined and sophisticated—light, fragrant, and wonderfully digestible, each separate grain so light and airy that a spoon is provided with which to eat it—that is, if you don't have the art of eating with your hands. It is the supreme achievement of the highly developed cuisine of Persia. For special occasions and for guests, the rice may be richly garnished with a number of exotic ingredients, but no matter how complex the additions, it is the rice itself that remains the fragrant centerpiece of the meal.

No guests would be entertained without a least one dish of steaming fluffy rice on the *sofreh* (serving cloth). This has given rise to the quite false belief that rice is the staple diet of Iran. It is not. Bread is the staple diet of the Iranians and wheat is their principal crop. Rice grows only in a few very limited areas, mostly along the narrow Caspian littoral in the north but also in some rare, lush valleys in the temperate regions of the south.

There are five main types of rice produced in Iran, the very best of which is called *Ambar-boo* (amber-scented). Grown only in a few small areas, it has a fine, very long grain, pointed at both ends; it is unbroken and pleasantly firm to the touch and the grains have a pale golden translucence. It has the loveliest fragrance, and when cooked the grains remain quite separate and become white, fluffy, and even longer. It was usually reserved for use by the imperial court; whatever remained was very hard to find and very expensive.

The *Darbâri* (imperial court) rice is also of an exemplary quality, hard, long-grained, and fragrant, affordable only for the very wealthy or for very special occasions. It was grown solely on the Shah's extensive rice plantations in Gilan.

The rice most commonly used for festivals and entertainment is the *Dom Siâh* (black-tailed), a variety of basmati. It too is very long-grained, hard, aromatic, and with a cream-colored transparency.

It is the *Sadri*, however, that is eaten by most urban families and by the rural poor on special occasions. It is a long-grained rice with a pleasant aroma and of reasonable quality. The *Sadri* rice was brought to Iran from India as recently as the nineteenth century by the then Prime Minister, Sadridowleh Mirza Agha Khan. It is not in the same league as the *Ambar-boo* or the *Darbâri* but is a perfectly adequate rice for most occasions and it makes a fine *polow*. Almost all the rice produced in Iran is consumed there, leaving none, sadly, for export.

The nearest thing to Iranian rice commonly available in the West is the basmati from India and Pakistan. This is very similar to the Iranian *Sadri*, and it responds well to the Persian methods of preparation. Sometimes the *Dom Siâh* variety can be found at Iranian and Indian stores. It is excellent and if spotted in any store should be snapped up without hesitation and kept for special occasions.

Finally, there is the *gerdeh* (round) or champa variety, a short-grained, almost round rice that breaks easily and is very starchy. It is used mostly for desserts, stuffings, and *koofteh* (meatballs).

Much of the success in producing a fine dish of rice lies in the selection of the rice. In Persia, rice is purchased once a year, a year after harvesting. Freshly harvested rice is not recommended for cooking. Great care is taken over the annual selection of rice for the family: the grains must be hard, very long, and pointed at both ends, and have a faintly golden translucence and a fine fragrance. There is a correct way to purchase rice, a ritual to be followed that is as skillful and serious as wine tasting.

It is best to visit a rice merchant in the northern provinces where the finest rice is grown. Here a very wide variety of rice in great sacks will be lined up ready for inspection. Some polite conversation begins the process, followed by a round of tiny glasses of tea. The formalities over, the serious business can begin. A hand is plunged deep into the recommended sack of rice and the grains allowed to run freely through the fingers. A handful is taken up and studied carefully for length, color, and aroma. A grain is rubbed free of starch for its luster and bitten for its hardness. And then the next sack is tried and tested. The experts will know from which area the rice comes, even from which field.

The best judge of rice, though, is usually the merchant himself, and each tiny improvement in the quality of the rice will be reflected in its price. For those of us less qualified (or less confident) to appraise the best rice, it is usually fairly safe to go for the most expensive, particularly if the merchant is trustworthy. This is certainly true in Iran. And it holds good here as well, even though there are no rice merchants and little choice.

When a new sack of rice is opened at home it is carefully sifted in a special colander to separate the broken grains from the whole grains. The whole grains are mixed with some table salt to keep them pure, then stored in a cool dark container for use in the finest dishes for entertaining and special occasions. The broken grains are used in soups.

Finally, each new sack of rice is test-cooked to establish the length of soaking and/or cooking time. The rice required for use in stuffings and *koofteh* (meatballs) as well as for desserts will almost certainly be *Champa*, which disintegrates quickly and is more glutinous. This too should be salted and stored in a cool dark place.

The lightness, subtlety, and immense variety of rice dishes have led the Persians always to select these dishes to put before their visitors and guests. And over the past several centuries, it is the rice dishes that have excited most comment from foreign travelers.

There were few European visitors to Persia before the seventeenth century and they were rather more concerned with trading than with feasting. Nevertheless, tales of the exotic extravagance and bounteous tables of the Persian court began to filter back to the capitals of Europe. In 1670, Sir John Chardin noted that the *chelow* in Persia was a "triumph of cooking" in the form of "a white pyramid of steamed rice, every grain of which is dry outside, but inside is full of juice." He noted that there were more than twenty sorts of *polow*. "It has," he said, "a wonderful, sobering, filling, and nourishing effect."

As more and more tales reached Europe, the merchants and diplomats began to look forward to the lavish entertainment offered by the Persians. They were rarely disappointed. One of the companions of the Holstein ambassador to Persia in the eighteenth century recorded their entertainment by the local governor in Isfahan when they arrived there. He described the feast course by course, and marveled when the "second course was brought in, consisting of fifty silver dishes with rice of all colours."

In 1824, another diplomat, James Morier, wrote:

> Here were displayed all the refinements of cookery. Rice, in various shapes, smoked upon the board; first the *chilau*, as white as snow; then the *pilau*, with a piece of boiled lamb, smothered in the rice; then another *pilau*, with baked fowl in it; a fourth, coloured with saffron, mixed up with dried peas; and at length, the King of Persian dishes, the *narinj pilau*, made with slips of orange peel, spices of all sorts, almonds and sugar.

Fifty years later, Augustus Mounsey wrote about his *Journey through the Caucasus and the Interior of Persia*. He too was captivated by the cuisine. "All Persians," he wrote, "have a notion of cooking, and the dishes they prepare are wonderful." He went on: "Of the merits of a *pilau* it is unnecessary to say anything further than that all European cooks ought to be sent to the East in order to learn how to boil rice."

In 1892 Lord Curzon himself proclaimed that "the rice especially was prepared in a manner than no Parisian artist could emulate." Ella Sykes, wife of a British diplomat, in 1910 wrote that the ability to cook rice to perfection is "a peculiarly Persian art."

Much more recently, in 1985, Claudia Roden, in her *New Book of Middle Eastern Food*, noted that "Persia has carried the preparation of rice to extraordinary heights of refinement."

A great deal has been written about the art of cooking rice, and many methods for producing "perfect rice" have been described. Of course, perfection, like beauty, is in the eye of the beholder, but if you like rice light and flavorsome, then it is best lightly parboiled, then strained and steamed to complete the cooking and to ensure light dryness. This is the method most favored by the Persians; rice cooked in this way is called *chelow* (steamed white rice) or *polow* (when it is mixed with vegetables, meats, fruits, and/or nuts).

Another way of cooking rice, which is quicker and less trouble, is to simply boil and then steam it without straining. Plain white rice cooked by the so-called "absorption method" is known in Iran as *katteh* and some of the mixed rice dishes as *dampokhtak* (steam-cooked) (this has become *dumpukht* in the Indian cuisine). They are richer and heavier and almost certainly "better for you" in that much of the starch and goodness of the rice and other ingredients are retained. It is the method favored in the northern provinces of Iran where rice is the staple diet and is eaten two or three times a day. It is of course more nourishing and also more fattening—both added attractions in more frugal times. Recipes for these dishes are given under *Katteh*.

A third method has become popular in the modern housewife's kitchen: an automatic *polowpaz*, an electric rice cooker that can produce, quite quickly and with a minimum of effort, an unfailingly well cooked rice with a crisp undercrust (*tahdeeg*). Unfortunately the rice is also unfailingly bland and characterless, giving no hint of the skill or imaginative art of the cook. And despite its name, it is almost impossible to produce in it a mixed rice (*polow*) of any rare delicacy or interest.

In this respect, it should be noted that there are two types of electric rice cookers available on the market. One is made in the Far East and produces a Japanese-style rice (rather sticky with only a hint of undercrust). To make Persian rice, be sure to get an Iranian-made one that produces Iranian-style rice (dry, separate grains and a crisp *tahdeeg*). They are very useful when catering for a large number of people, since they free up the stove top for other saucepans.

The addition of a little saffron to rice dishes greatly enhances the flavor and fragrance as well as the appearance of these splendid dishes. Its use is usually optional because of its expense. It is only used to garnish rice dishes on very special occasions. In one or two dishes only does it form an integral part of the meal, but there is no conflict here because such dishes are by definition festive.

Lastly, there is the perplexing question of how much rice is required to serve the ever-present (in recipe books at least) four to six people. The answer must lie in the nationality, age, and habits of the said four to six people. One pound of rice should be sufficient for the average group. However, if the people are teenagers who like rice and are eating only one course, it will be barely enough for two of them. If it is one dish among many at a buffet meal, it will account for six, as it will if it forms part of a three- or four-course meal for middle-aged people at a formal dinner.

The method of cooking rice also makes a difference. The "absorption method" (*katteh*) is far more filling than *chelow*, which is strained, rinsed, and steamed. Equally, when rice is mixed with other ingredients to make a *polow*, less rice is required. These differences have been allowed for in the quantities suggested for the various dishes. In Iran, the normal requirement for plain rice is just over half a pound per person, but it is rare to see anything less than 2 pounds of rice cooked, for one must always be prepared for the arrival of unexpected guests.

Happily, rice keeps well and lends itself to reheating without difficulty or much loss in texture or flavor. It is certainly ideal for "plate meals"—a single portion of *chelow khoresht* (rice with stew) on a plate can be sprinkled with a little water to compensate for dehydration and heated up in the microwave within two minutes. Larger amounts can be heated up in a saucepan over a low heat. After 10 or 15 minutes, add a tablespoonful or two of water, which will turn to steam the moment it filters to the bottom of the saucepan and thus effectively heat through the rice.

PREPARATION OF RICE, PERSIAN STYLE
Requirements for plain white rice for 4-6 people

Since rice plays such an important and festive role in the Persian cuisine, I feel I should relate a few old wives' tales (and a number of hints) about how and why the Persians first parboil and then steam their rice, and about how they serve and garnish it with saffron.

....

1 pound (2 cups) rice
4 tablespoons salt
⅓ cup vegetable oil

Crispy rice bottom (tahdeeg)
1 small egg
1 teaspoon yogurt
2 teaspoons liquid saffron (see page 36)

Garnish
2 teaspoons liquid saffron (see page 36)
¼ cup clarified butter

....

First, pick over the rice and remove any discolored bits or foreign matter. Wash clean in several changes of running water to remove all starch. This of course also removes much of the nutritional value, but in a country where rice is not the main source of nutrition and is consumed only occasionally, this seems relatively unimportant, given the resulting lightness of the end product.

To prevent the rice from breaking, set it to soak in fresh cold water to which 2 tablespoons salt have been added for each pound of rice. The water should stand at least 1 inch above the rice. Traditionally, chunks of rock salt were always used for this purpose. In Iran where the rice is hard and the climate dry, the rice is soaked for many hours, usually overnight, but basmati (and even *Dom Siâh*) does not require more than three to six hours. If it is soaked much longer, it will require less boiling and if soaked overnight, may quickly overcook and disintegrate.

Bring about 2 quarts water with 2 tablespoons salt to a rapid boil.

The soaked rice should be drained and the excess water poured off (thus removing excess salt) and then poured into the fast-boiling well-salted water (recommended saucepan sizes are given on page 61). Stir the rice carefully so that all the grains are free-floating and bring back quickly to boiling. If the rice is not of top quality, a tablespoonful of yogurt may be added to the boiling rice to improve its appearance and taste. Some people use the water from strained yogurt to cook the rice.

If the rice looks liable to break, add a tablespoon of lemon juice to prevent this happening.

After boiling for 3 minutes, the rice should be tested to see if it is ready. It is impossible to specify the exact length of time required to cook rice. It varies according to the fierceness of the heat, the thickness of the pan, and the amount of rice, a large amount requiring almost no boiling time at all, because it tends to cook as the water comes back boiling. It is best to test it frequently.

Scoop up a grain or two and test by pressing it between finger and thumb or by biting a grain between your teeth. It should be soft on the outside but still firm and slightly resistant in the center, but not hard or brittle. If not quite ready, try again in a moment or two, but while waiting, resist the temptation to stir the rice about: it serves no useful purpose (except in large saucepans over too small a source of heat) and can break the grains. When ready, strain immediately.

An ordinary vegetable colander is no good for straining because half the rice will disappear through the holes and down the sink. A mesh strainer is suitable provided it is free-standing so that the water can drain away immediately, but make sure it is large enough to prevent compression of the rice. The best and cheapest is a close-woven shallow wicker fruit basket about 12 inches across. It can be placed over an ordinary colander so that the water just swishes away, and it is adequate for up to 2 pounds of rice. If you intend to cook large amounts of rice frequently, it is advisable to invest in a free-standing rice colander, available in specialty kitchen equipment shops.

> Each house in Persia is thought to have its resident *jinni* (genie) who is the cause of many minor mishaps, losses and breakages. He is jealous of his home and he serves to keep other demons away and so merits a modicum of protection from the householder. When the rice is strained, it is feared that the scalding water may kill him and a more malevolent devil may take his place. A prudent housewife will therefore say *bismillah* (in the name of God) to make the *jinni* temporarily scamper away in fear (saying *bismillah* is the equivalent of holding up the cross) and so protect his life. After all, better the devil you know than the devil you don't.
>
> A Persian fable

Rinse the rice thoroughly with tepid water. This is best done by rinsing out the saucepan and pouring the water over the rice.

Return the rinsed out saucepan to the heat and pour in oil to generously cover the bottom. While the oil is heating, toss the rice carefully several times in the colander to remove excess moisture and separate the grains as much as possible. (If you wish to make an extra special crispy bottom, *tahdeeg*, please see page 61.) When the oil is sizzling hot, take the rice up gently in a skimmer or a large slotted spoon and sprinkle into the pan. Continue to do this, building the rice up into a conical shape. It is important throughout to sprinkle the rice. Never tip it all back in at once—this will squash and compress it. Make two or three holes in the rice by carefully poking the handle of a wooden spoon through it to the bottom of the pan. This releases the steam. Wrap the lid in a clean kitchen towel and put firmly on the saucepan so that no steam can escape. The kitchen towel absorbs the steam and prevents moisture from dripping back into the rice to make it soggy. Traditionally, some of the hot charcoals from the fire were piled on to the concave lid of the pot to give an even heat to dry and cook the rice. More recently, a *damkoni*, a round close-knit raffia "lid" covered in several layers of cloth, is used for the steaming process, but a kitchen towel wrapped over the lid will do as well.

The rice should be left on a high heat for a few minutes until it is steaming. Iranian housewives have a number of ways of ascertaining when the rice is steaming without actually removing the lid (which releases the steam and is thus ill-advised). Wet a finger and dab on the outside of the saucepan; if the wet patch sizzles and evaporates immediately, the rice is assumed to be steaming. But some experience with the same saucepan and burner soon leads to expertise. For those with less experience or confidence, a quick peek by lifting the lid slightly is sufficient to see if the steam is billowing. When it is, immediately lower the heat to medium-low to cook for a further 30 minutes (more for larger amounts), when the rice will be ready to serve. It can, however, be left on the very lowest heat of all for another hour or more without any deterioration, provided it is very gently steaming.

When ready to serve, put the hot saucepan on a cold wet surface or in the sink with an inch of water in it. This releases one last burst of steam, and also makes the crispy bottom (*tahdeeg*) easier to remove.

Take up a skimmer (or a large heaping slotted spoonful) of rice and mix carefully with the liquid saffron in a small bowl. Put to one side for garnish. Then gently take up the rice with the skimmer and sprinkle it on to a warmed dish, building the rice up into a symmetrical mound.

Sprinkle the saffron rice over the top. Melt some clarified unsalted butter and pour through the skimmer all over the rice to give it a sheen.

Finally, remove the crispy bottom of the rice, preferably in one or two pieces, and serve on a separate plate.

The crusty bottom of the rice (*tahdeeg*) is considered a great delicacy in Iran and is much sought after. It is rich, crisp, and tasty, and has a habit of disappearing in the kitchen before it ever reaches the table: the many helpers who always appear on the scene when the rice is being dished up exact a price for their assistance, which is often paid unwittingly with a crunchy piece of *tahdeeg*. Nevertheless, the cook usually prevails to keep most of it intact. It's important that she should because the golden *tahdeeg* is the ultimate proof of her ability to prepare perfect rice.

In some parts of the Middle East, the appearance of *tahdeeg* on the table is taken to mean that the bottom of the pot has been reached and the rice is finished. In Iran, it is too great a delicacy to deny to guests, and the entire pot will be turned out to get to it; everyone knows there is always lots more rice.

Tahdeeg results from putting the parboiled rice into the hot fat prior to steaming. There are a number of ways to ensure a specially thick and rich *tahdeeg*:

a) Beat an egg with a little yogurt and liquid saffron, mix in a skimmer of parboiled rice and add to the sizzling oil, spreading across the bottom of the pan. Sprinkle the rest of the rice on top.

b) Beat a small egg together with 1/2 teaspoon yogurt and 1 teaspoon tomato paste; mix in a skimmer of rice and pour into the hot oil.

c) Lay thinly sliced rounds of potatoes in the hot oil.

d) Lay a thin slice of Persian *lavâsh* bread (or pieces of filo pastry) across the bottom of the pan in the hot oil.

The saucepan (*deeg*) traditionally used for cooking rice in Persia is wide-based and slightly conical in shape, built to maximize the dying embers and to give a dry, even heat all around the steaming rice. It also has the advantage of producing large amounts of *tahdeeg*, delightfully out of proportion to the total amount of rice.

Suggested Saucepan Sizes

For easy reference, the following table gives relative saucepan sizes for cooking rice:

For Plain Rice*	For Mixed Rice**	Saucepan Size
1 cup	2 cups	2 quarts
11/2 cups	1 cup	21/2 quarts
2 cups	11/2 cups	3 quarts
3 cups	2 cups	31/2 quarts
4 cups	3 cups	4 quarts
7 cups	41/2 cups	5 quarts
9 cups	7 cups	Over 5 quarts

---

* The step-by-step recipe for plain rice begins on page 58.
** Recipes for making rice mixed with other ingredients appear in the recipes for *polow* on the following pages.

MASTER RECIPE FOR MIXED RICE

Polow is made exactly as *chelow* in that the rice is first parboiled then steamed. But in a *polow*, the various ingredients, which are prepared separately, are added in layers to be steamed together with the rice. I have first given the basic method for preparing the rice in brief, while the recipe for the additional ingredients appears on the following pages.

In most of the rice recipes, I have listed the ingredients for *tahdeeg* (the crusty bottom of the rice) and for garnish as optional extras. These always include saffron, which is very expensive, but since many of these dishes are, by definition, festive, it is pleasant to include it. Other choices of *tahdeeg* are given on page 61.

The Persians do not as a rule eat a great deal of meat and this *polow* section is particularly suited to the vegetarian. While many of these dishes include meat, poultry, or fish, they are rarely cooked together with the rice. *Polow* can therefore be (and often is) served with the meats on a separate dish, making it ideal for people of all tastes and beliefs.

As mentioned earlier, I do not include oil for frying in the list of ingredients, except when a specified amount is required. For most of the recipes below, a 3-quart saucepan is ideal.

> I must add besides, that the goodness of the Rice does not
> discover itself in the Sight nor Smell of it; the Proof lies in the
> Dressing of it, and consists in these three Things, That it boils
> quick, That the Grain remains intire; and that it swells.
>
> Sir John Chardin, *Travels in Persia 1673-1677*

MIXED RICE
Polow

Master recipe sufficient for 4-6 people

....

1 pound (2 cups) basmati long grain rice
4 tablespoons salt
½ cup vegetable oil

Garnish
4 teaspoons liquid saffron (see page 36)
¼ cup clarified unsalted butter

....

1. Pick over the rice, wash thoroughly in 5 or 6 changes of water, and let soak in water to cover by at least 1 inch for three hours or more. Add 2 tablespoons salt.

2. Prepare *polow* ingredients (see individual recipes on following pages).

3. Bring about 2 quarts of water with 2 tablespoons salt to a rapid boil in a 3-quart saucepan.

4. Pour off excess water from rice and pour into fast bubbling water. Bring back to a boil and boil for 2-3 minutes. After 2 minutes, test to see if rice is ready: the grains should be soft on the outside but still firm in the center. Strain and rinse with tepid water. Toss rice gently in colander.

5. Return the rinsed out saucepan to the heat and add oil and 2-3 tablespoons water. Heat until sizzling.

6. Sprinkle one layer of rice across the bottom. Then spread about a third of the prepared ingredients (see following recipes) over the rice, then another layer of rice and another layer of ingredients. Repeat once more, finishing with a layer of rice and building it up into a conical shape.

7. Poke two or three holes through the rice to the bottom with the handle of a wooden spoon. Wrap the saucepan lid in a clean kitchen towel and cover pan firmly.

8. Keep on high heat for 2-3 more minutes until rice is steaming, then reduce heat to low for at least 30 minutes. The rice can be kept warm and fresh on the very lowest heat for an hour or even longer.

9. Place saucepan on a cold wet surface and leave for a minute or two. While waiting, melt the butter and put aside for garnish. Lightly mix 2 or 3 tablespoons of rice with the liquid saffron in a small bowl; reserve for garnish.

10. To dish up, gently toss and mix the rice and ingredients and sprinkle lightly on to a warmed dish in a symmetrical mound. Garnish with the saffron rice, and pour the melted butter all over to give it a sheen.

11. Finally, remove the crusty bottom and serve on a separate plate.

RICE WITH HERBS
Sabzi Polow

This splendidly fragrant dish is the traditional meal of the spring festival, *No Rooz*. The first herbs of the New Year are a feast for all the gastronomic senses: a delight to see, a treat to smell, and a joy to savor. The breath of spring is the aroma that fills the kitchen when fresh cilantro, parsley, chives, and dill are being cleaned and chopped together.

The dark aromatic wedges of the herb omelet contrast perfectly with the delicate green and golden *polow*. The Gilan tradition of serving lightly fried fish as an accompaniment has been adopted by many modern Iranians who today have easy access to fresh fish. In any event, the first meal of the first day of the New Year should include eggs (the symbol of birth), herbs (the symbol of growth), rice (the symbol of bounty), and fish (the symbol of freshness).

The flavor and fragrance of fresh herbs are the very essence of this dish, but the quantities required are not always available, especially in March when *No Rooz* is celebrated. It is at such times that dried herbs come into their own. Packs of dried herbs, weighing only 2 ounces yet sufficient for up to just over 2 pounds rice, are available at a number of Iranian foodstores in big cities in the West. Some cooks take the best of both worlds, by using mostly dried herbs but adding a handful of fresh ones to give an added fragrance to the *polow*. The use of dried herbs, of course, does away with much of the work of cleaning, washing, and chopping. But many Iranian housewives find the preparation of fresh herbs an occupation full of memories: in Persia, it means the house is filled with excited children and happy friends and relatives gathering for the spring festival.

----

1 pound (2 cups) basmati long grain rice

4 tablespoons salt

1/2 cup vegetable oil

4 teaspoons liquid saffron (see page 36)

1/4 cup clarified unsalted butter

12 ounces fresh herbs*, equal portions of parsley, cilantro, dill, and chives (*or* leeks)

2 sprigs fresh fenugreek *or* 1/2 teaspoon dried (optional)

leaves of 2 fresh garlic *or* 1 clove dried

Prepare the rice to step 6 as given in the master recipe on page 63.

----

* If unavailable, use 1 ounce dried herbs, but add to the rice when it comes back to a boil. The rice and herbs will thus already be mixed when the rice is returned to the pan for steaming.

Clean and wash the herbs, removing any coarse stems. Shake dry (or put in a salad spinner), chop finely, then spread out on several thicknesses of paper towel to dry off. Cut garlic leaves into 1-inch lengths and add to the herbs (the bulbs may be kept and dried). If using dried garlic, chop finely and add to herbs.

When adding herbs to the rice at step 6, be sure they are quite free of excess moisture before sprinkling them in layers with the rice.

Serve with Herb Omelet (see page 193) and yogurt, or with fried fillets of white fish (see page 282).

RICE WITH FAVA BEANS
Bâghâli Polow

Fava beans and dill form a most happy partnership in the cuisine of Persia. The strong fragrance of dill wonderfully complements the pleasantly bland flavor of the fava bean.

It is vital to skin the beans as well as shell them. This requires both time and patience, but the flavor and texture of a skinned bean, unspoiled by a gray tough outer skin, is a delight. And the sight of a bowlful of the fresh, bright green beans makes the effort well worth while.

This dish is easily prepared in the West. Fresh fava beans are common in early summer while fresh dill is available in large urban centers and rural farmstands. Dill is a herb that dries particularly well, retains much of its flavor and color and is available dried the year-round, although the dried dill (or dillweed) on sale in small jars in large supermarkets is not suitable: it is too fine and powdery and often has dreary stale color and odor.

Commercially frozen fava beans work very well in this dish: blanching them first makes them easy to skin, and indeed this is also true of fresh fava beans, which can be shelled, blanched, skinned, and frozen for future use. Dried fava beans (which, if purchased in an Iranian store, will be already skinned) may also be used. They should be picked over and washed before being simmered in a little water for 30 minutes until almost cooked. But the *polow* is more fragrant made with fresh fava beans and fresh dill in season.

....

1 pound (2 cups) basmati long grain rice
4 tablespoons salt
½ cup vegetable oil
4 teaspoons liquid saffron (see page 36)
¼ cup clarified unsalted butter

4½ pounds fresh in the pod *or* 2 pounds frozen fava beans
2 bundles, about 12 ounces fresh dill *or* ½ ounce dried
1-2 cloves garlic *or* one medium onion
3 teaspoons liquid saffron (see page 36)

....

Prepare the rice to Step 4 in the master recipe on page 63.

Shell the fava beans, then blanch and skin them. (If using frozen, simply blanch and skin.) Finely chop the garlic or onion. Clean and wash the dill, removing any coarse stems. Shake dry (or put in a salad spinner), then chop finely and spread on a double thickness of paper towel to dry.

Add the beans (and the dried dill if using) to the rice when it comes back to a boil at Step 4, then strain together. Fresh dill and garlic or onion should be sprinkled in layers to steam with the rice at Step 6. Pour over the liquid saffron.

Serve with tender pieces of Poached Lamb (see page 281) and bowls of yogurt.

❂ ❂

RICE WITH BLACK-EYED PEAS
Loobyâ Polow

Replace the fava beans with 8 ounces black-eyed peas, which have been simmered in lightly salted water for 20-30 minutes until almost tender. Drain and add to the rice at Step 6, along with the dill and other flavorings.

RICE WITH CABBAGE
Kalam Polow

Cabbage does not have a long history in Iran. It is not a common ingredient in the soups and *shoorbâ*, Persia's most ancient dishes, nor does it appear as a popular ingredient in the recipes of the medieval Arabic cookbooks that include so many Persian dishes. Nor is it common in the dishes described in the cookbooks of the sixteenth-century Safavid court, although the author of one of the books notes in passing that "in Greece they also stuff cabbage leaves" as well as the grape leaves more commonly stuffed in Iran.

Three hundred years later, Dr. Wills was impressed by the size of the cabbages grown in Iran, but he called them "Turkish cabbages," which he said grew "to a size of 28 pounds per head and quite white, close and tender." This is the cabbage most familiar to Iranians today, and its leaves are commonly filled or stuffed to make *dolmeh*, the dish so popular all over the modern Middle East. But perhaps its most common use in modern Iran is in a *polow*.

Exactly when cabbage was first used in a rice dish is less clear. Dr. Wills mentioned *kalam polow* as a common dish in 1891, and it also appeared in the list of dishes served at a dinner in Kerman given in honor of Henry Savage, an English traveler, in 1900. Neither makes special reference to it as an unusual or new dish.

Any hint of a "cabbage smell" in *kalam polow* is dispelled with the addition of cinnamon and dried dill. Tiny meatballs (known as "sparrows heads" in sixteenth-century Persia) are mixed in with the cabbage and rice, and the whole is flavored with saffron.

1 pound (about 2 cups) basmati long grain rice
4 tablespoons salt
½ cup vegetable oil
3 teaspoons liquid saffron (see page 36)
¼ cup clarified unsalted butter

2 pounds white cabbage
1 large onion
4 teaspoons ground cinnamon
2 teaspoons crushed dried dill

Meatballs
1 pound lean ground lamb *or* veal
1 large onion
salt and pepper

Prepare the rice to Step 6 in the master recipe on page 63.

Shred the cabbage, cutting out hard stalks, wash well and let drain. Finely slice the onion and fry together with the cabbage in oil in a large saucepan until soft, golden brown and much reduced, stirring frequently to prevent burning. Sprinkle with salt, black pepper, 2 teaspoons powdered cinnamon, and the dried dill.

Meanwhile, make the meatballs by mixing the meat and onion together. Add salt and pepper, and knead well. Keeping your hands wet, make tiny meatballs. Fry in oil until nicely browned.

When layering the rice, cabbage, and meatballs at Step 6, sprinkle in the remaining cinnamon.

Rice with Green Beans
Loobyâ Sabz Polow

Loobyâ Polow is a dish with relatively modern roots. Green beans are not indigenous to Iran: John Fryer made no mention of them in his list of common vegetables in Persia in 1673, nor did Dr. Wills in 1899. They appear to have been brought to Iran by the Europeans at the turn of the century, along with the tomato, the other principal ingredient of this dish. Green beans and tomatoes are both native to tropical America.

This is not one of the classic dishes of Persia and is rarely served at formal dinners, but is none the less a tasty and attractive meal. The dish appears to have evolved in tandem with the burgeoning of the urban middle classes after the Second World War. It is largely unknown in the rural areas of the central Iranian plateau where green beans are still a rarity, but it is very poplar in urban areas, and also along the Caspian littoral where rice is much eaten and where beans are familiar to all those with a garden.

In the West it is an unusual and economical meal to make during the summer months since the principal ingredients are available in profusion. Tomato paste can be found in every kitchen and runner beans (or dwarf beans) freeze well, so it is a meal that can also be quickly produced at any time of the year when friends or relatives drop in unexpectedly. The commercial frozen sliced beans available in Western supermarkets are not suitable for this dish as the beans should be chopped not sliced.

No saffron is required for the garnish or the crusty bottom, since the color and flavor of the tomatoes make it unnecessary.

---

1 pound basmati long grain rice
4 tablespoons salt
½ cup vegetable oil
¼ cup clarified unsalted butter

1 pound boned lamb
1 large onion
1 heaping teaspoon *advieh* **No. 1 (see page 30)**
salt and pepper
2 tablespoons tomato paste
2 pounds runner, stick, *or* **dwarf beans**

Prepared the rice to Step 6 as given in the master recipe on page 63.

Trim the meat of all fat and cut into small pieces. Wash and leave to soak for a few minutes.

Chop the onion and fry briskly in oil until golden brown. Add the spices, salt, and pepper, stir, then add the drained meat. Stir and fry until meat is well browned.

Add the tomato paste, fry briefly, then add water to cover the meat, put on the lid, and simmer gently for about 20 minutes.

Meanwhile string and chop the beans into 1/2-inch lengths. Add to the meat, stir, cover, and simmer for 15 minutes. Remove the lid, stir well, and cook until the liquid is completely reduced.

Add the meat and bean mixture in layers to steam with the rice in Step 6.

✿ ✿

RICE WITH GREEN PEAS
Nokhod Polow

A modern dish, it can be made at any time of the year. Preparations are similar as that for Rice with Green Beans, above. Replace the green beans with 6 ounces fresh or frozen peas.

RICE WITH LENTILS
Addas Polow

When the Persians defeated the Romans in Carrhae (present-day Harran, Turkey) in 53BC, the Roman general Marcus Crassus blamed his defeat on the depletion of the wheat supplies to his troops. They had been forced to rely on a diet of lentils, which he maintained caused "a heaviness of body and a dullness of mind." The word lentil is, after all, derived from the Latin *lentus* (slow).

Lentils are one of the earliest foods known. The Egyptians used to give them to their children to "enlighten their minds, open their hearts and render them cheerful," while the Romans considered lentils to possess two uncommon virtues: mildness and moderation. The Persians too classify them as "cold" foods, which are good to slow the metabolism and calm a temperamental person.

Another truism that has come down over the centuries is that lentils should be eaten with caution unless properly prepared. They have a propensity for concealing tiny stones and grit and should be picked over with care. There is nothing new in this stricture: Zeno, the Eastern Roman Emperor from AD476 to 491, cautioned: "A wise man acts always with reason, and prepares his own lentils himself." Even today the Iranian army nickname for *addas polow* (rice with lentils), long one of the mainstays of army cooks, is *satchmeh polow* (rice with lead shot).

Lentils are cheap and tasty, and are frequently used in Persia as a thickening agent in vegetable soups. In this *polow*, they give a pink hue and a pleasant flavor to the rice. The addition of dates, golden raisins, and crisply fried onions combine to make a surprisingly delicious meal of great beauty. It is traditionally served at *nazr* (thanksgiving ceremonies) or at prayer meetings held to mark the death of Abol-Fazl Hazrat-e Abbas, (a Shi'ite Muslim "saint").

---

1 pound (2 cups) basmati long grain rice
4 tablespoons salt
1/2 cup vegetable oil
4 teaspoons liquid saffron (see page 36)
1/4 cup clarified unsalted butter

3/4 cup green lentils
1/3 cup golden raisins
1/2 cup pitted dates

Garnish
1 large onion

Prepared the rice to Step 6 as given in the master recipe on page 63.

Pick over the lentils, wash and simmer gently in lightly salted water until tender. Strain and reserve, adding the stock to the water for rice.

Clean the golden raisins and soak in a little warm water for 20 minutes.

Cut the dates across into two and fry briefly in a little oil.

At Step 6, sprinkle the lentils and golden raisins in layers to steam with the rice. The dates should be placed to one side on top of the rice to steam.

Thinly slice the onions and fry briskly in oil until golden brown and crisp. Sprinkle over the top of the dish as garnish. The dates may be put all around the dish at the base of the rice.

If you wish, tender pieces of lamb (see page 281) may also be served as an accompaniment.

RICE WITH SHRIMP
Maygoo Polow

This is a dish from the Persian Gulf, so it comes as no surprise to find that there is a hint of hot spices in the flavorings. The high temperatures combined with the influence of the Indian subcontinent set many of the southern dishes apart from the gentler tastes of the rest of the country. Nevertheless, the inclusion of onions and herbs gives this a unique Persian flavor.

1 pound (2 cups) basmati long grain rice
4 tablespoons salt
½ cup vegetable oil
4 teaspoons liquid saffron (see page 36)
¼ cup clarified unsalted butter

1 bundle cilantro, about 5 ounces
2-3 sprigs fresh fenugreek *or* 1 teaspoon dried
1 large onion
1 teaspoon turmeric
black pepper
1 teaspoon mild curry powder
1 pound peeled shrimp

Prepare the rice to Step 6 as given in the master recipe on page 63.

Wash and clean the cilantro and fenugreek, removing coarse stems. Shake or spin dry, then chop finely. Set aside to dry.

In the meantime, slice the onion and fry in oil until golden. Stir in the turmeric, black pepper, and curry powder, then add the chopped herbs. Stir briskly and fry for a few minutes.

Add the shrimp and stir-fry briskly for a minute or two. Remove from the heat.

Add the shrimp and herb mixture to the rice in layers to steam at Step 6.

RICE WITH NOODLES
Reshteh Polow

Pasta has existed for many centuries. The thirteenth-century Arabic cookbooks that contained many Persian dishes had numerous recipes calling for various sorts of noodle as well as flat sheets and shapes of pasta and even tiny balls. Today, only two are used with any frequency: short flat noodles (used in soups) and short rounded ones. Until well into the last century these simple noodles of flour and water were always made in the home, and even today many Persian housewives still prefer the homemade (for recipe, see page 285) to the commercially produced.

This dish calls for fine round noodles. If they are not available, the best replacement is fresh spaghetti. The Persian name for noodles is *reshteh*, which means thread or string. Dishes containing noodles are traditionally prepared at times of decision or change so that the "reins (of life) may be taken in hand" and the future given direction. *Reshteh Polow* is often served on the eve of the New Year as its threads intertwine in the same way that the family bonds are tied together.

---

1 pound (2 cups) basmati long grain rice
4 tablespoons salt
½ cup vegetable oil
4 teaspoons liquid saffron (see page 36)
¼ cup clarified unsalted butter

5 ounces fine noodles
3 ounces currants
peel of 2 oranges
1 teaspoon ground cinnamon
3 teaspoons liquid saffron (see page 36)

Prepare the rice to Step 4 as given in the master recipe on page 63.

Cut or break the noodles into 1-inch lengths and brown briefly in a frying pan, shaking and turning constantly, until they become a golden color. Set aside.

Pick over the currants and soak in a little warm water until puffed and shiny. Drain and set aside. Peel the oranges thinly (avoiding the pith) and cut into julienne strips. Cover with cold water, bring to a boil, and drain. Repeat twice more to remove all bitterness.

Add the noodles to the rice when it comes back to a boil (Step 4 of the master recipe), then strain together.

Layer in the orange peel and currants with the rice at Step 6, and pour over the liquid saffron. Serve with dates and crisply fried onions.

JEWELED RICE
Morasa' Polow

In 1824 James Morier described this dish as "The King of Persian dishes" and there is little doubt that it raises the humble grain of rice to regal heights. Of all the festive dishes in Iran, this is the one chosen to be served at wedding banquets: it is thought to augur well for the young couple and to bring sweetness to their new life together. Yet despite its festive elegance it consists of quite simple and easily available ingredients. It artistically blends the commonplace into pleasing harmony. At very extravagant weddings, this stunning dish with its golden saffron rice studded with gleaming "gems" (resembling diamonds, rubies, emeralds, and topaz) is sometimes served in a swirl of spun sugar, which gives a wonderful crunchy contrast to its soft textures and gentle flavors. It is an astonishingly beautiful and dramatic dish for special occasions and stands as shining testimony to the imaginative glory of Persian cooking.

1 pound (2 cups) basmati long grain rice
4 tablespoons salt
½ cup vegetable oil
4 teaspoons liquid saffron (see page 36)
¼ cup clarified unsalted butter

1 pound carrots
2 tablespoons granulated sugar
4 teaspoons liquid saffron (see page 36)
peel of 3 oranges
2 tablespoons each almond slivers, pistachio slivers, currants, and dried barberries (see page 25)
1 teaspoon *advieh* No. 3 (see page 31)
2 tablespoons crystallized sugar (see page 26) *or* crushed sugar lumps

Prepare the rice to Step 6 as given in the master recipe on page 63.

Peel the carrots and slice into julienne strips. Fry in oil over medium heat for 10 minutes, stirring constantly. Stir in a tablespoon of sugar, 2 teaspoons liquid saffron, and 2-3 tablespoons water, cover and cook for 4-5 minutes until liquid is reduced. Put into a bowl and set aside.

Peel the oranges thinly (best done with a potato peeler to avoid pith) and cut into julienne strips. Cover with cold water, bring to a boil and strain. Repeat twice more to remove bitterness. Set aside.

Soak and skin the pistachios and almonds and cut into slivers.

Brown 1 teaspoon of the almonds in a frying pan and put aside for garnish. Put remaining almonds and all pistachios into a small saucepan, cover with cold water, bring to a boil, strain, and set aside.

Bring the rest of the granulated sugar and 6 tablespoons water slowly to a boil and simmer gently for 10 minutes. Add the orange peel and the nuts, keeping back a teaspoon each of almonds and pistachios for a garnish, and boil for half a minute. Strain and reserve the syrup. Put the peel and nuts on one side.

Soak the currants in warm water for 10 minutes until puffed and shining. Strain and set aside, keeping back a teaspoonful for the garnish.

Pick over and clean the barberries, then gently fry for a minute or two in a little oil until a glowing red (take care not to let them burn). Set aside.

At Step 6, layer in the carrots, peel, nuts, and currants with the rice and sprinkle the *advieh* over each layer. Finally, just before making the holes in the rice, pour over the remaining liquid saffron and syrup.

At Step 10, garnish the rice with a sprinkling of almonds (both white and brown), pistachios, currants, and barberries before pouring the clarified butter over all. Finally, crush the crystallized sugar into small "diamonds," mix with half a teaspoon boiling water and sprinkle over the rice.

Serve with Saffron Chicken (page 283), Fried Chicken (page 284), or Stuffed Chicken (page 177).

RICE WITH ALMONDS
Shireen Polow

This famous dish is a less ornate version of the previous recipe, and is frequently served at fashionable weddings and celebrations. The Arabs along the Persian Gulf (an area which was formerly part of the Persian Empire) eat a simplified and sweeter version of this rice. It is a special favorite of the pearl divers who derive much needed energy from its sweetness. In this recipe, I have reduced the sweetness in line with modern eating habits.

Prepare as for *Morasa' Polow* in previous recipe, adding only 1/4 cup almonds, 1/2 cup unsalted pistachio nuts, the peel of 3 oranges, *advieh*, and liquid saffron, but omiting other "jewels."

RICE WITH CARROTS
Haveej Polow

Another striking dish that has a sweet delicacy, yet its ingredients can be found at any supermarket throughout the year. It is a popular banquet dish at some of the less opulent weddings in Persia.

Prepare as for *Morasa' Polow* on page 76, adding only 1 1/2 pounds carrots, peel of 2 oranges, sugar, and liquid saffron.

RICE WITH SOUR CHERRIES
Âlbâloo Polow

The sour cherry (*albâloo*) of Persia is very similar to the morello cherry. In this *polow* the cherries retain their warm color and make a most beautiful and striking dish.

The season for sour cherries is sadly very short. In Iran when the fruit is gathered, the women of the neighborhood meet together to pit and preserve large amounts of *âlbâloo* to be used both in this lovely *polow* and as a syrup for a sherbet. Working together, the task is quickly and affably completed, and each woman will have enough sour cherries to last her through the year.

If you manage to find some of these bright little cherries in the shops, snap them up. It is well worth the effort to preserve this tart summer flavor for dull winter days. *Âlbâloo*, like most fruit in Iran, is also dried and can usually be found in Iranian stores. While the dried cherries do not retain the exquisite color, the flavor remains excellent.

....

> **1 pound (2 cups) basmati long grain rice**
> **4 tablespoons salt**
> **¹/₂ cup vegetable oil**
> **4 teaspoons liquid saffron (see page 36)**
> **¹/₄ cup clarified unsalted butter**
>
> **1 pound fresh morello cherries *or* 8 ounces dried**
> **   *âlbâloo* cherries**
> **²/₃ cup sugar**
> **2 teaspoons liquid saffron (see page 36)**

....

Prepare the rice to Step 6 as given in the master recipe on page 63.

Wash the cherries and pit them. (If using dried, soak them for at least an hour, then pit and use as fresh.) Put the cherries in a pan with the sugar and leave for an hour, then add a little water, cover, and simmer gently for 15 minutes until most of the liquid has been reduced, stirring from time to time. Remove from heat and set aside.

At Step 6, put in alternate layers of rice and cherries to steam. Pour over any remaining syrup and the liquid saffron. Serve with Saffron Chicken (page 283) or Chicken Kebab (page 153).

RICE WITH DRIED FRUIT AND NUTS
Ajeel Polow

A rice dish with a long and noble history, this is a festive dish, served for celebrations and special occasions. One of the main ingredients, the sour cherry, *âlbâloo*, is not easily available in the West, though dried *âlbâloo* can be found in most Iranian stores. It is well worth seeking them out to make this rich and colorful dish. In season, morello cherries make an excellent replacement. I am grateful to my sister-in-law, Batul, for giving me her lovely recipe.

....

1 pound (2 cups) basmati long grain rice
4 tablespoons salt
1/2 cup vegetable oil
4 teaspoons liquid saffron (see page 36)

1/4 cup clarified unsalted butter
1/2 pound ground lamb *or* veal
1 onion, grated
1 teaspoon *advieh* (see page 31)
1 cup dried sour cherries
1/2 cup currants
1/2 cup dried apricots
3/4 cup ground walnuts
crisply fried onion slices
salt and pepper

....

Prepare the rice to Step 4 in the master recipe on page 63.

Make the meatballs by mixing the meat and onion together. Add salt and pepper and knead well.

Keeping your hands wet, make tiny meatballs. Fry in oil until nicely browned.

Soak and pit the dried cherries, clean and soak the apricots and currants. Mix the fried meatballs with the dried fruit, walnut, and crisply fried onion slices.

Add the meatballs and dried fruits in layers to steam with the rice in Step 6.

RICE WITH DRIED APRICOTS
Gheisi Polow

Known as *zardaloo* (yellow plum), apricots originated in Armenia on the northwestern frontier of Persia where they have been cultivated for more than 2,000 years. When the Romans invaded Persia, they so appreciated the delicious juiciness of the apricot that they took it back to Rome with them in the first century AD. It is the first of the summer fruits and the Romans called it "praecox" (precocious) because of its early ripening. Within a few years the first orchards of apricot trees were planted in Italy and then all over Europe.

The European apricots, though, even those from the sunnier climates, never seem to attain the same sweet flavor as those of Isfahan, where an apricot, freshly picked and still warm from the hot sun, is a succulent and irresistible mouthful of juicy fragrance. Dr. Wills, who visited Persia in the late nineteenth century, was of the opinion that "the finest apricots in the world are certainly produced in Isfahan."

If possible, try to get hold of dried Iranian apricots, usually available from Iranian and Greek stores. They are less colorful than the Californian but much richer in flavor and better suited to this delectable dish. They imbue the rice with a rich golden hue and a delicate sweet-savory flavor. As Claudia Roden has pointed out in her *Book of Middle Eastern Food*, apricots seem to have a special affinity with lamb.

----

1 pound (2 cups) basmati long grain rice
4 tablespoons salt
$\frac{1}{2}$ cup vegetable oil
4 teaspoons liquid saffron (see page 36)
$\frac{1}{4}$ cup clarified unsalted butter

1 pound boned leg of lamb
1 large onion
$\frac{1}{4}$ teaspoon nutmeg
1 teaspoon cinnamon
salt
$\frac{3}{4}$ cup dried apricots
$\frac{1}{4}$ cup golden raisins
2 teaspoons liquid saffron (see page 36)

Prepare the rice to Step 6 as given in the master recipe on page 63. Trim the meat of all fat, cut into small pieces and wash.

Chop the onion and fry in oil until soft and golden. Add the nutmeg, cinnamon, and salt, stir, then add the drained meat. Stir and fry until meat is nicely browned. Add just enough water to cover, simmer gently with the lid on the pan until the meat is tender and the liquid completely reduced. Set aside.

Wash the dried apricots, pat dry, cut each into six pieces and fry in oil for 5 minutes, until softened. Set aside.

Put the golden raisins to soak in warm water for 10 minutes until puffed up. Strain and set aside.

At Step 6, layer the cooked meat, apricots, and golden raisins with the rice. Pour over the liquid saffron.

RICE WITH BARBERRIES
Zereshk Polow

The essence of this dish lies in the high quality and the perfect balance of its simple ingredients. The saffron rice is dotted throughout with the bright, ruby-colored barberries so loved by the Persians for their mouth-watering piquancy. The delicate flavor of chicken lightly poached in lemon juice and saffron complement and complete this elegant and very typically Persian dish.

Barberries were once common in the West. Small, red, and sour, they contributed a pleasing tartness to many a bland dish in medieval times. In Iran, the barberry is still very popular. The berries are dried and stored, and are a common standby in every Persian kitchen. They serve to add a brilliance and a refreshing sourness to a number of dishes throughout the year.

When buying dried barberries, make sure they are a light maroon color. They may be cleaned and stored in the freezer where they retain their fresh color and bite. The previous season's barberries are frequently dark and lusterless and barely worth bothering with.

> 1 pound (2 cups) basmati long grain rice
> 4 tablespoons salt
> 1/2 cup vegetable oil
> 4 teaspoons liquid saffron (see page 36)
> 1/4 cup clarified unsalted butter
>
> 2 tablespoons dried barberries (see page 25)
> 1/4 cup unsalted clarified butter
> 1 tablespoon sugar
> 2 teaspoons liquid saffron (see page 36)

Prepare the rice to Step 6 as given in the master recipe on page 63.

Pick over the barberries and remove stems. Wash, pat dry, and fry briefly in butter, stirring constantly (take care, for they easily burn). Stir in the sugar and liquid saffron, remove from heat, and set aside.

At Step 6, layer the barberries with the rice and pour over the liquid saffron. The accompanying meat for this dish is Saffron Chicken (page 283).

BAKED RICE
Tahcheen

The following recipes are prepared slightly differently than the previous ones. The steaming process can be completed in a nonstick pan or hot oven. Ideally, preparations for each of the next three recipes should start the previous day.

Tahcheen (which means "laid on the bottom") is always perceived as something very special in Persia. A classic dish, it contains rice and meat (both traditionally festive items) and also a generous enhancement of the costly saffron. It used to be made in wide-bottomed saucepans, which were placed in the hot coals of the baker's oven and left for many hours to bake, so that a wonderfully disproportionate crusty layer of rice would result.

This dish can also be made in an ovensafe bowl, as explained in the following recipe.

1 pound (2 cups) basmati long grain rice
4 tablespoons salt
1/2 cup vegetable oil
4 teaspoons liquid saffron (see page 36)
1/4 cup clarified unsalted butter

1 pound boned shoulder *or* leg of lamb
2 medium onions
1/4 teaspoon turmeric
salt and pepper
1/2 cup yogurt
2 eggs
4-6 teaspoons liquid saffron (see page 36)

Trim the meat of all fat, cut into 2-inch cubes, and wash. Slice one of the onions finely into a pan, add the turmeric, the salt and pepper, the meat, and 2 tablespoons water, cover and simmer on a low heat for an hour or two until the meat is very tender. Leave to cool.

Grate the second onion into the yogurt, beat in the eggs, liquid saffron, salt, and pepper until the yogurt is smooth and golden. Strain the meat and add to the yogurt mixture to marinate for at least 8 hours.

Prepare rice to Step 5 of the master recipe on page 63. Add extra oil to the pan and put on to heat.

Remove lamb from marinade. Mix about a third of the rice in the marinade then pour into the hot oil and spread across the bottom of the pan and up the sides. Lay the lamb on top, then sprinkle over the rest of the rice. Cut the butter into pieces and dot over the rice. Cover and proceed as in step 7 of the master recipe, page 63. Alternatively, you can bake this in the oven. Pre-heat oven to 375°F. Cover casserole tightly with a piece of oiled foil and bake in the oven for two hours.

To serve, sprinkle the white rice on to a warmed dish, then garnish with the meat and wedges of the thick, crusty bottom.

BAKED RICE WITH SPINACH
Tahcheen-o Esfenâj

This pretty layered *tahcheen* dish is thought to come from Isfahan. Certainly a dish very like this was served at the court of Shah Abbas in the golden days of seventeenth-century Isfahan. Spinach has long been grown in the gardens around Isfahan and has always been highly esteemed.

As with so much of Persia's produce, spinach first arrived in Europe with the Arabs in the seventh and eighth centuries; by the eleventh century it was already commonly grown in Spain. Its Persian name made a relatively short transition through Arabic and Spanish into English. When it first arrived in England, it was frequently served as a dessert as well as a savory, reflecting its Eastern origins.

The texture and strong flavor of the spinach contrasts well with the delicately flavored saffron rice. It can be baked in an oven with great effect. A 2-quart ovensafe bowl is required for the quantities given below. A clear-glass bowl makes it easy to see when a golden crust has formed evenly all over.

---

1 pound (2 cups) basmati long grain rice

4 tablespoons salt

1/2 cup vegetable oil

12 ounces boned shoulder *or* leg of lamb

2 medium onions

1/2 teaspoon turmeric

salt and pepper

1 cup yogurt

2 medium eggs

6 teaspoons liquid saffron (see page 36)

1 1/2 pounds fresh spinach *or* 10 ounces frozen
  chopped spinach

1/2 cup butter, cut into pats

At least 12 hours before you wish to serve, trim and wash the meat and cut into 2-inch chunks. Slice one of the onions finely into a pan, add the turmeric, the salt and pepper, the meat, and water to half cover. Cover and simmer gently for an hour or so until the meat is tender. Allow to cool.

Beat the eggs, saffron, salt, and pepper into the yogurt until smooth, then add the strained meat and leave to marinate for at least eight hours, preferably overnight.

Slice the second onion finely and fry in oil until soft and golden.

Add ¼ teaspoon turmeric and fry. Wash and chop the spinach and add to the onion along with salt and pepper to taste. Fry for 10-15 minutes, stirring constantly. Remove from heat and allow to cool.

Prepare rice to Step 4 of the master recipe on page 63 and preheat the oven to 375°F.

Pour the oil into the casserole, turning to coat the sides. Remove meat from marinade. Mix half the rice with the marinade and pour it all into the casserole, spreading across the bottom and up the sides as much as possible. Place the meat carefully in a layer over the rice, then spread the spinach over the meat. Lastly, add the rest of the rice, leveling it off. Cover closely with a piece of oiled aluminum foil and bake in the oven for two hours.

Remove from oven. Lift the foil, scatter the pats of butter over the rice, and replace the foil. Leave for five minutes. Invert bowl onto a warmed plate. This is delicious served with Cucumber and Pomegranate Salad (see page 211).

BAKED RICE WITH CHICKEN
Tahcheen-o Morgh

This is a beautiful party dish. It looks wonderful and can be prepared in advance. Despite its exotic air, it is well suited to a modern kitchen, for it is baked in an oven with entirely authentic results.

For extra special occasions, the quantities can be increased by half so that two shallow bowls (one smaller than the other) may be baked together in the oven and the smaller one turned out on top of the larger one. This is a very dramatic presentation, and one that increases the proportion of crusty rice. When cut, the rice inside the golden casing has a lovely marbled appearance. For the rice below, I use a shallow oval ceramic bowl so that the rice can be turned out like a golden cake on to the usual dish for serving. Alternatively, it can be made in an ovensafe bowl and turned out onto a large round plate.

In Iran, this dish is rarely served to the family on its own, but rather forms part of a selection of dishes for a dinner party. It is in fact a most useful dish for a buffet dinner, for it can be prepared in advance and kept in the bowl for several hours before it is cooked in the oven. It needs little last-minute attention. Mrs. Fatimeh Khorsandi gave me this recipe.

> 1 pound (2 cups) basmati long grain rice
> 4 tablespoons salt
> 1/2 pound chicken breasts
> 1 medium onion
> salt
> 3/4 cup yogurt
> 2 medium eggs
> 3-6 teaspoons liquid saffron (see page 36)
> 1/4 cup clarified unsalted butter

At least 12 hours before you wish to serve, wash and skin the chicken breasts, and cut lengthwise into three or four pieces each. Slice the onion finely into a pan, add salt and chicken, add water to half cover, put on the lid and simmer very gently for half an hour until tender. Let cool.

Beat the eggs into the yogurt along with the saffron, and salt to taste. When smooth and golden, place the drained, cooled chicken pieces in it to marinate for at least 8 hours, preferably overnight.

Preheat the oven to 375°F, and prepare the rice to Step 4 in the master recipe on page 63.

Add the rice to the chicken and marinade, along with the oil, and mix gently and thoroughly. Pour into a 2-quart casserole or bowl and cover with the lid, or with a piece of oiled aluminum foil.

Bake in a hot oven for 2 hours. Remove from oven. Lift the lid or the foil, scatter the butter, cut into pieces, over the rice, and cover again. Leave for five minutes. Invert bowl onto a warmed dish or plate.

BOILED WHITE RICE
Katteh

The approach to rice in the northern provinces of Iran is one of intimate familiarity and daily practicality, far removed from the social significance given to it in the rest of the country. The rice, although boiled and steamed, is not strained after parboiling; it thus becomes a more substantial dish. Of course, for special occasions, the same varieties of light and airy *polow* as in the previous recipes are produced, but for everyday meals the quick and nourishing *katteh* is the order of the day.

This method of cooking rice is very popular in the Caspian littoral, the only region in Iran where rice is the staple food. Here it is eaten two or three times a day, even at breakfast, and is the sustaining meal of all classes. It can be eaten hot with accompanying sauces and meats (see following section), or it can be cooled and cut with a knife to be eaten in place of bread with cheese or jam. It can be molded into balls to be carried on a journey. Indeed, until well into the twentieth century the Persians from the Caspian area considered rice altogether far superior to bread, while in the central plateau the word *katteh* is still used in a disparaging way to describe badly prepared rice.

The fact is, when good-quality rice is cooked with care in this way, *katteh* can be very light and pleasing. I have found a nonstick saucepan to be ideal for this method, but it is not essential. As a general rule, double the amount of water as rice is required.

....

2 cups basmati long grain rice
4 cups water
2 teaspoons salt
¼ cup unsalted butter

....

Pick over and wash the rice thoroughly in running water until the water runs clear. Drain well and put into a pan along with the salt and water. Leave to soak for up to two hours.

About an hour before you want to eat, bring rice and water quickly to a boil, then immediately reduce heat and simmer uncovered over a medium heat for about 10-12 minutes until the water has disappeared, and holes appear in the rice.

When water can no longer be seen bubbling in the holes, cut up the butter and scatter over the rice, wrap the saucepan lid in a clean kitchen towel and put on firmly. When steaming, reduce heat to very low and let cook gently for 40 minutes.

Remove pan from the heat and leave for 5 minutes without removing lid. Then slide a knife down the sides of the pan to ease the rice away and invert it on to a warmed plate. Alternatively, dish up the rice onto a warmed plate, remove the crusty bottom, cut into pieces, and arrange them over the top.

STEAMED RICE WITH FAVA BEANS
Dampokhtak

This dish originated in the Caspian region where both fava beans and rice are grown. When it was taken to India by the Moghuls in the sixteenth century, the fava beans were replaced with lentils and it became known as *khichri*. The English in India found this nourishing dish so delicious that they adopted and adapted it, adding smoked fish and boiled eggs, and brought it back home with them, calling it kedgeree.

In Persia, it underwent no such changes and still remains a favorite family dish. Indeed it is so quick and easy to prepare that it is never served to formal guests, for it might appear that they were not expected.

In Iran, dried fava beans are frequently used to replace fresh fava beans. The dried beans, like fresh ones, are always skinned before they are dried, so they quickly become soft when reconstituted and cooked. Various kinds of dried fava beans can be found here in health food stores.

In many parts of Iran, this dish is eaten with Pickled Stuffed Eggplant (see page 218), but in the Caspian region it is sometimes served with fried eggs.

---

1 cup basmati long grain rice

1½ cups dried (skinned) fava beans

1 medium onion

2 teaspoons turmeric

salt and pepper

2 tablespoons butter

Garnish
crisply fried onion slices

Pick over and wash the rice until the water runs clear. Leave to soak in cold, lightly salted water for about half an hour.

Pick over and wash the fava beans and let soak for a few minutes more.

Slice the onion and fry in oil until golden brown in a 2-quart saucepan (preferably nonstick). Stir in the turmeric, salt, and a generous sprinkling of black pepper, then the drained fava beans. When well mixed, add enough hot water just to cover, put on the lid, and simmer gently until the beans are half cooked (about 15 minutes), adding more water if necessary.

Drain the water from the soaking rice and add to the pan with sufficient water to cover by 1 inch, ensuring the rice is level. Boil without a lid for 5-7 minutes until the water has disappeared and the rice is pitted.

When water can no longer be seen bubbling in the holes, cut up the butter and scatter it over the rice, wrap the saucepan lid in a clean kitchen towel and put on firmly. When steaming, reduce heat to very low and leave to cook gently for 30 minutes. This will keep warm and fresh for another hour or more on the lowest heat.

Dish up the rice onto a warmed dish. A crispy crust is an integral and delicious part of this dish. Carefully remove it, cut into wedges, and heap on top of the rice. Garnish with crisply fried onion slices, and serve with pickles.

❂ ❂

RICE WITH DILL
Sheveed Polow

This recipe is taken from *The Art of Cooking in Gilan* by Zari Khavar, who recommends serving it with lashings of butter and pieces of salted fish.

Traditionally, much of the plentiful fish from the Caspian Sea was preserved either by smoking (it would be hung high in the rafters over the central fireplace) or by salting. For this dish, the heavily salted fish would be reconstituted by placing it in a bowl of fresh water placed on top of the steaming pot of rice to warm through. When dishing up, the salt water would be discarded and the fish broken up into pieces to be eaten with the rice. It really is a delicious combination and very popular in the northern provinces of the Caspian region.

Prepare as for *katteh* (see page 90), but add 1 heaping tablespoon dried dill when soaking the rice in step 1, or preferably, a large bunch of chopped fresh dill when bringing the rice to a boil in step 2.

In some parts, a cup of diced potatoes is added to the rice.

RICE WITH TOMATOES
Istambooli Polow

This is a modern dish, its two principal ingredients, potatoes and tomatoes, being newcomers to Iran. They both arrived at the beginning of this century from the West via Istanbul, hence the name of the *polow*.

It is a cheap and cheerful dish, and is a family favorite in urban Iran today. Yet it rarely appears on a festive table for special guests, despite its colorful appearance and popularity.

New potatoes are best for this dish or any waxy type, such as red-skinned potatoes, that hold their shape. Potatoes that quickly disintegrate are no good as they spoil the texture of the dish.

---

3 cups basmati long grain rice
12 ounces boned leg of lamb
1 medium onion
½ teaspoon turmeric
1 teaspoon *advieh* No. 1 (see page 30)
salt and pepper
2 medium potatoes
3 tablespoons tomato paste

Garnish
crisply fried onion slices

Pick over and wash the rice in several changes of water. Soak in cold water with ½ tablespoon salt for about an hour.

Trim the meat of all fat, cut into small pieces, wash and soak for a few minutes.

Slice the onion and fry in oil until soft and golden in a 3-quart saucepan. Stir in the turmeric, *advieh*, salt and pepper, and fry, then add the drained meat. Stir and fry until well browned. Stir in the tomato paste, and add enough water just to cover. Put on the lid and simmer gently for half an hour until the meat is almost tender.

Peel the potatoes and cut into ¾-inch cubes. Add to the stew.

Drain the rice and add to the stew, stir carefully, and add boiling water to cover ¾ inch. Adjust seasoning, and boil rapidly, uncovered, for 4 minutes. Reduce heat to medium and boil for another 6 minutes, until water is reduced and the rice pitted.

When water can no longer be seen bubbling in the holes, wrap the saucepan lid in a clean kitchen towel and put on firmly. When steaming, reduce heat to very low and leave to cook gently for 30 minutes. This will keep warm and fresh for another hour or longer when on the lowest heat.

Serve up on a warmed dish, and garnish with fried onion slices.

STEWS AND SAUCES

It is a curious fact that although *khoresht* is the Sassanian (pre-Islamic Persian) word for a sauce served with rice, there is not one recipe for *khoresht* in the Safavid court cookbook published in 1547. There are, however, more than thirty recipes for *ghaliyeh*, the Arabic word for stew, a clear indication of the extensive influence of the Arabic language on medieval Persia. In the last three or four centuries, *khoresht* has once again come into common usage, except along the Persian Gulf where many of the fish stews are still called *ghaliyeh*.

In truth, *khoresht* is more of a stew than a sauce. Rich with herbs, fruits, or vegetables, it closely resembles a stew, yet its purpose is that of a sauce to accompany the main dish of white rice.

Each region in the vastness of Persia has its own speciality: the fish stews from the Caspian littoral in the north are herb-based, while those of the Persian Gulf are influenced by the hot spices of the Indian subcontinent. The central provinces combine lamb with the fruit and legumes of the high plateau to produce such classics as *khoresht-e beh* (quince stew) while the northern provinces make much use of herbs to produce the splendid *ghormeh sabzi* (lamb with herbs).

Today, it is the best from each of these regions that forms the standard repertoire of the Iranian housewife, although she will certainly have one or two favorites from her childhood that she will make regularly for her own family, as well as adaptations of her own.

The common factor in all these stews is a sour flavor, most usually derived from the addition of lemon juice or of whole and powdered dried limes. In season, verjuice or tiny unripe grapes are sometimes used, while tamarind is popular along the Persian Gulf, sharp oranges in the Caspian littoral, and barberries or tart pomegranates in the central plateau. Sometimes sour green plums or sumac are also used.

In the West, dried limes (*limoo amâni*, see page 26), both powdered and whole, are available at Middle Eastern stores. Tiny, unripe grapes can also be found at Iranian supermarkets in season, and, better still, a homegrown grapevine gives a good supply in the summer.

Traditionally, the stews contain very little meat. Meat has always been scarce and expensive in Iran, and so whenever a stew was served, the meat would be piled high in the center of the dish. This has now become the usual way to serve a *khoresht*. During this century, however, increasing affluence has led to a greater consumption of meat, most particularly among the Iranian community in exile in those countries where meat is plentiful and herbs are scarce and expensive. It must be said, though, that too much meat in a *khoresht* upsets the balance of the meal and is not authentic.

Most Persian housewives buy meat on the bone, and then after boning, trimming, and dicing the meat, will add the bone to the *khoresht* for flavor, removing it just before serving. Much care is taken in trimming every scrap of fat off the meat. It is also thoroughly washed and soaked briefly in fresh water, before being drained and added to the stew. This practice stems from the requirements not only of hygiene but also of religion and flavor, since it washes out the blood, which is forbidden to Muslims, and results in fresh, clean meat that is free to absorb all the subtle flavors of the spices.

Fried onions are an important ingredient. Indeed, they are vital in most Iranian recipes not only for their flavor but also as a thickening agent or a garnish. Fried onions serve many purposes: as a basic ingredient in stews, as a garnish on a number of soups, stews, omelets, and rice dishes, and as a stuffing for meat dumplings. Persian housewives often have a "fry-in" (or perhaps a "cry-in"?), when large quantities of onions are fried crisply and kept for future use. They are, incidentally, always sliced downward for Persian recipes. For garnish, the onion slices are separated into separate "new moon" shapes, and dropped into a plentiful amount of hot oil and cooked until golden. Drain immediately, then sprinkle onto a paper towel to absorb excess fat. They should be separate, golden, and crisp.

It is said that when a girl can fry onions well, so that they are crisp and evenly golden, she is ripe for marriage. In other words, her childhood training for her future life as a wife has been satisfactorily completed.

The consistency of a *khoresht* should never be too thin, though there should be enough sauce to pour over the rice. Most importantly, all the ingredients should be well blended, or, as the Persians say, *jâ oftâdeh*, which means "well matured" or "ripened." The sauce is thickened by reduction and with the use of onions (but *never* flour). Some housewives believe that making the *khoresht* the day before eating gives it a richer and more settled flavor, but others feel that the ingredients taste fresher when served the same day.

Khoresht is normally served with plain rice (*chelow* or *katteh*), although some are equally delicious eaten with bread: *gheimeh* (split peas with limes), for instance, is thick enough to be eaten with fresh Persian bread, but *fesenjân* (chicken with walnuts), though thick, is far too rich and would be unthinkable without white rice.

Whenever guests are expected (which is most of the time in Iran), a housewife will always make at least two stews that contrast in flavor and color, to serve with plain rice. And she will of course ensure that the correct balance between "hot" and "cold" ingredients (see page 8) is maintained in order to keep her family healthy and cheerful.

MIXED HERB STEW
Khoresht-e Ghormeh Sabzi

In a country famed for its herb stews and soups, this mixed herb stew is the epitome of them all. The simple combination of fresh herbs cooked with lamb and dried limes results in a mouth-watering, rich flavor. Its aroma during preparation is so tantalizing that it is likened to the scent of political intrigue.

While not difficult to prepare, cleaning, chopping, and drying the herbs can be time-consuming. Perhaps it is for this reason (and also because it is so delicious) that an Iranian man is the envy of all his friends and neighbors when his wife can produce the perfect *ghormeh sabzi*.

There are a number of different versions: in Tehran and Tabriz, red kidney beans are used for their contrasting beauty, while in Khuzistan and other southern provinces black-eyed peas are preferred for their finer flavor. In the central province, parsley, cilantro, and chives are the main herbs, while in the south, dill is also used. In any case, a small amount of fenugreek leaf and a generous amount of dried limes must always be included to give the dish its unique and rare bitter-sour flavor.

Parsley and scallions are both easily available most of the year, while fresh fenugreek is available in the summer months and dried fenugreek leaf the year-round in specialty shops. Cilantro can be replaced with parsley if necessary, or spinach may be used to bring up the quantity of herbs. It is also possible to buy packs of dried *ghormeh sabzi* herbs in Iranian stores in the West. Half a pack is required for this recipe: soak overnight, squeeze dry, and fry as fresh. The fried herbs may be cooled, wrapped, and kept in the refrigerator for up to thirty days or in the freezer for up to three months. (For further hints on herbs, see page 40). If dried lime powder is difficult to find, use extra fresh lime or lemon juice.

¾ **cup red kidney *or* black-eyed peas**

4 tablespoons fresh fenugreek *or* 2 tablespoons dried

1 large bunch parsley

1 large bunch cilantro *or* parsley

3 tablespoons dill (optional)

12 ounces boned leg of lamb

1 medium onion

2 tablespoons dried lime powder

4 whole dried limes

salt

juice of 2 lemons *or* 4, if dried limes are not available

If using red kidney beans, leave to soak for several hours, preferably overnight. Then boil fast for ten minutes, drain, and rinse well. Put to one side.

Clean and wash the herbs, removing coarse stems, drain, and shake dry. Chop finely.

Fry the herbs (sprinkling in the crushed dried fenugreek leaf, if using) in a little oil over a moderate heat, turning constantly, adding more oil when necessary until the herbs darken (about 30-40 minutes). Remove from heat and set aside.

Trim and cut the meat into large pieces, 2½ inches, wash and leave to soak while you slice and fry the onion until soft and golden. Add the drained meat and brown well on all sides.

Stir in the herbs. Add the beans, lime powder, and enough water to cover. Cover the pan and simmer gently for an hour.

Pierce the dried limes in several places with a sharp knife and add along with the dried lime powder and salt.

Simmer gently for another hour or until the meat and beans are tender and the whole sauce well blended. Add lemon juice to taste.

Dish up into a warm serving dish and serve with white rice.

STEW WITH SPINACH AND PRUNES
Khoresht-e Esfenâj-o Âloo

The very word "prunes" is apt to strike terror into the hearts of all respectable people who were brought up to know their time and place. There is something dark and sinister about them. They are rarely seen except on hotel breakfast tables, where they lurk despondently next to the much loved, freshly-squeezed orange juice. It was not always this way.

Before the year-round availability of great varieties of fresh fruit, the prune was a popular and useful fruit in the kitchen. It appeared in savory dishes as well as in desserts and puddings. A famous old Lancashire dish, "hindle wakes," has chicken stuffed with prunes and served with lemon juice—a strangely Persian group of flavors to find in the north of England—while recipes for beef and prune casserole and goose stuffed with prunes are classics of Central European cooking.

In Persia, prunes have always had a very different air about them. They come in a variety of colors and sizes. This stew would be made with small yellow plums (known as *âloo bokhârâ*), which have an appealingly tart flavor, but I have had much success with the dark pitted prunes found at every supermarket in the West. The contrasting flavors of prunes and lamb blend perfectly in a thick spinach sauce. This delicious dish gives the despised prune a truly glamorous air. Served with plain rice, it makes a surprisingly elegant meal.

> **1 pound boned leg of lamb**
> **2 medium onions**
> **1 pound fresh spinach** *or* **1 package frozen chopped spinach**
> **2 small leeks** *or* **6 scallions**
> **4 teaspoons dried lime powder**
> **juice of 2 lemons** *or* **4, if dried limes are not available**
> **salt and black pepper**
> **10 pitted prunes**

Trim all the fat from the meat, cut into 1 inch cubes, wash, and leave to soak in cold water for a few minutes.

Slice the onions and fry in a little oil until soft and golden.

Drain the meat, add to the onions, and stir-fry until meat is well browned. Add enough water to cover, sprinkle in the dried lime powder, cover the pan, and simmer gently for an hour.

Meanwhile, thoroughly wash and drain the spinach, toss dry and chop finely. Keep to one side.

Thoroughly wash the leeks or scallions, chop finely and fry

lightly in a little oil until soft. Add the spinach and stir-fry for 5-10 minutes until soft and well mixed.

Add to the stew with lemon juice, salt and pepper to taste. Simmer for another 15 minutes.

Wash the pitted prunes, cut in half, and add to the stew 5 minutes before serving.

Dish up into a warm bowl and serve with white rice.

RHUBARB STEW
Khoresht-e Reevâs

According to the Zoroastrian religion of ancient Iran, the human race was born of the rhubarb plant, which in turn grew from the first creation of Ahura Mazda, *Gâyomard* (Mortal Life). Its Persian name *reevâs* comes from the Old Persian word *reev*, meaning a shining light. From ancient times, rhubarb has always been considered good for cleansing the blood and purifying the system.

When it first arrived in England, its medicinal properties were also highly valued. Only in the last century was it consumed for pleasure, when it was welcomed as the first fruit of summer—even though technically it is a vegetable.

In Safavid times, rhubarb was used as a thickening agent in a rich *khoresht* of lamb and celery. But in modern Iran, parsley and mint give substance to the sauce while the rhubarb is added minutes before serving. This basic parsley and mint sauce serves as the basis for a number of stews including celery, cardoon, and eggplant.

All the ingredients for this stew are easily available, especially for anyone with a garden. What country garden does not have a crown of rhubarb, a patch of parsley, and a clump of mint, all delightfully fresh in the early summer? Even without a garden, such ingredients are not difficult or expensive to obtain from the local supermarket.

Khoresht-e reevâs is a pretty dish, the pink and red rhubarb affording a lovely contrast to the dark green herbs. Traditionally, it is served in Iran to aid digestion. It is reassuring to know that a dish that is so "good for you" is also such a pleasure to eat.

---

1 pound boned leg of lamb
2 medium onions
1 bunch fresh parsley
1 bunch fresh mint
10-12 stalks rhubarb

Trim the meat of all fat, cut in 2-inch cubes, wash, and leave to soak while you slice and fry the onions in oil until golden brown. Add the drained meat and brown on all sides. Add enough water to cover, put on the lid, and simmer gently for half an hour.

Clean and wash the parsley and mint, removing coarse stems, shake dry and chop finely. Fry in a little oil, turning constantly for 10-15 minutes. Add the fried herbs to the stew and continue to stew gently for an hour or so until the meat is tender and the stew well blended.

Wash rhubarb, trim and discard leaves, chop into 1/2-inch lengths. A few minutes before serving, add the salt and the rhubarb. Do not allow the rhubarb to overcook or disintegrate. Serve with white rice.

CELERY STEW
Khoresht-e Karafs

A delectable way to serve celery. Wash and cut about 2 pounds (about 1 bunch) celery into ½-inch lengths and fry in a little oil for 10-15 minutes until golden. Add to the stew with the parsley and mint (to which have been added some fresh green celery leaves). The celery should remain slightly crunchy. Add the juice of 1 lemon.

CARDOON STEW
Khoresht-e Kangar

Cardoons are found all over Iran, but are specially tender from the mountains near Shiraz. Be sure to remove the sharp thorns, and use as celery as above.

GREEN PLUM STEW
Khoresht-e Gojeh Sabz

Hard round green plums eaten with salt are a favorite with children. They can be found at Iranian stores in early summer, and give this stew a delightfully piquant flavor. Omit the mint and use 2 bunches of parsley and 6-8 stems tarragon. Briefly fry about 2 pounds green plums and add to the stew 20 minutes before serving.

NORTHERN EGGPLANT STEW
Nâz Khâtoon

A popular dish in the northern province of Gilan. Wash, top, and tail 4½ pounds eggplant, then bake in a medium oven for an hour or until tender. When cool, peel and cut up into cubes and add to the stew with the parsley and mint. Add sour grapes or verjuice instead of lemon juice.

EGGPLANT STEW
Khoresht-e Bâdenjân

The eggplant has come to epitomize Middle Eastern cooking. Known as the poor man's caviar, it appears in so many dishes from Morocco to Egypt and from Greece to Turkey that it is hard to believe that it was virtually unknown in the Mediterranean region until the seventh and eighth centuries.

The Arabs fell under the spell of the *badin-gân*, as it was called in Old Persia, when they conquered Iran in the seventh century. Not having a hard "g" in their alphabet, they called it *al-badinjân*. They introduced it to all the countries on their conquering path along the North African coast and up into Spain, where it became known as *berenjena*.

But just as the Arabs came to a halt in Spain, so did the eggplant, and it wasn't until the fifteenth century that it finally found its way into Italy, the eighteenth century into France, and the twentieth century into England and the US. As Elizabeth David commented in *Italian Food*, it seems strange that despite the development of the fine cuisines of Italy and France during these centuries, neither country came up with any dishes that can compare with the delicious and varied methods of preparing eggplant found all over the Middle East.

If possible, buy small eggplant for this dish as they should be sliced in half for frying. Very small ones can be left whole, and are considered very delicious. However, you will probably have to make do with large ones, which should be cut lengthwise into 1/4-inch slices.

All eggplant absorb enormous amounts of fat when fried, and while this was not thought to be a bad thing in the old days, it bothers weight-conscious people nowadays. I have found it best to place the fried eggplant slices in a colander over a bowl so that the excess fat can drain away (and be used again).

---

4 pounds eggplant
1 pound boned leg of lamb
2 medium onions
1 teaspoon turmeric
3 tablespoons tomato paste
3-4 medium tomatoes
3/4 cup small unripe grapes (see page 37)
juice of 1 lemon
salt and pepper

Peel the eggplant and cut into 1/4-inch thick slices. Spread them out, sprinkle with salt, and leave for at least half an hour. Wipe dry and fry in a generous amount of oil until golden brown. Leave to drain.

Trim the meat of all fat, cut into 2-inch cubes, wash, and leave to soak in fresh water for a few minutes.

Slice the onions and fry briskly in oil until golden brown. Add the turmeric, salt, and pepper, then the drained meat and stir-fry until well browned.

Stir in the tomato paste, the skinned and finely chopped tomatoes, sour grapes, and lemon juice with water to cover. Put on lid and simmer gently for 30 minutes.

Add the drained eggplant and a little more water if necessary, cover and simmer for another 30 minutes or until the meat is tender and the sauce well blended.

Serve in a warmed vegetable dish, arranging the eggplant slices around the dish and heaping the meat on top in the middle. Serve with white rice.

One day, Nasser ed-Din Shah was eating a dish of eggplants and, turning to his chamberlain, remarked, "What an excellent vegetable the eggplant is!"

"Yes, indeed, Your Majesty," replied the chamberlain, "it is the most delicious of vegetables. It is at once appetizing, nourishing, and tasty."

The next day, His Majesty, having over-indulged his appetite the day before, was suffering from a stomach ache and observed, "What an unpleasant vegetable the eggplant is…"

The chamberlain broke in, "Yes indeed, Your Majesty, the eggplant is the worst of vegetables. It causes wind and flatulence, it is quite unwholesome."

The Shah looked at him in astonishment, "Didn't you tell me yesterday that the eggplant is an excellent vegetable? Why have you changed your mind?"

"Your Majesty," replied the chamberlain, "I am the servant of the Shah not of the eggplant."

Persian Folk Tale

CUCUMBER STEW
Khoresht-e Khiyâr

This is a delightful stew with a light summery flavor. Replace the eggplant with small cucumbers (available in adventurous supermarkets and Middle Eastern stores), or with English cucumbers cut into quarters and seeds removed.

GREEN BEAN STEW
Khoresht-e Loobyâ

This is a modern dish, using as it does vegetables that first appeared in Persian markets only at the beginning of this century. Not being a classic dish it is rarely served on formal occasions, but it is a firm favorite especially among the urban young. Replace the eggplant with 2 pounds chopped green beans (dwarf, runner, or stick) and omit the sour grapes.

OKRA STEW
Khoresht-e Bâmieh

This is a stew from the southern Persian Gulf region, the okra entering Iran from Africa in the nineteenth century. Be sure to use very fresh young okra. Replace the beans with 2 pounds young okra, topped and tailed. Add verjuice or dried sour grape powder to taste.

ZUCCHINI STEW
Khoresht-e Kadoo

Replace the eggplant with zucchini.

POTATO STEW
Khoresht-e Seebzamini

Replace the eggplant with peeled, diced potatoes and add 1 bunch chopped fresh cilantro or parsley and omit the sour grapes.

TURNIP STEW
Khoresht-e Shalgham

Replace the eggplant with peeled, diced turnips, add 1 bunch chopped fresh cilantro or parsley and omit the sour grapes.

Fava Bean Stew
Khoresht Gol dar Chaman

Garlic is an integral part of this famous Caspian dish, as it is of many dishes from the coastal regions. It is believed to be effective against rheumatism, an affliction of the damp and humid regions of the country.

Garlic makes only a fleeting appearance in the dishes of the central provinces where the air is pure and dry. There are few rheumatic pains there to require garlic, and, besides, the smell is so much more potent in the dry air of the high plateau. The aroma of one small clove of garlic carries for miles and hangs about for days there, but seems to be absorbed more quickly by the heavy moist air of the seashore.

This recipe comes from Zari Khâvar's *Art of Cookery in Gilan*. She recommends a delicious vegetarian version where the meat is replaced with extra fava beans.

---

1 pound boned leg of lamb
2 medium onions
1-2 cloves garlic
½ teaspoon turmeric
2 large bunches fresh dill *or* 3 tablespoons dried dill
1 pound fava beans *or* 1 cup dried skinned fava beans
3-4 eggs
salt and pepper

Trim the meat of all fat, cut into ¼-inch cubes, wash and leave to soak in cold water for a few minutes.

Fry the sliced onion and chopped garlic in oil until golden. Stir in the turmeric. Add the drained meat and stir-fry until it is well browned. Just cover with water, put on the lid, and simmer for 45 minutes.

If using dried dill and beans, pick over them and soak separately for at least 30 minutes. Shell, blanch, and skin fresh beans and set aside. Wash the fresh dill, removing coarse stalks, shake dry and chop finely. Drain the dried beans and squeeze out excess water from the dried dill, if using.

Add the dill and beans to the meat, with a little extra water if required, and simmer gently for 10-15 minutes, until the beans are just tender.

Break the eggs into a cup one by one and slip whole into the stew.* Cook gently for another two or three minutes.

Dish up into a warm bowl, arranging the whole eggs on top of the stew if using. Serve with plain white rice.

---

* Or the eggs may be beaten together and stirred into the stew.

SPLIT PEA AND LAMB STEW
Khoresht-e Gheimeh

This is a very Persian dish, a dish of the people that is equally at home in the courts of kings, the mosques of mullahs, and the homes of the humble. In days gone by, it was made of cooked meat dried and preserved in oil but nowadays it is always made with fresh meat.

The simple combination of ingredients (meat, onions, split peas, and dried limes) is perfectly balanced. The split peas absorb the oil of the preserved meat, the fried onions give a pungent flavor and the dried limes a tart freshness. Simple and economical to make, the ingredients were, and still are, commonly available in every Persian housewife's kitchen throughout the year.

White rice and *gheimeh* is commonly served to congregations at mosques during prolonged prayer meetings, passion plays, and memorial services. This timeless dish, so cheap and easy to prepare, is an obvious choice when a large number of people need to be served a hot and satisfying meal.

Today, the basic ingredients of *gheimeh* have been extended to include the two most famous newcomers to Iran: tomatoes and potatoes. Tomatoes serve to enhance the color and flavor and it is very rare nowadays to find this dish made without the addition of tomato paste. Fried potatoes are added as a garnish in many parts of the country.

> **12 ounces boned leg of lamb**
> **1½ cups yellow split peas**
> **2 medium onions**
> **1 teaspoon turmeric**
> **3 tablespoons tomato paste**
> **2 tablespoons dried lime powder**
> **3-4 whole dried limes**
> **salt and pepper**
> **juice of 1 lemon**
> **2-3 potatoes**

Trim the meat of all fat and cut into small ¼-inch cubes, wash and leave to soak in cold water for a few minutes.

Pick over and wash the split peas. Put to one side.

Slice the onions and fry in a little oil until a rich golden brown. Stir in the turmeric and some pepper, then add the drained meat and stir-fry until brown.

Add the tomato paste, fry briefly, then add the split peas, and cover generously with water. Add the dried lime powder, stir, cover, and leave to simmer gently for 20 minutes. Stir from time to time, adding more water if necessary.

Pierce the whole dried limes and add them, the salt, and lemon juice to taste. Simmer until the meat is tender and split peas soft (but not disintegrating).

In the meantime, peel and dice the potatoes into small cubes, not more than 1/2 inch. Deep-fry briskly until crisp and golden.

Dish up into a warm bowl, with fried potatoes piled on top. Serve with white rice.

Split Pea and Eggplant Stew
Gheimeh Bâdenjân

This dish is popular throughout Iran. Follow the previous recipe, but cut the meat into 2½-inch cubes. Instead of potatoes, prepare and fry 3 pounds eggplant as in the recipe for Eggplant Stew (see page 103) and add 20 minutes before serving.

Gheimeh bâ qâf neest, bâ ghain neest,
Gheimeh bâ goosht-o lappast.

Gheimeh's not with "q" or "gh,"
Gheimeh's with meat and split peas.

One day a schoolgirl asked her mother if the correct way to spell *gheimeh* was with a "q" or a "gh." Her mother, who was illiterate, very practically replied: "It's not with a 'q' or with a 'gh,' it's with meat and split peas."

DUCK WITH WALNUTS AND POMEGRANATES
Khoresht-e Fesenjân

The ancient Persians esteemed the walnut tree so highly that its fruit was reserved solely for the delectation of the king. When, in a period of peace, the king of Persia sent some of his prized walnut trees to the king of Greece, they were in turn kept entirely for the Greek king's pleasure. They were later cultivated with honor in Greece. From there, inevitably, they found their way to Rome where the tree "was placed under the protection of the most powerful of the [Roman] gods." Walnuts came to stand for abundance and prosperity.

It is walnuts that give *khoresht-e fesenjân* its unique flavor and texture. Popular in Persia for centuries, this aristocratic sauce of walnuts and pomegranates is usually made with duck, chicken, or game birds. A *fesenjân* of meatballs is also delicious, the exquisite sauce making a noble meal of the mundane meatball. And in Gilan they make a delectable *fesenjân* with fish cutlets and even with eggplant slices, which gives vegetarians a chance to sample these lovely dishes (see next two recipes).

The sauce is very rich and the darker meat of duck or game birds is better able to hold its own in the thick sauce. I have experimented with two pairs of pheasants accompanied by tiny meatballs (a combination reminiscent of the Safavid court) and this resulted in an excellent meaty *fesenjân*. Since the dish is an autumnal one, traditionally served at the onset of winter, pheasants seem ideally suited to the season and the meal.

Let us not break too far from tradition, though. Our winters are much longer in the West than in Persia and the season for pheasants is very short. So I have opted for a large duck that produces more meat, and more than enough fat to prepare the entire meal. The dish may be garnished with tiny meatballs to give it a romantic Safavid air, and at the same time extend the meat content. It is best to start preparation of this meal the day before.

> 1 large duck
>
> 2 medium onions
>
> 1½ cups shelled walnuts
>
> 3-5 tablespoons pomegranate paste (see page 33) *or* reduce about 2 quarts fresh pomegranate juice
>
> 6 ounces ground lamb *or* veal (optional)
>
> salt
>
> 2-3 tablespoons sugar (if using pomegranate paste)
>
> 1 lemon (if using reduced pomegranate juice)

Wash and cut up the duck, then put the wings, legs (cut into two pieces), and the breasts (cut into two or three pieces) into a container, cover and keep in the fridge until required.

Simmer the carcass with half an onion for several hours to produce about 1 quart stock. Strain and reserve stock. Discard carcass.

Pick over and chop the walnuts, then put them through a grinder (or use a food processor). Fry the walnuts in oil, stirring constantly, until they change color and darken (about 15 minutes). Put to one side to cool. Excess fat may then be removed.

Fry the duck pieces on all sides for a few minutes. Remove with a slotted spoon and when cool enough to handle, remove the skin. Meanwhile, chop the second onion and fry until soft and golden in the same pan. Return the skinned duck pieces, add enough of the cooled duck stock to just cover the duck, put on lid, and simmer gently for 20 minutes.

Add the walnuts with a little more stock and simmer gently for another 20 minutes, stirring from time to time.

If desired, mix the ground meat, the remaining onion and a little salt together and with wet hands make into tiny meatballs. Fry until nicely browned.

Stir in the pomegranate paste or juice and continue to simmer gently until the duck is tender. Add salt and sugar (if using pomegranate paste) or lemon juice (if using pomegranate juice). Add the meatballs, and simmer for a few minutes more.

Dish up the stew into a warm bowl, and serve with plain white rice.

FISH WITH WALNUTS AND POMEGRANATES
Khoresht-e Mâhi Fesenjân

The *fesenjân* dishes of the northern provinces of Gilan and Mazandaran are always very dark brown, almost black in color. This is mostly achieved by the pomegranate juice, which in the Caspian region is reduced to a thick black paste. They are also cooked in a copper pan to intensify the dark color. In most parts of Persia, the very dark sauce is deemed to be the most desirable, and everywhere it is classed as an elegant dish suitable for the most distinguished of guests.

This recipe comes from Zari Khavar's *The Art of Cooking in Gilan.* The walnuts are not fried first (as in the previous recipe) but must be cooked for at least an hour before the pomegranate paste and fried fish are added.

1½ cups shelled walnuts

2 pounds fresh white fish (cod *or* haddock) cut into
  1-inch thick steaks

2-3 tablespoons thick pomegranate paste

salt and pepper

Put the walnuts through the grinder twice, then put into a saucepan with 2 cups of water. Simmer gently for at least an hour until the oil of the walnuts rises to the surface, stirring from time to time.

In the meantime, fry the fish steaks in oil until lightly browned.

Add to the walnuts and simmer gently for a few minutes.

Add a little water to the pomegranate paste and stir into the stew. Add salt and pepper, and simmer gently for 5-10 minutes until the fish is cooked through.

Dish up into a warm bowl and serve with white rice.

EGGPLANT AND POMEGRANATE STEW
Sheeshandâz

Replace the fish steaks with 3 pounds large eggplant, peeled and cut across into 1-inch thick slices. Salt, fry, and drain, and add to the stew with ¼ teaspoon each of turmeric and ground cinnamon.

SHRIMP STEW
Ghaliyeh Maygoo

The deep waters of the Persian Gulf have been bustling with soldiers of trade and fortune since the beginning of time. The Greeks and the Romans both knew these waters. The Arabs and the Indians have traded across the Gulf with the Persians for centuries, and African caravans and European colonialists have all stopped off at the Persian Gulf ports.

These southern shores have seen more foreign visitors than any other part of the country and the food of the Persian Gulf region reflects this influence. In this stew, the curry powder and tamarind of India are combined with the herbs of mainland Persia to make a rich pungent sauce for the splendid king prawns found in the Persian Gulf.

---

4 ounces tamarind paste

1 large bunch cilantro *and/or* parsley

½ cup fresh fenugreek

2 medium onions

1-2 cloves garlic

¼ teaspoon nutmeg

1 teaspoon mild curry powder

black pepper

1½ tablespoons tomato paste

2 pounds large peeled shrimp

Put the tamarind to soak in about 1½ cups water for 15 minutes. Strain the paste through a fine sieve. Put the liquid to one side.

Clean and wash the herbs, shake dry and chop finely. Set aside.

Finely chop the onions and garlic and fry in oil until golden. Stir in the nutmeg, curry powder, and pepper, then add the herbs. Fry, stirring constantly, for 5 minutes. Add the tomato paste and sufficient tamarind water to cover. Put on the lid and simmer gently for 30 minutes.

In the meantime, peel and wash the shrimp, pat dry and fry in a little oil until they change color. Five minutes before serving, add the shrimp to the stew and salt if necessary.

Dish up into a warm bowl and serve with plain white rice.

FISH STEW
Ghaliyeh Mâhi

This really is a lovely way to prepare fresh fish. The herbs, tamarind, and garlic give the dish a very distinctive Persian Gulf flavor.

4 ounces tamarind paste
1 large bunch parsley
1 large bunch scallions *or* 2 medium leeks
½ cup fresh fenugreek
2-3 cloves garlic
2 tablespoons all-purpose flour
1 teaspoon curry powder
¼ teaspoon turmeric
½ teaspoon red chili powder
2 pounds large white fish (cod *or* haddock) cut
   in 1-inch thick steaks
salt and pepper

Put the tamarind to soak in about 1½ cups water for 15 minutes. Squeeze the paste in the fingers, discarding the thorns, and strain through a fine sieve. Put the liquid to one side.

Clean and wash the herbs, shake dry, and chop finely. Chop the garlic, add to the herbs and put to one side.

Brown the flour in the saucepan, add a little oil, and stir in the curry powder, turmeric, and chili powder. Fry briefly, then add the herbs and garlic and fry, stirring constantly for 5 minutes. Add the tamarind water, cover, and simmer gently for 20 minutes.

Add the fish steaks and simmer very gently for another 10 minutes or so until the fish is cooked through. Add salt and pepper to taste.

Dish up into a warm bowl and serve with plain white rice.

But there is not, I believe, in all the World, a Place so full of Fish
as the Persian Gulph, they Fish twice a Day along the Shore,
and take all the Sorts of Fish which Europe affords, but it is
much better, more delicious and in greater Plenty.

Sir John Chardin, *Travels in Persia* 1673-1677

BARBERRY AND ALMOND STEW
Khoresht-e Zereshk

A famous wedding dish from Kermanshah, this tart sauce is laden with symbolism. While most wedding dishes in Persia are sweet to ensure a happy start for the young couple in their new life together, barberry and almond stew is one of contrasts. Sweet and sour, soft and crunchy, it is a warning to the newlyweds that life too is filled with both sadness and happiness. This saffron-perfumed stew contrasts with any of the sweet rice dishes.

....

1 pound boned leg of lamb
2 medium onions
1½ cups almond slivers
1½ cups pistachio slivers
½ cup dried barberries (see page 25)
¼ cup sugar
salt and pepper
4 teaspoons liquid saffron (see page 36)

....

Trim the meat of all fat, cut into ¼-inch cubes, wash, and leave to soak in cold water for a few minutes.

Slice the onions very finely and fry in oil until a soft golden brown.

Add the drained meat and stir until well browned. Add water to cover, put on the lid, and simmer for 40 minutes.

Put the almond and pistachio slivers in a small pan, cover with cold water, and bring to a boil. Drain immediately and add to the stew. Continue simmering for another 20 minutes.

Pick over the barberries, wash, pat dry, and fry briefly in oil, stirring constantly (take care they don't burn). Sprinkle over the sugar, mix well, then add to stew.

Add salt and pepper and, just before serving, the liquid saffron.

When thickened and reduced, dish up into a warm bowl. This may be served with plain white rice or with *shireen polow* (see page 78) or *haveej polow* (see page 78).

ORANGE STEW
Khoresht-e Nâranj

Oranges, known by the ancient Persians as *nârang*, have been grown in the Caspian region for at least 2,000 years. After the Arab conquest of Iran, these oranges found their way along the Mediterranean shores and up into Spain. The Arabs called them *nâranj* (not having a hard "g" in their alphabet) while the Spaniards called them *naranja*, and the French orange. These early oranges were all very sour.

It was not until the early sixteenth century that the sweet orange became known both in Persia and in Europe, when the early Portuguese explorers first brought it from China. Stopping off to pick up provisions at the Persian Gulf port of Hormuz, the Portuguese traded spices and sweet oranges from the East for water and provisions. Despite the hot and arid climate of the Persian Gulf, the new fruit trees did rather well in the nearby desert oases. Today, the sweet and juicy oranges of the oasis town of Bam acknowledge their history in their name of *portoghâl*.

Today, the sour *nâranj* is available in some US supermarkets for only a brief few weeks in January, when it appears as the Seville orange for marmalade making. It can, however, be found in Iranian stores in the West throughout February and even into March.

In Iran, there are still two distinct fruits available in the winter months: the sharp *nâranj* and the sweet *portoghâl*. The Old Persian name is still recalled in the tangerine, which is known as *nârangi* or "orange-colored."

The Persians never let the easy charms of the sweet *portoghâl* blind them to the attractions of the *nâranj*. The *nâranj* blossoms are so deliciously perfumed they are made into a delicate jam, its aromatic skin is dried for use in flavoring rice dishes and stews, its wonderfully sharp juice is used in beverages and desserts or to give a lift to fried fish and meat patties, soups, and pastes. The whole fruit is steeped and preserved in syrup; it is made into jams and marmalades, slices are used for garnishing sweet and savory dishes. For the Persians, the *nâranj* is irreplaceable. The *portoghâl*, though delicious, is just one of many seasonal sweet and juicy fruits.

The sour *nâranj* or Seville orange is preferable for this classical stew from the orange groves of the northern provinces. If sweet oranges are used, add lemon juice. It alters the flavor slightly, but is still a very pleasing and rather special dish.

---

1 large chicken, about 4-5 pounds
2 medium onions
1 teaspoon cinnamon
3 Seville *or* other oranges

3 large carrots

½ teaspoon liquid saffron (optional) (see page 36)

2 tablespoons sugar *or* juice of 1 lemon if using
   sweet oranges

salt and pepper

Garnish

2 teaspoons pistachio slivers

2 teaspoons almond slivers

Cut the chicken into pieces (wings, legs into two, and the breasts into four). Wash and pat dry. Fry in a little oil until nicely browned. Remove with slotted spoon and put to one side.

Finely slice the onions and fry in some oil until soft and golden brown. Stir in the cinnamon, add the chicken and enough water to cover. Put on lid and simmer gently for 30 minutes.

In the meantime, peel the oranges thinly (with a peeler) and cut into julienne strips. Put in small pan, cover with cold water, bring to a boil and drain. Repeat twice more and leave to drain.

Peel the carrots and cut into julienne strips. Fry in oil for 20 minutes then add to stew with the orange zest. Simmer for another 25 minutes.

With a sharp knife remove the pith from the oranges and the skin from the segments.

A few minutes before serving, stir in the liquid saffron (if using) and the sugar (or lemon juice if using sweet oranges), and add the orange segments.

Simmer for a minute or two and dish up into a warm bowl. Garnish with almond and pistachio slivers if desired and serve with plain white rice.

SOUR CHICKEN STEW
Khoresht-e Morgh-Torsh

A recipe from the city of Resht in the Caspian littoral. This was traditionally made with the juice of Seville oranges, but they are rare in the US, so replace with fresh lime juice. This recipe was kindly given to me by my sister-in-law, Batul.

---

1 chicken, about 3½ pounds
1½ tablespoons yellow split peas
10 cups fresh herbs (equal quantities of leeks, parsley, mint, and cilantro)
1 *or* 2 cloves of garlic
2 tablespoons rice flour
1 cup orange juice
salt and pepper to taste
4 medium eggs

Wash and cut up the chicken, then put it in a pot with the split peas and just cover with water.

Bring to a boil, cover, and simmer gently.

Meanwhile, clean the herbs, keeping the mint and cilantro separate. Spread to dry. Mince the garlic and pound with the mint and cilantro into a paste. Chop the leeks and parsley, then fry all the herbs and garlic together for 10 minutes. Add to the chicken and continue to simmer.

Blend the rice flour with a little cold water, then add slowly to the stew, stirring continuously.

Add salt and pepper to taste and the orange juice.

Just before serving, beat the eggs and add slowly to the simmering chicken.

Dish up into a warm bowl and serve with white rice.

Opposite: Jeweled Rice (*morasa' polow*)

QUINCE STEW
Khoresht-e Beh

Do not be misled by the appearance of the quince. Although it looks like a large, hard, dull-skinned, misshapen apple, it has, when cooked, a wonderful deep pink color and the most aromatic flavor. Indigenous to Persia, it is used in many dishes, both sweet and savory. In this stew, it imparts a lovely color and a sweet fragrance to the simple split pea stew.

12 ounces boned leg of lamb
2 medium onions
vegetable oil
½ teaspoon turmeric
⅓ cup yellow split peas
2 large quinces
salt and pepper
2 tablespoons sugar

Trim the meat of all fat, cut into small pieces, ¼-inch square, wash, and leave to soak in cold water for a few minutes.

Slice and fry the onions in oil until golden brown. Stir in the turmeric, then add the drained meat, and stir until well browned.

Stir in the cleaned and washed split peas, add water, cover, and simmer for 30 minutes, adding a little more water if necessary.

Peel and core the quinces, cut into eight segments and halve each segment across. Add to the stew and simmer for another 30 minutes until all is soft and tender.

Just before serving, add sugar, salt, and pepper to taste.

Dish up into a warm bowl and serve with plain white rice.

APPLE STEW
Khoresht-e Seeb

Replace the quince with apples, but add them 15 minutes before serving.

Opposite: top right, Duck with Walnuts and Pomegranates (*khoresht-e fesenjân*); top left, Split Pea and Lamb Stew (*khoresht-e gheimeh*); bottom right, Eggplant Stew (*khoresht-e bâdenjâh*); bottom left, Mixed Herb Stew (*khoresht-e gormeh sabzi*)

SOUPS
Through Thick and Thin

Most of the hearty "soups" in this section are a far cry from the light broths and bouillons that fall into the category of soups in the West. They are very substantial meals and have much in common with a French *potage*.

There are several groups of soup commonly featured in the Persian cuisine, the pre-eminent being *âsh*, a soup of legumes and herbs. Its importance in Iran can be measured by the fact that a cook is called *âshpaz* (soup cook) and the kitchen *âshpaz khâneh* (soup cook house). The varieties of *âsh* are wide-ranging and numerous, and the ingredients dictated not only by the season and the regions but also by the medical requirements and metabolic needs of the family. In times of sickness, the herbs and cures are blended in a delicious soup of comfort and remedy.

But *âsh* is not just for the sick-room. It is a meal of celebration and is an important feature in family gatherings, neighborhood get-togethers, prayer meetings, and seasonal celebrations. It is the main sustenance of the poor during the winter months, but can be frequently found on the tables of the rich. The myths and legends surrounding it reveal more of the people's warmth and wisdom than all the volumes written about the nation's long history.

The sixteenth-century cookbook of the Safavid court contained nearly fifty recipes for *âsh*. These were broken down into three groups, one containing meat, another wheat and barley, and a third (by far the largest group) having a sour flavor.

The first group had the richest combination of ingredients—and the most exotic names: Jeweled Soup, Sparrow Tongue Soup, Darling's Hair Soup, Cummerbund Soup, and Ear Ring Soup. But most of the *âsh* popular today come from the second and third groups, which while not meat-based do sometimes include meat, whose simple names are derived from the principal flavoring ingredients.

Much more recently, in a Persian book on food, *Khorâk-e Shenâkhteh*, written by Dr. Jazareri in 1981, *âsh* was broken down into three quite different groups, based on pasta, cereals, and rice. Dr. Jazareri discusses the relative merits of each group in medical terms, suggesting that the popular garnish of *kashk* (dried yogurt) and/or vinegar in *âsh* serves to aid digestion and reduce flatulence. He also looks at the balancing of "hot" and "cold" ingredients (see page 287), a factor that is very important to the Persian housewife in caring for her family.

The *âbgoosht* (literally, meat juices) group of soups contains meat as its main ingredient. Do not be misled, however, into supposing that *âbgoosht* never contains herbs or vegetables because it always does. There is some variety within this group, but the basic recipe is much the same all over the country.

Another group includes both *shoorbâ* and *haleem*. The word *shoorbâ* (or *shorbâ*) is originally Old Persian meaning "salted water" or broth. The food historian Charles Perry notes in *Petits Propos Culinaires* that *shorbâ* has come to mean "soup" in all the Arab countries of the Middle East as well as in many countries influenced by Islam: the Balkan countries, Ethiopia, Central Asia, Pakistan, and northern India, as well as the eastern provinces of China. Ironically, in Persia today, *shoorbâ* simply means a plain rice and herb broth usually made for invalids and convalescents.

As for *haleem* (or *harriseh*, as it used to be called in the sixteenth century) this thick elastic concoction barely falls into the category of soup at all, being more akin to a thick porridge. Indeed, in Iran *haleem* serves as an early morning winter meal, a dish that is both sweet and savory and very sustaining. This too can be found in many other countries of the Middle East.

Shoorbâ and *haleem* are much the same all over Iran. But the other soup dishes vary slightly from one region to another, even from one district to another. Although most provinces and even some towns claim a speciality, the regional differences these days are rapidly becoming less easy to discern. It is said that the best *âbgoosht* is made by the housewives of Azerbaijan in northwest Iran, while the central provinces of the high plateau claim supremacy in their varieties of *âsh*.

But fine *âsh* comes from many regions: from Mazandaran comes *âsh-e sak*, a soup of spinach with split peas, tiny meatballs, and sweet marjoram, and from the mountains of Azerbaijan comes *âsh-e goosh barreh*, an ancient recipe of ravioli. Tehran is famed for its *âbgoosht bozbâsh*, made of lamb, beans, tomatoes, cilantro, and lime juice, but a soup made with very similar ingredients is found in many other parts of Iran when it is often called *âbgoosht deezee*.

The garnishes too are intriguing: a soup of mung beans, herbs, and turnips is strewn with a mixture of fried ground meat, split peas, and tomatoes, or a soup of beans and noodles is garnished with dried mint softened in hot fat with crisply fried onions, or perhaps sour cream is blended with turmeric. A summer soup is garnished with tiny rose petals and chopped mint. The permutations are often exotic and endlessly surprising.

I have given the recipes in order of consistency, the first, *goosh barreh* (see "Lamb's Ear" Soup, page 122), being a fairly thin broth, through the *âbgoosht* and on to the thick vegetable soups and finally to the dishes of *haleem* that are so thick as almost to warrant the title of paste. This is only a representative selection of the vast range of soups enjoyed in Persia today. I have tried to include the most popular as well as one or two that are less well known.

Meat stock or whey (the liquid from strained yogurt) may be used instead of water in all the recipes in this section unless otherwise stated.

"LAMB'S EAR" SOUP
Goosh Barreh

According to the food historian Charles Perry, "boiled stuffed pasta" was known in Persia more than 1,500 years ago, when this particular dish was known as *jooshpâreh* or "boiled pieces." One thousand years later, in sixteenth-century Isfahan, the Safavid court cookbook gave four different versions of *jooshpâreh*: the little pasta parcels could be steamed or boiled in water and served with a sauce, or boiled in meat stock, or boiled with tiny meatballs (known as "sparrow's heads").

Goosh barreh also means "lamb's ear," and many people think the dish is so named because the little pasta parcels have more than a passing resemblance to lambs' ears. Coincidentally, the factory-made pasta shells (gnocchi) are commonly known in modern Iran as *gooshvâreh* (earrings).

Mrs. Khavar has a recipe in *The Art of Cookery in Gilan* for *doshvâreh* that calls for stuffed pasta parcels to be boiled in water, drained, and served with a sauce. But the recipe below (given to me by Miss Iran Doorandish, who comes from the northwestern province of Azerbaijan) says the parcels should be boiled in a well-flavored meat stock and dished up altogether as rich soup. She says that the soup should have a slightly hot, spicy flavor. Miss Doorandish tells me *goosh barreh* is still very popular in the bitter winters of Azerbaijan, and with very good reason.

Stock
6 fresh tomatoes *or* 3 tablespoons tomato paste
about 1½ quarts good meat *or* chicken stock
½ teaspoon red chili powder
salt and pepper
1 cup chopped fresh parsley
2-3 sprigs of fresh oregano *or* ½ teaspoon dried oregano

Filling
1 medium onion
½ pound ground meat

Pasta
3½ cups pasta flour
½ teaspoon baking powder
1 medium egg
about 1 tablespoon oil

Skin and chop the tomatoes and add to the stock with the chili powder, salt, and pepper. Leave to simmer for at least 30 minutes.

Grate the onion into the meat and mix well together. Fry in a little oil until cooked through, adding salt and pepper to taste. Set aside to cool.

Mix the flour with the baking powder and a pinch of salt and, with a fork, stir in the egg and oil, adding a little water slowly to mix to a fairly stiff dough. Knead well until it is pliable and smooth.

Roll out thinly on a floured board and cut out 2¹/₂-inch rounds with a pastry cutter. Cup the rounds in your hand, place a small teaspoon of meat mixture in the center, and pinch and twist both ends to seal. Dredge with flour and drop each one into the gently simmering soup. Work quickly so that the early ones do not overcook. Stir from time to time.

Simmer for 1 hour, stirring occasionally to make sure the "lamb's ears" do not stick to the bottom.

Ten minutes before serving, add the chopped parsley and oregano.

Dish up into a warmed tureen and serve with warm bread and fresh herbs.

✿ ✿

ONION SOUP
Eshkeneh

Legend has it that the name of this broth is derived from the Ashkanians, the ancient Persian Arsacid dynasty that held sway over Parthia in 230BC. The Persians and the Greeks both believed that onions gave men courage and fortitude, and the pots of onion soup, filled to the brim with broken pieces of dried bread, were the mainstay of the Ashkani foot soldiers serving King Arsaces.

While it is impossible to prove the myth beyond doubt, there is no reason why it should not be true nor why so simple a dish should not have survived unchanged. Similar dishes, which might have descended from this broth, or, more likely, developed independently over the years, can be found in other parts of the world. French onion soup, for example, is remarkably similar, even to the addition of croutons.

In Iran, this soup has generally been dismissed as a humble peasant dish. Served with dried bread soaked in it, it has served as a tasty and filling meal for villages cut off by snow, avalanche, or flood in the hard winter months.

In recent years, however, it has gained some credence among westernized Iranians looking back to their roots. In the 1960s and 1970s, it became fashionable in Tehran to serve *eshkeneh* as a first course. The enforced exile of many Iranians in the 1980s has given this simple dish an air of nostalgic respectability.

....

3 large onions
1½ tablespoons all-purpose flour
½ tablespoon dried fenugreek leaf
1 teaspoon turmeric
salt and pepper
3 medium eggs
dried bread (Persian *lavâsh or taftoon or* croutons)

....

Finely slice the onions and fry them slowly in oil until softened and golden brown.

Stir in the flour and the dried fenugreek, then add the turmeric, salt, and pepper, and, stirring, constantly, add about 1 quart water. Cover, bring back to a boil, then simmer gently for at least an hour.

Just before serving, increase the heat and pour the beaten eggs slowly into the boiling broth, or slip whole eggs directly into it.

Dish up into a soup tureen and add the dried bread, broken into small pieces. Serve with fresh bread and vinegar. Have some Pickled Stuffed Eggplant (see page 218) on the side.

LAMB SOUP
Âbgoosht-e Koobideh

Âbgoosht is popular among all classes, and during the winter months especially it is the meal that sustains the poor of the cities and villages alike. It forms a complete two-course meal, the meat and the beans being strained and pounded into a coarse purée to be eaten with bread, onions, and pickles while the strained broth is served as a separate appetizer—rather like the celebrated bouillabaisse of Marseilles, which can likewise be served as two courses. Bouillabaisse also contains saffron.

These two common features in two otherwise totally dissimilar soups testify to the ancient historical links between the French Mediterranean port of Marseilles and the distant Persian desert. When the Persians first conquered the Greek settlement of Phocaea (near present-day Turkish Izmir) in 600BC many of its inhabitants fled westward along the shores of the Mediterranean, finally establishing a western outpost by the name of Masilla (the modern Marseilles). Four hundred years later the Persians and Greeks together, with the help of the Massilians, defended Phocaea against the invading Romans. Clearly there were extensive contacts between the ancient Persians in Ionia and the peoples of the western Mediterranean ports. Today, of course, the connection can only be seen as tenuous. Yet it must also be said that old eating habits die hard.

In Persia today, saffron has been replaced mostly by the equally colorful and infinitely cheaper turmeric and, much more recently, by the ubiquitous tomato. *Âbgoosht* is a working man's dish, cooked in great quantity and sold in small individual cooking pots called *deezee* that have a curved base to sit snugly in the charcoal fire. The pots have given their name to the dish, for *âbgoosht* is equally well known by the name of *deezee*.

In days gone by, a piece of *roghan-e donbeh*, tail fat (see page 28) would have added extra richness. (There are tales of poor young men who would smear their mouths with fat so that others would think they had just dined lavishly on a fine bowl of *âbgoosht*.)

This nourishing dish is also popular in the home. Substantial quantities are made, and the meat paste is served with bread as a hot or cold snack. Faced with a sudden and unexpected increase in the number of guests to feed, a housewife can simply add extra water. *"Âb-e deezee-râ ziyâd kun"* ("Add extra water to the soup") is a famous refrain.

The lid should fit the pot closely so that all the flavors of the meat and vegetables are retained during the long slow cooking. Flurry and hurry are the natural enemies of this dish. A good Persian *âbgoosht* is best made when the cook is at peace with herself and the world.

1¼ cups chickpeas
1¼ cups pinto beans
2 medium onions
1 pound lamb on the bone
1 heaping teaspoon turmeric
½ teaspoon cinnamon
2-3 teaspoons dried lime powder *or* the juice
   of 2 lemons
1 pound tomatoes
1-2 tablespoons tomato paste
salt and pepper

Garnish
1 small onion, thinly sliced in rounds

Pick over and wash the peas and beans and leave to soak in warm water for an hour or so.

Chop the onions coarsely. Trim the meat of excess fat and wash.

Put the peas, beans, onion, and meat in a large pan with the turmeric, cinnamon, and dried lime powder (or lemon juice). Cover generously with about 2 quarts water, put on the lid, and bring to a boil slowly, then simmer gently for 2-3 hours until all is tender.

Skin the tomatoes, chop coarsely, and add to the soup with the tomato paste, salt, and pepper. Simmer for another 20 minutes.

To dish up, strain the meat and vegetables and put to one side. Serve the broth with fresh bread and herbs.

Separate the meat from the bone, then mash the meat and vegetables together to make a coarse paste. Adjust the seasoning. Pile the paste on a plate and garnish with fresh onion rings. Serve with warm bread, fresh herbs, and pickles.

LAMB AND HERB SOUP
Âbgoosht Bozbash

Replace the tomatoes with one bunch each fresh parsley and scallions, finely chopped, and add 1 tablespoon dried fenugreek.

CABBAGE AND CARROT SOUP
Âsh-e Kalam-o Haveej

It is hard to imagine the ubiquitous carrot, so cheap, cheerful, and commonplace, having its prehistoric origins in the far eastern reaches of the Persian Empire. During its long migration, it has been treated with both delight and disdain.

The early dark purple carrot was one of the spoils of war of Alexander the Great when he conquered the Persian Empire. From the marauding Macedonians to the philosophic Greeks and hence to the Romans was a relatively short journey. But the Romans showed little enthusiasm for the carrot and its westward journey stopped short for several centuries. The Arabs recognized its true worth and transported it along the north coast of Africa and up into Spain, from where it spread to the rest of Europe, changing from a dull color to its familiar orange in seventeenth-century Holland.

In Persia, the carrot is rarely regarded as common root vegetable but, rather, as an uncommon sweet. It is conserved and preserved in jams and syrups. Partnered with orange peel and almonds, it makes an elegant contribution to stews and rice dishes, and it adds color and flavor to this light and tasty soup.

I am indebted to Mrs. Pouran Ataie for this recipe. She tells me it was popular in Azerbaijan in her childhood, and remains one of her favorites today, and with good reason. It is quick and easy to prepare and the ingredients are available everywhere.

....

> **1 medium onion**
> **⅓ cup short grain rice**
> **1½ tablespoons tomato paste**
> **salt and pepper**
> **1 quart good meat *or* chicken stock**
> **2-3 medium carrots**
> **2 cups chopped white cabbage**
> **3-4 cups fresh spinach *or* 10 ounce pack of chopped**
> **frozen spinach**
> **1 bunch parsley**
> **1 bunch cilantro *or* extra parsley**
> **1 tablespoon sour cream (optional)**

....

Slice the onion finely and fry in a little oil until golden.

Pick over and wash the rice, and stir in with the onion. Add tomato paste, salt, pepper, and the stock, and simmer gently for 30 minutes.

Peel the carrots. Cut into large julienne strips and add to soup.

Clean and wash the spinach and herbs, shake dry, and chop finely. When cabbage and carrots are tender, add herbs to soup and simmer for 15 minutes more.

Just before serving, stir in the sour cream and bring back to a simmer.

Dish up into a warmed tureen and serve with warm bread and fresh herbs.

CREAM OF BARLEY SOUP
Soop-e Jo

I suspect that this soup entered Iran in the early part of this century, along with the White Russians fleeing the Bolshevik Revolution. Its Persian name *soop* implies an alien background. But over the past seventy years, it has become a firm favorite in the smarter restaurants and homes in Tehran where it is served as a first course—unlike the Persian potages, *âsh*, which constitute an entire meal.

It is quite delicious, especially when made with a good meat stock. The addition of lemon juice and sour cream gives a piquant Persian flavor to this rich and comforting soup.

----

1 cup pearl barley
2 medium leeks
2 medium onions
salt and pepper
about 1½ quarts good meat stock
1 large carrot
juice of 2 lemons
2 tablespoons sour cream

Garnish
chopped parsley

Wash the barley and leave to soak for 30 minutes.

Wash the leeks well, chop finely, and set aside.

Chop the onions and fry in a little oil until soft and golden. Stir in the salt and pepper and add the drained barley and leeks. Stir until all are coated with oil, then add about 1½ quarts of good meat stock. Cover, bring back to a boil, then simmer gently for two hours. Stir from time to time, adding a little more stock if necessary.

Grate the carrot and add to the soup with half the lemon juice. Continue simmering until the barley is completely soft.

Just before dishing up, stir in the sour cream and lemon juice to taste.

Dish up into a warmed tureen and garnish with chopped parsley.

NOODLE SOUP
Âsh-e Reshteh

This soup is thought to be one of the earliest known. In ancient Zoroastrian Persia it used to be known as *shuli*; its main green vegetables were spinach and fresh clover. Instead of noodles, the flour and water were mixed to a thin paste and poured directly into the soup to thicken and enrich it. In later years, water was flicked on to the flour that was rolled into tiny balls (known as *omâj*), which were then added to the soup. But by the Sassanian period (AD500) the flour and water were being made into noodles, as they still are today.

In pre-Islamic times, noodle soup used to be eaten on the first day of each month, a habit that was carried over into Muslim Iran, for it is still served at the first prayer meeting of every month.

Noodle soup, or *âsh-e pushteh-pâ* (pilgrim's soup) as it is sometimes called, is also served on the eve of departure of a loved one on the long and arduous journey to Mecca or of a cherished son setting off into the world. It is served as the main evening meal for all the relatives and neighbors who gather to bid farewell and to pray together for their safe return.

Noodle soup is one of the dishes made for religious pledges (*nazr*). These pledges are made as a thanksgiving to God for benign intervention in the affairs of the family: the miraculous recovery of a child from a long and serious illness or the safe return home of a much-loved family member after many years absence.

Such pledges involve the sharing of the family's joy and celebration and are often made on an annual basis, so that on the same day each year bowls of this delicious soup are brought to the door by a devout neighbor. Even in modern apartment buildings in Tehran, a family's happiness will be shared with all the residents of the block. (And when the bowls are returned, they should always contain a sample of the housewife's cooking from that day.) Such visits mark the passing of the years, and also serve to bring a community closer together, for no person can remain a stranger long among these constant reminders of shared celebration.

Noodle soup is specially favored for pledges since the tangle of noodles is thought to resemble the tangle of paths in one's life. They symbolize a fresh new start, and this is why noodle soup is often chosen to simmer on the stove during the transition from the old year to the new.

....

⅓ cup kidney beans*
⅓ cup chickpeas*
1 medium onion
½ teaspoon turmeric
salt and pepper

⅓ cup mung beans
⅓ cup whole brown lentils
juice of 1 lemon
sprinkling of dried dill and oregano
1 large bunch parsley *and/or* cilantro
1 bunch scallions *or* 1 medium leek
2 cups loosely packed spinach *or* beet greens
1 cup Persian noodles**
1 tablespoon *kashk* (see page 26) *or* sour cream

Garnish
1 tablespoon *na'nâ dâgh* (see page 42)
1 medium onion, sliced and crisply fried
1 teaspoon *kashk or* sour cream
sprinkling of turmeric

Pick over and wash the kidney beans and chickpeas and leave to soak separately for at least 3 hours, preferably overnight. Before using, bring the kidney beans to a rapid boil for ten minutes, then drain.

Slice the onion and fry in oil in a large saucepan until golden brown. Stir in the turmeric, salt, and pepper, then add the drained kidney beans and chickpeas. Cover with about 1½ quarts stock or water, put on the lid and bring to a boil, then simmer gently for 1 hour.

Carefully pick over and wash the mung beans and lentils. Add to soup with the lemon juice, dill, and oregano. Stir and simmer for another hour, adding a little more stock if necessary.

Clean, wash, and shake dry the herbs. Chop coarsely and add to soup. Simmer for 20 minutes more.

Add the noodles and simmer for another 5-10 minutes, stirring fairly frequently at this stage. Stir in the *kashk* or sour cream.

Dish up into a warmed tureen and, if liked, garnish with scallop-shaped swathes of *na'nâ dâgh* around the edge, then sprinkle fried onions around the scalloped circle. Put a couple of swirls of *kashk* or sour cream in the center and sprinkle just a little turmeric over them.

If liked, serve with extra bowls of *na'nâ dâgh* and fried onions. Vinegar and warm bread should be on the table.

---

* 15-ounce cans of kidney beans and chickpeas may be used and should be added at the same time as the mung beans and lentils.
** Persian soup noodles (*Reshteh-ye âsh*) are available from Iranian stores, or can be made at home (see page 285). Flat Chinese or Italian noodles may also be used, but must be broken into short lengths before being added.

MUNG BEAN SOUP
Âsh-e Mâsh

Mung beans have been familiar in Persia for centuries, so that when the Zoroastrians fled to India during the Arab conquest they continued to make use of these beans. Today, the most famous Parsee (Persian) dish in Bombay is *dhansak*, which always contains mung beans.

In Persia today, mung beans are also still used to thicken soups. This soup, unlike *dhansak*, contains little or no meat or any of the hot Indian spices. It relies solely on the fresh taste of herbs and turnips (and, of course, the mung beans) for its flavor.

This soup (sometimes also known as *âsh-e shalgam*) is served to anyone suffering with a cold, for young turnips are highly regarded for their fresh peppery flavor and beneficial effects. For those of a cold temperament also, "hot" spices such as cinnamon, ginger, and pepper are added to give warmth and energy as well as relieve congestion. Mung beans are full of goodness and the herbs and spinach brim with vitamins.

The mung beans are often boiled separately in a little water. After about 15 minutes, when extra water is needed, add a little cold water. The green skins pop off and rise to the surface. Skim them off and add the beans (and the cooking liquid) to the soup. This is recommended when feeding invalids as the skins are believed to be constipating.

½ cup short grain rice
¾ cup mung beans
1 medium onion
½ teaspoon turmeric
salt and pepper
juice of 1 lemon
4 cups loosely packed spinach *or* beet greens
1 large bunch parsley *and/or* cilantro
1 bunch scallions *or* 1 leek
2 tablespoons fresh dill *or* ½ teaspoon dried fenugreek
1 pound turnips

*Garnish**
1 small onion
¼ pound lamb, diced very small *or* ground
2 tablespoons yellow split peas
1 teaspoon tomato paste
1 teaspoon liquid saffron (optional)
salt and pepper

Wash and put the rice to soak for 30 minutes.

Pick over and wash the mung beans and simmer in a little water for 15 minutes. Add cold water when necessary and skim off the green skins as they rise to the surface.

Slice the onion and fry briskly in oil until golden brown. Stir in the turmeric, salt, and pepper. Add the drained rice, the mung beans with their cooking liquid, lemon juice, and about 1½ quarts stock or water. Simmer for 30 minutes.

Clean, wash, and shake dry the spinach, scallions, and herbs. Chop finely and add to soup and simmer for 15 minutes.

Peel and dice the turnips and add to soup. Simmer for about 30 minutes until turnips are tender.

Meanwhile make the *gheimeh* garnish: chop and fry the onion in a small pan until golden, stir in the meat and fry until browned. Add the washed split peas, tomato paste, and enough water just to cover. Simmer, adding more water only if necessary. Cook until split peas and meat are tender: the *gheimeh* should be fairly dry. Add the saffron if using and stir in salt and pepper to taste.

Dish up the soup in a warmed tureen and strew the *gheimeh* garnish over it. Serve with warm bread and fresh herbs.

---

* Alternatively, grind ¼ pound lamb with 1 onion, salt, and pepper, make tiny but firm meatballs and drop in the soup at the same time as adding the stock.

POMEGRANATE SOUP
Âsh-e Anâr

The pomegranate bush is very beautiful. It has pretty little leaves edged in scarlet, and tiny delicate blooms in a deep shade of cerise. The young pomegranates first appear as graceful pale green droplets that slowly turn red as they swell and fill. The outer skin of the mature fruit becomes like a leather orb, which, when fully ripe, breaks open to reveal a ball of shining rubies, glistening and bursting with juice beneath. It thrives in the hot dry air of the foothills surrounding the central Persian desert.

The pomegranate has many uses in Persia. It is one of nature's loveliest and most permanent dyes; the seeds run with a rich tart juice that is made into a popular drink; it cools and cleanses the system and aids digestion, and is excellent for pregnant mothers. The juice is reduced to a dark, sharp syrup, which for centuries has been added to stews and soups to enhance the flavor and color—as in this popular winter soup.

To find such a fruit in the arid plateau of Iran must have seemed nothing short of a miracle to the ancient Persians. This may explain its importance in human history, for it vies with the grape and the fig in legend and myth. Iranians believe that Eve was tempted with a pomegranate in the Garden of Eden. Cyrus the Great, King of the Persians, is said to have wished for a number of good generals equal to the number of seeds in a pomegranate, while the Prophet Mohammed commanded, "Eat the Pomegranate, for it purges the system of envy and hatred."

The Arabs brought the pomegranate and its reputation westward in the seventh century. The kings and queens of Europe endowed the pomegranate with the attributes of fertility and, in medieval England, it became a popular flavoring and garnish.

....

½ cup short grain rice

¾ cup yellow split peas

2 medium onions

½ teaspoon each turmeric and cinnamon

salt and pepper

½ pound ground meat

1 bunch scallions

1 bunch parsley

1 bunch cilantro *or* extra parsley

3 sprigs fresh mint

6 tablespoons pomegranate syrup

3 tablespoons sugar

Garnish
1 tablespoon *na'nâ dâgh* (see page 42)
1 small onion, sliced and crisply fried

....

Pick over and wash the rice and split peas and leave to soak separately in water for at least half an hour.

Slice one of the onions and fry in oil until golden. Add the turmeric, cinnamon, salt, and pepper, then stir in the drained rice and peas. Add about 2 quarts stock or water, cover, and simmer for an hour.

In the meantime, grate the second onion into the meat, add salt and pepper, and with wet hands make tiny but firm meatballs. Drop directly into the soup as you make them.

Clean and wash the herbs, removing any coarse stems, shake dry and chop finely. Add to the soup and simmer for another 30 minutes, stirring from time to time, adding more stock if necessary.

Stir in the pomegranate syrup and sugar.

Dish up into a warmed tureen, and garnish with fried onion slices and swirls of *na'nâ dâgh*. Serve with warm bread and fresh herbs.

FRUIT SOUP
Âsh-e Meeveh

Soup made with fruit has an altogether different air about it. Such soups come from the central plateau and are often made during the winter months when a well-stocked kitchen comes into its own. The herbs, beans, and dried fruits are all blended into a heart-warming soup laden with the flavors of summer. For special occasions, meatballs would be added to the soup for extra flavor, but the soup is no less authentic if served without them.

⅓ cup chickpeas
⅓ cup red kidney beans
1 medium onion
½ teaspoon turmeric
salt and pepper
1 cup each parsley, cilantro, spinach, and chives
3 sprigs fresh mint *or* sprinkling of dried mint
¼ cup short grain rice
¼ cup pitted prunes
¼ cup dried apricots
¼ cup golden raisins
1 tablespoon dried barberries (page 25) *or* fresh sour grapes
juice of 1 lemon

Pick over and wash the chickpeas and kidney beans, then leave to soak in fresh water for at least three hours, preferably overnight. Boil the kidney beans rapidly for ten minutes, then drain.

Finely slice the onion and fry in oil until golden brown. Stir in the turmeric, salt, and pepper, then add the drained peas and beans. Cover with about 1 quart water or stock and simmer for two hours.

Pick over and wash the herbs, removing any coarse stems, shake dry and chop finely. Add to the soup and simmer for another 15 minutes.

Pick over and wash the rice and add to the soup. Add the halved and pitted prunes and dried apricots and simmer for another 30 minutes.

Wash the golden raisins, dried barberries, and sour grapes and add along with the lemon juice.

Dish up into a warm tureen and serve with warm bread and fresh herbs.

SPINACH SOUP
Âsh-e Sak

In her splendid *Vegetable Book*, Jane Grigson relates that in AD647, the great Chinese emperor T'ai Tsung asked tributary rulers to send him their best plants. The King of Nepal sent him spinach, which had just recently arrived from Persia. Mrs. Grigson concludes that today the Chinese name for spinach, *poh ts'ai* (Persian vegetable), reflects its origins.

As of course does the English word for spinach, which is derived, via the Arabs, from the Persian word *espenâj*. It is strange, therefore, that this Persian soup, which has spinach as its main component, should be called *âsh-e sak*. *Sak* or *saag* is the Indian word for spinach, so one would assume that this soup must have come from India, possibly via the Persian Gulf or the southeastern province of Baluchistan. Yet it is thought to have originated in the Caspian region. In any event, it is quite delicious and full of rich goodness and Persian piquancy.

---

1 medium onion
1 pound spinach
1/2 teaspoon turmeric
salt and pepper
1 cup split peas
1 cup rice flour
1/2 cup Seville orange juice *or* lemon juice

Meatballs (optional)
1/2 pound ground lamb *or* veal
1 medium onion

Slice and fry the onion gently in a little oil until golden.

Wash the spinach thoroughly, shake dry, chop finely. Set aside.

Pick over and wash the split peas and stir into the onions. Add the turmeric, salt, pepper, and spinach. Stir over heat for half a minute, then add 1 1/2 quarts water or stock. Cover and simmer for 45 minutes.

If including meatballs, grate the onion into the ground meat, add salt and pepper, and with wet hands, make small but firm meatballs. Drop directly into simmering soup and cook for 15 minutes.

Blend the rice flour with 2 tablespoons water until smooth. Pour slowly into the soup, stirring constantly. Add the orange juice and simmer for 2 or 3 minutes more.

Dish up into a warmed tureen. Serve with warm bread and fresh herbs.

"PLEDGE" SOUP
Âsh-e Nazri

Like noodle soup, *âsh-e nazri* (or *âsh-e sholleh ghalamkâr*, literally scribe's soup, as it is sometimes called) is frequently chosen to serve at prayer meetings for the recovery of a sick child or the safe return of a loved son departing on a long journey. All the ingredients for the soup must be donated by those who wish for the return of the child (to health or to home) so that the rich are not accused of bribery or the poor excluded through poverty.

Neighbors, friends, and family each bring a portion of legumes, meat, or herbs, and assist with the stirring. A great deal of loving effort always goes into the making of a "pledge" soup, and such is the concerned and neighborly confusion surrounding the cook on the day of preparation that any hubbub is often likened to *sholleh ghalamkâr* by Iranians. There should always be more than enough soup to distribute to all the neighbors as well as to the poor.

If the prayers are answered, the soup will be made annually as pledged, usually on the nearest saint's day. Mrs. Khavar, in *The Art of Cookery in Gilan*, gives a recipe for *âsh-e nazri* that calls for 2¼ pounds each of the legumes, 9 pounds of wheat, and 18 pounds of meat. It is a staggering quantity to contemplate in any domestic kitchen; so that in the recipe below I have replaced each pound with one ounce, which will serve 12 people very nicely.

Mrs. Khavar recommends each ingredient be cooked separately, probably because each neighbor would prepare her own contribution before bringing it to the central cooking pot. In the recipe given here, I instead suggest adding each ingredient to the soup according to its cooking time.

----

1 cup wheat berries
⅓ cup chickpeas
⅓ cup kidney beans
1 pound lamb on the bone
2 medium onions
vegetable oil
⅓ cup lentils
⅓ cup fava beans
⅓ cup pinto beans
⅓ cup mung beans
⅓ cup short grain rice
4 cups herbs (chives, cilantro, spinach, and dill)
salt and pepper
½ cup *kashk* (see page 26) *or* sour cream

Garnish
1 small onion
½ teaspoon turmeric
salt and pepper
¼ pound ground meat
⅓ cup split peas
2 teaspoons liquid saffron (see page 36)

Soak the wheat berries for 24 hours. Soak the chickpeas and kidney beans separately overnight. Boil kidney beans rapidly for ten minutes before using in the soup.

Strain the wheat berries, cover with fresh water, add a little salt, and bring to a boil. Reduce heat and simmer gently until cooked. (As the wheat berries soften, the soup will need constant stirring.) Add more water if necessary. When the wheat berries are cooked, strain to remove husks. Reserve both wheat berries and stock.

Wash the meat, sprinkle with salt and pepper, cover with water, and simmer gently until very tender. Strain, keeping the stock. Discard the bones and pound the meat (or put in a food processor). Set aside.

In a large pot, slice the onions and fry in a little oil until golden brown. Add the meat, wheat berries, drained chickpeas, and kidney beans and generously cover with both the wheat berries and meat stock and more water. Bring back to a boil and simmer gently for two hours, stirring frequently.

In the meantime, make the *gheimeh* garnish. Chop the onion and fry in a little oil. Add the turmeric, salt, pepper, and ground meat. Stir until well browned, then add the washed split peas, cover with water, and simmer gently until meat and peas are tender, adding more water only if necessary. The garnish should be fairly dry. Put on one side.

Pick over and wash the lentils, fava, and pinto beans. Add to the soup. Simmer for another hour, with frequent stirring.

Pick over and wash the mung beans. Put in a small pot with a little water to simmer gently. After 15 minutes, add cold water to make the skins pop off. Skim off the skins, then add beans and cooking water to soup.

Pick over and wash the rice. Add to soup and simmer, stirring, for 20 minutes more.

Clean and wash the herbs, removing any coarse stalks. Shake dry and chop finely. Add to soup and simmer for 30 minutes, still stirring.

Add salt and pepper to taste. The soup should be well amalgamated, quite thick and rather viscous. Just before serving, stir in cream or *kashk*.

Dish up into a warmed soup tureen. Garnish with the split pea and meat preparation. Pour the liquid saffron over all. Serve with warm Persian (or pita) bread and fresh herbs. Persian pickles and a tarragon vinegar should be on the table.

BARLEY PORRIDGE
Haleem

It is said that this dish, like many others, was invented by the sixth century Persian King Khosrow and that when the Muslims conquered Persia a century later, it became a firm favorite of the prophet. Its fame and popularity were thus assured and it spread all over the Middle East.

In many Arab countries today it is known as *harriseh*, and is indeed still sometimes called that in the southern regions of Persia, where it has long been regarded as the finest winter breakfast dish. The specialty restaurants that make barley porridge start their preparations in the evening and stir the porridge through the night to ensure the right consistency. Their first customers arrive well before dawn.

This porridge used to be a special treat for breakfast on Friday (the weekly holiday). A young member of the family would be prevailed upon to set off before sunrise to buy a great bowl of porridge and some fresh thick crusty bread, *nân-e barbari*. With such a meal under one's belt, the whole day took on a new meaning.

....

1 cup wheat berries*
1 pound lamb *or* turkey on the bone
1 medium onion
½ teaspoon turmeric
salt and pepper
⅓ cup chickpeas (optional)

Garnish
3 tablespoons clarified unsalted butter
powdered cinnamon
superfine sugar

....

Put the wheat berries to soak for 24 hours. Strain, add fresh water and a little salt, bring to a boil, then reduce heat and simmer gently for two hours. When the wheat berries begin to soften, stir constantly and cook for at least another two hours, adding more water if necessary.

In the meantime, wash the lamb or turkey and put in a saucepan with the coarsely chopped onion, turmeric, salt, pepper, and chickpeas, if using. Cover with water, bring to a boil, then reduce heat and simmer gently until the meat is very tender. Strain, keeping the stock and discarding the flavorings (except the chickpeas, which may be kept for a garnish if wished).

Separate the meat from the bones, discard the bones, and pound the meat in a pestle and mortar (or in a food processor) until the meat is smooth. Set aside.

When the wheat berries are soft, strain through a cheesecloth to remove husks, then return to pan (with any liquid) and heat through very gently, stirring constantly, until thick.

Take a little of the wheat berry soup and mix it into the meat until all is well blended and smooth, then stir in the simmering wheat berries, stirring constantly. The meat stock should be added only if necessary and after the meat and wheat berries are thoroughly blended. The porridge should be homogenous and slightly elastic.

Dish up into a warmed bowl (or individual bowls) and garnish with melted butter and the chickpeas. Sprinkle with cinnamon and sugar. Have extra cinnamon and sugar on the table along with plenty of warm crusty Persian bread.

---

*There are a number of shortcuts. Cream of oats or rolled oats are fine substitutes, which are quick to prepare and dispense with the need for hours of stirring.

MUNG BEAN AND RICE SOUP
Âsh-e Sholleh Mâsh

This is one of a number of dishes known as *sholleh*, in which short grain rice is cooked until it is soft and thick. According to the culinary historian Charles Perry, *sholleh* was brought to Persia by the Mongolians in the thirteenth century. Three hundred years later, some fifteen *sholleh* dishes, mostly savory, were listed in the Safavid cookbook.

Today, however, *sholleh* has all but disappeared from the cuisine of Persia, except for two or three soup dishes (*sholleh ghalamkar* on page 138 being the most notable), and one very celebrated dessert, *sholleh zard* (see page 254).

3/4 **cup short grain rice**
1 **cup mung beans**
2 **medium onions**
1/2 **teaspoon turmeric**
salt and pepper
1/2 **pound ground lamb** *or* **veal**

Pick over the rice, wash, and leave to soak in water for about 30 minutes.

Pick over the mung beans, wash and put on to simmer in a little water. When necessary add a little cold water, then skim off the green skins and discard. Set aside the beans and cooking liquid.

Slice the onions finely and fry in oil until soft and golden. Stir in the turmeric, salt, and pepper, add the meat and fry, stirring, for 5 minutes.

Add the drained rice and the beans, stir thoroughly, then add about 1 quart stock or water. Cover and simmer for an hour or more until rice and beans are soft. Stir from time to time, adding more stock or water if necessary.

Dish up in a warmed tureen and serve with warm bread, fresh herbs and vinegar.

EGGPLANT PORRIDGE
Haleem Bâdenjân

If eggplant is the "poor man's caviar," then this dish must be the "poor man's paté." It is delicious eaten with warm bread or hot toast, and is economical and easy to make, and very nourishing too. I am indebted to Mrs. Parvin Zeineddin for allowing me to use her lovely recipe.

---

1 pound lean boneless lamb
1¼ cups black-eyed peas *or* lentils
2 medium onions
vegetable oil
salt and pepper
½ teaspoon turmeric
1 pound eggplant
2 tablespoons *kashk* (see page 26) *or* sour cream

Garnish
2 teaspoons *na'nâ dâgh* (see page 42)
1 small onion, sliced and crisply fried
1 tablespoon chopped walnuts

Trim and dice the meat and leave to soak for a few minutes. Pick over and wash the legumes and leave them to soak for a few minutes also.

Slice and fry the onions in a little oil until golden. Add the drained meat and peas or lentils, salt, pepper, turmeric, and about 1 quart water. Bring to a boil, then simmer gently for an hour or so until the meat and beans or lentils are quite tender, adding a little more water if necessary.

In the meantime, peel and cut the eggplant into ¼-inch thick rings and sprinkle with salt. After half an hour, dry off and fry until golden.

Add the eggplant slices and pound together with the meat and beans or lentils with a wooden meat pounder, if necessary adding up to 1 cup water to keep the mixture soft but not liquid. Stir over a gentle heat, until all the liquid is absorbed and the mixture begins to come away from the sides of the pan. Remove from heat and beat in the *kashk* or sour cream until well blended.

Pour into a shallow bowl and garnish with *na'nâ dâgh*, crisply fried onions, and chopped walnuts.

GRILLS

Beneath the Bough

Cooking over open flames is almost as old as the discovery of fire itself. Grilling, broiling, toasting, and roasting are all words that originally meant cooking over an open fire and they all entered the English language from Saxony and Normandy a very long time ago. Much more recently, another word for the same method, barbecue, was introduced through the word *barbacoa*, which was originally Spanish, meaning to cook a whole carcass on barbs over a fire. It has since come to mean any grilled food cooked out of doors.

The latest addition to our vocabulary, kebab, comes from the Persian word *kabâb*. Its use spread from Iran across the Middle East in the seventh and eighth centuries and into northern India in the seventeenth century. It has only become commonly accepted into the English language over the past thirty years or so.

In Persian, *kabâb kardan* simply means "to grill." In Persian poetry, *jeegar kabâb kardan* (literally "to grill liver") means to break someone's heart with love or grief. In the past the kitchen was known in some parts of Iran as *kabâb-khâneh* (kebab house).

Today, kebab has come to mean any food threaded on a skewer and grilled over charcoal. Steaks and hamburgers, though grilled, are not kebabs because they are not on a skewer, though in all other respects the method of cooking is the same.

In Iran, the art of *kabâb*-making has reached a high point of sophistication, despite the fact that grilling is a relatively primitive method of cooking. The "national dish" of Iran is *chelow kabâb* (rice with lamb kebab). The simple ingredients of this dish—plain white rice with grilled lamb—belie the skill of its preparation and the subtlety of its flavors.

To serve *chelow kabâb* at home with all the accompaniments needs careful planning and the services of an assistant. Good organization is vital when serving: two pairs of hands are necessary to grill the kebabs and to dish up the rice simultaneously.

The *chelow* should be prepared as in the recipe given on page 58. Since each person must mix the rice with a generous pat of butter, a fresh raw egg yolk (which cooks in the hot rice during mixing), and a liberal sprinkling of sumac, it is important that all these accompaniments are prepared beforehand.

The fresh eggs should be broken and the whites removed so that only the yolks remain in the shell, which may be stood in egg cups, or, as is done in traditional Persian restaurants, wedged upright together on a plate of salt. (This should be done no earlier than 15 minutes before serving.) Cut the butter into pats and put on the table along with a

144

"shaker" of sumac. Prepare a large jug of *âb-doogh*, the traditional yogurt and mint drink (see page 243). A bowl of fresh herbs and some fresh bread are always to be found on a Persian *sofreh* (dining cloth).

While all this is going on, the charcoal should be lit at least half an hour before you wish to serve (or according to the instructions on the charcoal bag). When all is ready, start grilling the kebabs and at the same time (this is where the second pair of hands comes in) dish up and serve the rice.

For formal meals, the rice should be garnished with saffron and served on a large dish in the center of the table. The kebabs too should be presented on a single dish and passed around.

In the old days, when the specialty restaurants offered as much *chelow kabâb* as you could eat, waiters would go around the restaurant with skewers of hot kebabs held high, ready to serve immediately anyone who wanted more.

As far as traditional medicine (see page 8) is concerned, this is considered to be the perfect meal: the "cold" rice is balanced with "hot" eggs while the "cold" sumac balances the "hot" lamb. At the same time, the sourness of the sumac not only adds piquancy to the juicy lamb, but aids the digestion. The butter gives an extra rich creaminess to the rice. In summer and early autumn, a skewer of tiny grilled tomatoes add a touch of seasonal freshness.

It can be seen that such a meal has nothing in common with the chunky bits of rubbery meat, green pepper, and onion accompanied by a scoopful of glutinous rice that is so often served as a Middle Eastern delicacy in this country. The difference is greater than that between fresh whipped cream and collapsing aerosol cream.

Today, in the West there is a staggering variety of equipment for barbecues and grills that would astonish the average cook in Iran, where the simple *manqal* reigns supreme. A *manqal* is a tin box standing on four little legs with the bottom pierced with holes. It is portable, adaptable, very cheap, and extremely effective. If no *manqal* is available, then a few well-placed bricks will serve as well.

The skewers are a different matter. They are long, made of aluminum and come in three widths: $1/8$-inch, $3/8$-inch, and 1-inch wide. Each width is for a different type of *kabâb*. Round narrow skewers like knitting needles with pretty handles should not be taken seriously. The meat twists around and around on the skewers, the handles get hot, and in any case, in Iran, the kebabs are never served on the skewer but are slid off on to the plate ready for eating.

The best kebabs are made on metal skewers, for the metal conducts the heat to cook the meat quickly and evenly from inside as well as out. The aluminum ones keep their shape and are easy to clean. The narrow skewers are used for chicken, liver, kidneys, sturgeon, and *tikkeh kabâb*. The medium width is used for *kabâb barg*, and the widest is for the ground meat kebabs.

When grilling Iranian kebabs, it is essential to remove the grid that normally is supplied with barbecues in the West. The skewers should be long enough to extend from one side of the charcoal to the other. Ideally, the kebabs should be 7-9 inches long, though this depends on the width of the grill and should be held about 4-6 inches above the charcoal.

Always use real charcoal for a truly authentic flavor. Let the coals burn well, then when the flames have died down and the coals are ash-white, spread them evenly across the *manqal*. The temperature may be raised, if needed, by fanning the coals until they glow red.

> Kazem soon produced a saucepan—our only tureen—half full
> of nearly boiling soup. Chicken and rice came next, and
> Kazem to my surprise, declared that he had cutlets of mutton
> "quite ready" and an omelet "to follow." He had accomplished
> all this, including potatoes, with nothing but three big stones
> for his fire place.
>
> Arthur Arnold, *Through Persia by Caravan*, 1877

FILLET KEBAB
Kabâb-e Barg

Kabâb-e barg (literally leaf kebab) transcends all other kebabs. The lamb is cut as thin as a leaf, delicately flavored with lemon juice and traces of onion, lightly grilled over glowing charcoal and basted with saffron and butter. The result is unfailingly tender and succulent.

With care and a little experience, it is not difficult to make this delicate kebab at home. Indeed in this country the hardest part is acquiring the correct cut of meat. *Kabâb-e barg* is made from lamb tenderloin, not a common cut in the West where it more usually appears cut across with the bone as lamb chops. With some fore-warning, a cooperative butcher will sometimes take out a lamb (tenderloin) fillet for you. Nowadays, too, some Iranian shops in the West have lamb tenderloin available in their refrigerators, and here, you can even get the meat cut into kebab-shaped pieces.

The tenderloin will seem quite expensive, but do not be deterred as a medium-sized fillet, properly cut, will make three large kebabs which, along with rice and accompaniments will be more than enough for four people. If, as is usual, Ground Meat Kebabs (see page 149) are also served, then you will have enough for a substantial meal for six or eight people.

If you cannot get a trimmed tenderloin of lamb, neck fillets are the best replacement. You will need at least two because they are much fattier and smaller than a tenderloin.

---

1 pound fillets of lamb tenderloin per person

Marinade
2 medium onions
juice of 2 lemons

Basting sauce
1 medium onion
¼ cup unsalted butter
juice of 1 lemon
salt and pepper
1 teaspoon liquid saffron (optional) (see page 36)

Accompaniments **(for the rice) per person (see page 144)**
1 egg
1 tablespoon unsalted butter
½ onion
1-2 teaspoons powdered sumac

Trim the lamb of all fat so that only the long "eye" of the fillet remains. Cut into three or four equal wedges (two for neck fillets). With the hand, press each wedge firmly on a wet board to flatten slightly, then with a very sharp knife, and holding the meat firmly with the palm of your hand, slice almost through the meat horizontally, but do not sever completely. Turn the wedge over and repeat the process, slicing from the opposite side, as shown below. Straighten out the meat to a long thin fillet, beat lightly with the blunt edge of a large knife. Leaving on the board, weave a medium-width skewer through the length of each one, as shown below. (It is not necessary to cut into pieces, for they will pull apart easily when cooked.)

Lay the skewers across a shallow oven tray, sprinkle with the juice of two lemons, cover (with an inverted oven tray), and leave to marinate for an hour or so.

An hour before grilling, grate two onions over them and leave to marinate.

For the basting sauce, melt the butter and mix with the juice from the onion and the lemon. Add the liquid saffron, salt, and pepper.

When the charcoal is burning white, grill the kebabs for a minute on one side, turn and baste, using a pastry brush. After a minute or two, turn and cook on the other side, continuing to baste.

When cooked, slide the kebabs off the skewer and serve immediately with the white rice explained on page 58 (see also description on page 144).

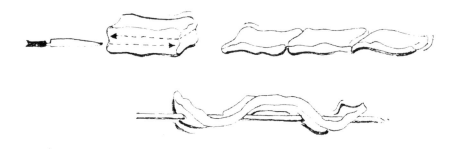

GROUND MEAT KEBAB
Kabâb Koobideh

Kabâb koobideh is the Persian equivalent of the American hamburger and is the favorite "take-out" food of the urban middle classes. It is served wrapped in warm Persian *sangak* bread (see page 50), and eaten with *torshi-ye leeteh* (see page 217), fresh herbs and a liberal sprinkling of sumac. It is also frequently served as part of the national dish *chelow kabâb* (see previous recipe). These ground kebabs are splendid affairs. They are large and well browned on the outside with a soft and succulent interior. *Chenjeh kabâb* are similar but smaller in size, while the tiny *looleh kabâb* are served as a light snack wrapped in bread.

The preparation of ground meat kebabs, as its Persian name implies (*koobideh* means pounded or kneaded) requires a fair amount of kneading. This is vital to achieve the necessary elasticity for the kebab mixture to adhere to the skewers. Some people try to cut a corner and add an egg to the mixture, but it shouldn't be necessary. Making use of the dough blade of a food processor for a few minutes saves a lot of aching arms. Kneading the mixture over slight warmth also helps a lot but be careful not to allow it to get too warm. The meat should be quite fatty so I suggest using lamb from the shoulder.

---

1 pound boned shoulder of lamb
1 medium onion
1 teaspoon dried breadcrumbs
salt and pepper
¼ teaspoon turmeric
¼ teaspoon baking powder

Grind the meat finely, first on its own, then with the onion. Place in a large heatproof bowl, adding the remaining ingredients, and knead well together for 15 minutes, partly over the low heat for a minute or two, until the mixture is smooth and sticky.

Wash your hands free of fat. Have a bowl of fresh cold water nearby and keeping your hands wet, take a medium handful of the mixture and mold all around an inch-wide skewer, pressing the mixture lightly with the fingers, making indentations all the way down the skewer; press firmly to the skewer at both ends. The kebabs should be about 7-8 inches long.

Grill the kebabs for two or three minutes on each side, turning twice. When nicely browned and cooked through, slip off the skewer onto some warm Persian (or pita) bread. Cover with bread to keep warm.

Serve immediately, with pickles and fresh herbs, or serve with rice as in the previous recipe.

CUBED LAMB KEBAB
Tikkeh Kabâb

Tikkeh means "small piece" in Persian, a most apt description of this kebab since traditionally it is made of small pieces of freshly-slaughtered lamb.

When the family bought a sheep for slaughter to celebrate the Feast of the Sacrifice, a professional butcher would be invited to perform the ritual slaughter in the courtyard of the family home. He would immediately cut the carcass into serving pieces and strip out the tenderloin. This would be cut into small pieces and threaded onto skewers, alternated with pieces of onion and tail fat (see page 28). Quickly grilled and sprinkled with salt, it was a tasty meal of celebration, the very freshness of the meat ensuring its tenderness. The remaining meat and sometimes the offal would be distributed to friends and neighbors.

Since it is often impossible to acquire such fresh meat, especially lamb tenderloin, *tikkeh kabâb* is usually made from any lean cut of lamb (trimmed leg, shoulder, or neck fillet) cut into small pieces of equal shape and well marinaded.

Various forms of this simple kebab are popular all over the Middle East and the subcontinent and have become familiar in the West in recent years via the Greek, Turkish, and most especially Indian restaurants. In the latter, "tikka" is now usually taken to mean spicy hot grilled chicken pieces.

1 pound lean boned lamb

Marinade
2 medium onions
juice of 2 lemons
salt and pepper

Basting sauce
¼ cup unsalted butter
juice of 1 lemon
½ teaspoon liquid saffron (optional) (see page 36)

Trim the meat of all fat, cut into neat cubes and wash. Grate the onions into a bowl, add the lemon juice, salt, pepper, and the drained meat. Mix well together, cover, and leave to marinate for at least 8 hours.

Opposite: Chicken Kebab (*joojeh kabâb*)

While the charcoal is burning through, prepare the basting sauce by mixing the melted butter, lemon juice, and liquid saffron (if using) together.

Thread the pieces of meat on to narrow skewers and grill over the charcoal, turning and basting until nicely browned and cooked through.

Serve with Persian (or pita) bread, fresh herbs, lemons, and sumac.

Opposite: Rice with Lamb Kebab (*chelow kabâb*)

SHISHLIK
Sheesh Kabâb

I suspect that this particular version of the familiar lamb kebab is a relative newcomer to Iran. *Sheesh* is Turkish for skewer (the Persian word is *seekh*) and it seems likely that it entered Europe, the US, and Iran from Turkey. Large green peppers are not indigenous to Iran and have become common only in recent years. The marinade is also different with its blending of oil and lemon juice. In Western restaurants, this kebab is frequently served with small amounts of rice, but in Iran it is eaten simply with bread, fresh herbs, and lemon juice.

---

1 pound lean boned lamb
2 large green peppers
4 medium onions
8 small tomatoes (optional)

Marinade
juice of 2 lemons
4 tablespoons oil
salt and pepper

Trim the meat of all fat, cut into neat 1-inch cubes and wash well and put in a bowl. Marinate in the lemon juice, oil, salt, and pepper for at least 3 hours, preferably overnight.

Cut up the green peppers into 1-inch squares, discarding the seeds. Cut the onions into quarters.

Thread the meat, pepper, onions, and tomatoes alternately onto a fine skewer and grill over glowing coals, turning frequently and basting them with the marinade.

When cooked, push the kebabs off the skewers onto a warmed dish and serve immediately.

Chicken Kebab
Joojeh Kabâb

If ever proof were required that atmosphere is an important part of the joy of eating, it is to eat *joojeh kabâb* in a Persian garden restaurant in Tehran on a summer's evening. The breeze from the snow-capped mountains just north of the city are a refreshing relief after the awful heat of the day. The sound of splashing fountains and tumbling streams drowns the distant roar of traffic. The scent of jasmine fills the air, except for the occasional drifting aroma of grilled chicken. The normal sounds of a restaurant are lost in the soft night air, and any cigarette smoke is filtered through the bowers of vines that give a pleasant privacy.

Such restaurants serve only *joojeh kabâb*, otherwise known as chicken kebab although in truth *joojeh* actually means pullet or young hen. Each portion consists of one whole pullet, carefully cut into eight pieces and threaded onto a single medium-sized skewer.

Young hens are available from good butchers and for an authentic *joojeh kabâb* they should be no bigger than 1½ pounds. Chicken pieces are also quite suitable. Quantities for one person.

1 whole young hen

Marinade
½ medium onion
juice of ½ lemon
salt and pepper

Basting sauce
½ teaspoon liquid saffron (see page 36)

Cut off the wings and legs and cut the latter into two pieces. Cut out the backbone, flatten the breast as much as possible, and cut across into two pieces. Wash, pat dry, and put in a bowl. Grate the onion over the chicken pieces, add the lemon juice, salt, and pepper, mix well until the chicken pieces are all coated. Leave to marinate for at least 3 hours, preferably overnight.

While the charcoal is burning through, thread the chicken pieces onto a fine skewer (wing, drumstick, thigh, two breasts, thigh, drumstick, and wing).

Grill gently, basting frequently with the marinade juices mixed with the liquid saffron.

When cooked thoroughly, slip the chicken off the skewers onto a warm plate. Serve with lemon juice, bread, and fresh herbs.

STURGEON KEBAB
Kabâb-e Ozunborun

The sturgeon of the Caspian Sea is fabled for its splendid caviar. As long ago as 300BC, Aristotle commented on the remarkable quality of sturgeon eggs, but it is from Russia that caviar has acquired its reputation as a rare and costly delicacy. It has been known in the West for at least 400 years but has only recently become available on a relatively wide scale, since the introduction of refrigeration and rapid transportation.

Caviar has never been fully appreciated by the Persians. The reasons for this are quite simple: sturgeon is so plentiful in the deep waters of the southern Caspian Sea that its caviar is eaten with salt by the local inhabitants with great pleasure, but with little regard to its worldwide luxury status. It would have been unthinkable in the past to transport such a commonplace and perishable commodity to the hot central plateau beyond the high Elborz mountains. And so it remained in the northern provinces of Gilan and Mazandaran: a cheap and delicious snack, rich in protein, plentiful in its season but impossible to keep for long by salting, smoking, or drying.

Things were different in Russia. Most of the northern Caspian Sea is very shallow. It is also very accessible to the flat, cold hinterland to the north, so that in Russia, sturgeon was not only less easily available close in to the shore, it also had a larger market to satisfy. Scarcity raises the price and leads to appreciation.

The Caspian is the largest inland sea in the world. It has been slowly evaporating for centuries, an occurrence that has been accelerated by the construction of dams on the Volga in the Soviet Union and the Sefid Rud in Iran. But the lowering level of the sea is more keenly felt in the northern shallows than in the deep southern waters along the Iranian coast. The great beluga sturgeon (which produces the most and the best caviar) prefers the deep waters and it is thus being driven inexorably southward away from the Russian shores.

In the meantime, in the early part of this century, Iran learned from the Russians how to commercially wash, salt, and pack caviar. Today Iran exports almost as much first-class caviar as Russia. The Iranians themselves eat very little of it, for the majority never acquired the taste. It was too expensive and too alien. As for the local population that had formerly eaten caviar in great quantity, it had suddenly become too expensive.

And yet for all that, the Persians gave their own Old Persian (or Pahlavi) word for sturgeon roe—khâveeyâr—to the rest of the world, except the Soviet Union where it is called ikra. Khâyeh in Pahlavi means eggs.

The flesh of the sturgeon, however, remains popular in the northern provinces and there are a number of recipes for its preparation from the Caspian region. One of the most delicious is grilling over charcoal. Its firm, slightly oily flesh lends itself very well to this method as it retains its shape and remains moist during cooking. Although sturgeon is not easily available here, a salmon will serve just as well.

The recipe below first appeared in *The Art of Cookery in Gilan* by Mrs. Zari Khavar, who kindly allowed me to reproduce it here.

---

1 sturgeon *or* salmon, about 3 pounds

Marinade
1 cup lemon juice
2 medium onions
black pepper

Basting sauce
2 tablespoons lemon juice
1½ tablepoons melted unsalted butter
1½ tablespoons tomato paste

Clean, scale and wash the fish, then remove the central bone and cut into 1-inch cubes.

Put in a bowl, grate the onions over the fish, add the lemon juice and pepper, and leave in a refrigerator to marinate overnight.

Make the basting sauce by mixing the lemon juice, melted butter, and tomato paste together in a small pan, bring to a boil, and keep to one side.

Thread the cubes onto thin skewers and grill over hot charcoal, basting two or three times during cooking.

LIVER KEBAB
Jigarak

Early on a crisp winter's morning in Tehran when the rising sun casts a pink glow over the snowy mountains and the frost glistens along the tree-lined avenues, the street vendors do a brisk trade in freshly grilled liver kebabs. A tantalizing smell rises from the corner *jigaraki* (liver kebab vendor) as he threads pieces of liver (and sometimes lamb's heart and kidneys as well) on to small skewers and fans the burning coals. As each kebab cooks and browns, it is salted, thrust off into a flap of warm bread and rolled into a delicious "sandwich" for immediate consumption. A breakfast to set you up for the day.

These inviting rolls are not only served as an early winter breakfast but also as late night snacks on a warm summer's evening. A night out at the cinema, followed by a stroll along the tree-lined boulevards while consuming a roll of grilled liver is the stuff of which fond memories are made.

½ pound lamb's liver per person
salt and pepper

While the charcoal is heating through, wash and cut the livers into small cubes and thread onto fine skewers.

Grill for two minutes on each side.

When nicely browned, slip off skewer straight onto a piece of Persian *taftoon* or pita bread and sprinkle with salt. Serve immediately. Fresh herbs and pickles should be on hand.

HEART AND KIDNEY KEBAB
Del-o-Golveh Kabâb

Cut up 2 lamb's kidneys and 1 heart (per person) into small squares and thread alternately onto skewers. These need 3-4 minutes grilling per side.

MEAT DUMPLINGS
Hidden Treasures

The word *koofteh* is usually translated as meatballs, but they are really more akin to meat dumplings. Meat is pounded with rice and/or legumes until the mixture is elastic and paste-like, then it is formed into the shape of a ball, often enclosing dried fruit and nuts, and simmered gently in a good meat stock.

The name *koofteh* is derived from the method of making the meatballs, i.e., the pounding together of the ingredients. The Persian verb "to pound" *koobidan* or *koftan* (past tense: *koobidand*) has given its name to several dishes in Iran and neighboring countries. Apart from the *koofteh* dishes in this section, *kabâb koobideh* (Ground Meat Kebab, see page 149) and *âbgoosht-e koobideh* (meat soup with paste, literally, or Lamb Soup, see page 125) are two Persian dishes that reflect their method of preparation, while the *kibbeh* of Lebanon and Syria, the *keftedes* of Greece, the *kofteh* of northern India and Pakistan and the *kofta* of Turkey are all derived from this same Persian word.

By definition, all *koofteh* (from *kibbeh* to *koobideh*) require much pounding and kneading, an exhausting job that today can thankfully be done in a fraction of the time with a food processor. There are purists who maintain that nothing can replace the pestle and mortar for the correct consistency, but if a food processor is used with care, the results are very good, and these splendid meat dumplings (which in the past were made only rarely by the most dedicated cook) now make a frequent and very welcome appearance at many a Persian meal.

The stock in which these dumplings is cooked should be kept at a gentle simmer. At formal meals in some regions, the meat dumpling was served on its own, the stock appearing as a simple broth. In other regions, the stock was reduced to serve as a sauce with the leftovers on the following day. Either way, *koofteh* make a rich and satisfying dish for the winter season.

TABRIZ MEAT DUMPLINGS
Koofteh Tabrizi

The Tabrizi meat dumpling must be the largest dumpling in the world. Average-sized *koofteh Tabrizi* are about 8-10 inches in diameter but they are often very much larger. These enormous dumplings are the pride of housewives from Tabriz and the whole northwestern province of Azerbaijan.

Previously, considerable strength and stamina were required to pound the ingredients together into a sticky mixture. One lady from Tabriz told me to knead the mixture until my arms fell out. If the mixture isn't pounded properly, she said, the dumpling will break open when put in the stock and disintegrate as it cooks. Clearly doubting my stamina, she advised me to bind the dumpling in cheesecloth to hold it together, and added darkly that many a hastily-made Tabriz meat dumpling had ended up as a thick soup. In fact, the whizzing dough blades of a good food processor enabled me to produce a remarkably large dumpling that held together in all its glory.

The other great joy of a Persian meat dumpling is the treasure hidden in its center. In the case of a Tabriz meat dumpling, boiled eggs and fried onions, or prunes and walnuts are inserted into the center of the dumpling. Occasionally, as in the recipe below, a whole chicken, itself stuffed with dried fruits and nuts, is concealed in its depths. Such inner delights elevate the Persian meat dumpling to a rare height of sophistication.

It is as well to start preparation of a Tabriz meat dumpling the day before you plan to serve it, since the preparation of the stuffing and the slow simmering take time. Nothing smaller than a 5-quart saucepan will do.

---

1 small chicken, no bigger than 2 pounds
2 tablespoons butter
2 teaspoons liquid saffron (optional) (see page 36)

Stuffing
1 small onion
vegetable oil
½ cup walnut halves
½ cup dried apricots
3-4 teaspoons dried barberries (see page 25)
salt and pepper

Stock
2 medium onions

4 tomatoes, chopped
2 tablespoons tomato paste
1 teaspoon turmeric
salt and pepper
about 4 quarts good meat *or* chicken stock

Dumpling
¾ cup short grain rice
1½ cups yellow split peas
2 medium onions
4 ounces each scallions and parsley
3 sprigs tarragon
4¼ pounds ground veal *or* lamb
2 small eggs
salt and pepper

Garnish
1 teaspoon each almond and pistachio slivers
crisply fried onion slices
chopped parsley

....

First make the stuffing. Chop the onion and fry in a little oil until soft and golden. Chop the walnuts and apricots, add and sauté for a minute, then stir in the barberries, salt, and pepper. Mix and put to one side to cool.

Bone the chicken, stuff with the prepared mixture and sew up, drawing the chicken into as compact and round a shape as possible. Daub over with the butter and liquid saffron and wrap the chicken in aluminum foil. Roast in a pre-heated oven (350°F) for an hour and a quarter, opening the foil for the last half an hour. Leave to cool, then remove trussing strings.

Next prepare the stock. Slice and fry the onions in oil in a large saucepan until soft and golden. Stir in the turmeric, salt, pepper, and tomato paste, add the chopped tomatoes, fry for a moment, add the meat stock or bouillon cube. Bring to a boil and then simmer for at least half an hour.

Now prepare the dumpling. Pick over and wash the rice and leave to soak for at least half an hour. Simmer in enough lightly salted water to cover until cooked and the water absorbed. Put in a large mixing bowl to cool.

Pick over and wash split peas, then simmer in lightly salted water to cover until well cooked but not mushy. Strain off any excess water and add peas to rice to cool.

Slice the onions and fry until crisp and golden. Add to rice to cool.

Clean and wash scallions and herbs, shake dry, and chop finely. Add to rice along with the ground meat, eggs, salt, pepper, and crushed dried oregano.

Mix well and pound and knead well for half an hour until it is sticky. (This can be done in 1-2 minutes with the dough blade of a food processor or mixer, but finish off by hand.)

Have a bowl of water ready. Keeping hands wet, mold the mixture around the chicken, smoothing and adding more until the chicken is completely and thickly encased. It will become quite heavy, so it is best to complete the molding process on a wet baking sheet.

Ensure the stock is on a slow simmer, and with a large skimmer lift the dumpling and slip it gently into the stock. Cover and simmer very gently for 2 hours or until the ball rises to the surface.

Dish up the meat dumpling onto a suitable warmed round dish. Garnish the top with fried onion slices, almond and pistachio slivers, and chopped parsley. The stock may be slightly reduced and served as a broth, or reduced rapidly and served as a sauce with the slices of dumpling. The dumpling is also delicious eaten cold with a salad.

❂ ❂

Fava Bean Meat Dumplings
Koofteh Bâghâli

The use of uncooked rice (which expands within the dumpling) gives a pleasant, open consistency to these dumplings that are enhanced with the addition of fresh summer dill and fava beans. Preparations should start the day before.

Meatballs
1 cup short grain rice
2 pounds fresh fava beans *or* 12 ounces frozen
1 bunch fresh dill *or* 3 tablespoons dried
½ pound ground lamb *or* veal
salt and pepper

Stock
1 medium onion
vegetable oil
½ teaspoon turmeric
1½ quarts meat *or* chicken stock
2 teaspoons chopped fresh herbs (dill, oregano, and tarragon)

Pick over and wash rice, then put to soak in salted water overnight. Next day, prepare the stock as in the previous recipe, adding herbs.

Shell the beans and blanch them, fresh or frozen, by dropping into boiling water and straining them. Skin when cool enough to handle.

Clean the dill, removing coarse stems, wash, shake dry, and chop finely.

Drain the rice and put into bowl with ground meat, chopped dill, and salt and pepper to taste, and knead for 20 minutes by hand (or 30 seconds in a food processor) until sticky. Add the fava beans and knead by hand a few minutes more.

Keeping the hands wet, make 2-inch balls and drop them one by one into the barely simmering stock. After half an hour, increase the heat slightly and simmer for another hour until the dumplings have risen to the surface and are well cooked through.

Dish up the dumplings into a warm tureen and keep warm. The stock may be reduced a little and served as a broth, or greatly reduced and served as a sauce with the dumplings. Serve with warm bread and fresh herbs.

RICE MEAT DUMPLINGS
Koofteh Berenji

The first evidence of Persian meatballs appears in one of the early Arabic cookbooks. Known as *naranjiya*, they consisted of finely ground, well seasoned lamb, made into orange-sized balls, which were cooked and glazed in saffron and egg yolk three times. This method was later adopted in the West under the name of gilding and endoring.

While the meatballs below are not actually endored, they are the size of a small orange and when the saffron-flavored stock is reduced and poured over, a golden glaze results.

Stock
1 medium onion
½ teaspoon turmeric
1½ tablespoons tomato paste
salt and pepper
2 quarts good meat *or* chicken stock
2 teaspoons liquid saffron (optional) (see page 36)

Stuffing
1 small onion
2 walnut halves
1 tablespoon dried barberries *or* 2 pitted prunes

Meatballs
1 bunch each fresh dill *or* 1 tablespoon dried
2 tablespoons fresh oregano *or* 1 teaspoon dried
1 cup each chopped parsley and leeks *or* scallions *or* chives
¼ cup short grain rice
⅓ cup yellow split peas
1 medium onion
1 pound ground lamb and veal
salt and pepper

Garnish
1 teaspoon each almond and pistachio slivers

First prepare the stock. Slice the onion and fry in oil until soft and golden. Stir in the turmeric, tomato paste, salt, and pepper, add the stock, bring to a boil, then leave to simmer gently. After 30 minutes, add saffron.

Next prepare the stuffing. Slice and fry the onion in oil until a crisp golden brown; stir in the chopped walnuts, then the barberries or prunes. Draw to one side to cool.

Clean and wash the herbs and leeks, shake dry, and chop finely. Spread to allow excess moisture to dry off.

Pick over and wash the rice, bring to a boil in a little lightly salted water. Boil for half a minute, then strain and put the rice into a large bowl to cool.

Grate the onion into the meat and add to the rice along with the herbs. Add salt and pepper and knead well together for at least 20 minutes by hand or 3-4 minutes in the food processor.

When sticky, divide the mixture into four and form each into a ball. Poke a hole into the center and insert a quarter of the stuffing. Close over and mold into as firm a ball as possible. Drop one by one into the barely simmering stock. Leave to simmer gently (if the water is simmering too fast, the balls may break open). After half an hour, the heat may be raised a little. Cook for another hour.

Dish up into a warmed tureen, garnish with almond and pistachio slivers, and keep in a warm place. The stock may be reduced slightly and served as a broth, or greatly reduced and served as an accompanying sauce. Accompaniments are warm bread, fresh herbs, and lemon juice.

BULGHUR MEAT DUMPLINGS
Koofteh Bulghur

Replace the rice with bulghur wheat and proceed as for *koofteh berenji* above.

RICE PATTIES
Kobbeh

Since the next several recipes also require some pounding and kneading, I have included them in this section. Indeed, the Persian name for this dish, as already noted, is derived from the root of the Persian verb to pound. These patties, though, are all fried and not simmered in stock.

This is a popular dish among the Arabic-speaking Iranians of the southern province of Khuzistan on the Persian Gulf. I am indebted to my sister-in-law, Batul, for this lovely recipe.

Filling

2 tablespoons split chickpeas

1 small onion

2 tablespoons finely diced *or* ground lamb

¼ teaspoon turmeric

¼ teaspoon *advieh* No. 1 (see page 30) *or* mild curry powder

salt and pepper

1 tablespoon golden raisins

2 tablespoons fresh cilantro *or* parsley

Patties

¾ cup short grain rice

1 small onion

½ pound ground meat

salt and pepper

½ teaspoon *advieh* No. 1 *or* mild curry powder

2 medium eggs

Prepare the filling. Pick over and wash the chickpeas, pour boiling water over them and leave to soak for half an hour. Bring to a boil and simmer for an hour or more until well cooked. Strain and leave to cool.

Chop the onion and fry in oil until golden. Add the chopped meat, turmeric, *advieh*, salt, and pepper. Cover with a little water and simmer until meat is tender.

Clean and soak the golden raisins for 10 minutes, drain and cut in half. Clean and wash the cilantro, drain, and chop finely.

Then add the chickpeas, golden raisins, and cilantro to the meat and set aside to cool.

Prepare the patties. Pick over and wash the rice, boil in salted water until well cooked. Strain and put in a large bowl to cool.

Grate the onion into the meat (or grind together) and add to the rice with the flavorings. Knead well (in a food processor if wished) until the mixture becomes sticky.

Beat the eggs together in a shallow bowl.

Keeping your hands wet, divide the mixture into balls the size of a small orange. Poke a hole through to the center, put in a teaspoon of the filling and mold the ball into a round patty with the filling well covered.

Beat the eggs, slip each patty into the egg, and fry in hot oil on both sides until cooked through and golden.

Serve hot with warm bread and fresh herbs.

SOFT RICE MEAT DUMPLINGS
Kofteh Sholleh

In sixteenth century Persia, the royal cooks of the Safavid court had a list of eight *sholleh* (soft rice) dishes in their repertoire. Today, no more than three or four (see page 142) remain popular. In this dish, which is a speciality of Rezaiyeh in the northwestern province of Azerbaijan, the soft rice meat dumplings are prepared and served in their own rice broth. Indeed, this dish could as well be called a soup.

Made with lots of oregano (a herb popular in the northwestern provinces of Iran), it often includes a touch of red pepper or paprika to give extra piquancy. As with all meat dumpling dishes, the cooking should be slow and gentle. Great care must also be taken during the latter stages of cooking as the dumplings and the rice stock tend to stick to the bottom.

This recipe was given to me by Mrs. Pouran Ataie from Azerbaijan.

1¼ cups short grain rice

3 medium onions

vegetable oil

2½ quarts meat *or* chicken stock

6 fresh tomatoes

4-5 tablespoons tomato paste

3 tablespoons dried oregano

1 teaspoon paprika *or* ½ teaspoon red chili powder

salt and pepper

1 pound lean lamb *or* veal

Garnish

crisply fried onion slices

Pick over the rice and leave to soak for a few minutes.

Slice the onions and fry in oil until soft and golden. Drain the rice and stir in with the onions. Add enough water to cover, boil gently until water has been absorbed. Remove three heaping tablespoons of this mixture and keep to one side.

Add the stock to the remainder and stir in the skinned and chopped tomatoes, tomato paste, half the oregano and paprika, salt, and pepper. Cover and simmer gently.

Grind the meat together with the reserved rice, the remaining oregano and paprika, salt, and pepper. Mold into about ten balls of even size and carefully add to the slowly simmering soup. Cook gently for two hours, stirring occasionally, especially during the last half hour.

Dish up the meat dumplings into a warmed tureen and pour the stock over them. Garnish with crisply fried onion slices. Serve with warm bread.

CHICKPEA PATTIES
Shâmi Pook

Shâmi is the Middle Eastern name for Syria, so it would seem that these patties originally came to Persia a very long time ago from Damascus. Similar patties are now found all over the Middle East.

The traditional method of making these small round patties with the distinctive hole in the middle (not unlike a flat doughnut) is unique. A clean piece of wet cheesecloth is stretched across a saucer and a small amount of the patty mixture (about the size of a walnut) is pressed and spread across it to form a round flat disc. A hole is poked through the middle to ensure that the patties are well cooked through and light. This has led to them being called *pook* (hollow).

Today they are more usually molded in the hand or on a lightly floured board, but great care must be taken to keep the patty mixture as light as possible. They should be fried in oil deep enough to cover them until they are an even golden color. They make a nourishing lunchtime snack or supper and are served with pickles, bread, and fresh herbs.

---

1 pound lean lamb

2 medium onions

1 teaspoon *advieh* No. 1 (see page 30)

salt and pepper

1 teaspoon baking powder

4 cups roasted chickpea flour*

1 large egg

2 teaspoons liquid saffron (optional)

Trim the meat, wash and leave to soak while you peel and chop the onions. Put the onions, the drained meat, *advieh*, salt, and pepper, with sufficient water to cover, into a pan and bring to a boil. Simmer gently until meat is tender and the liquid reduced. Leave to cool.

In a large bowl, mix the baking powder and the chickpea flour, then slowly stir in about 1/2 cup warm water to blend to a smooth paste.

Put the cooked meat and onions through the grinder, add to paste with the egg, salt, pepper, and liquid saffron, if using, and knead well together.

Taking a walnut-sized ball, flatten it and form into a flat round patty, gently making a hole through the middle with your little finger.

Slip into hot fat deep enough to cover them and fry briskly for four minutes, turning after two, until they are evenly golden brown and fairly crisp on the outside.

---

* Roasted chickpea flour is available at Middle Eastern stores.

POTATO PATTIES
Cottlet Seebzamini

It is said that potatoes were first introduced into southern Persia in 1827 by the British ambassdor, Sir John Malcolm, and that for some years they were known as *aloo-ye Malcolm* (Malcolm's plums). Until well into this century, potatoes were still called *aloo* in the south. Some years later, however, potatoes also began to make an appearance in the north of Iran, arriving from the west via the port of Istanbul. The growing French influence meant that these new vegetables finally came to be called *seebzamini* (earth apples, or *pommes de terre*) all over the country.

This may explain the curious fact that in Iran where potatoes have been known for little more than a century, there are two distinct types of potato on sale for different purposes: one is firm and waxy and is known as *Istambooli* (which clearly reveals its western origins). It is used in *Istamboli Polow* (page 94) and *Salad Olivieh* (page 213). The other is a dry floury type (probably Malcolm's potato) that is used in omelets (page 196) and patties such as this. It is important that a floury potato is used; new potatoes will not do.

Filling
1 large onion
½ teaspoon turmeric
1 teaspoon *advieh* No. 1 (see page 30) *or* a mild curry powder
salt and pepper
1 pound ground lamb *or* veal
½ bunch fresh cilantro

Patties
3 baking potatoes
1 large egg
salt and pepper
½ teaspoon *advieh* No. 1 (see page 30) *or* a mild curry powder
½ teaspoon turmeric
2 medium eggs

First prepare the filling. Chop and fry the onion, add the turmeric, *advieh*, salt, and pepper, then the meat and fry until nicely browned. Add 1 cup water and cook gently until the water is completely reduced, being careful the mixture doesn't stick. Turn off the heat, add the chopped cilantro, and set aside.

Boil the potatoes in their skins until tender, peel, and put through the grinder. Add the egg, salt, pepper, *advieh*, and turmeric and mix well.

Take a handful of the potato mixture and flatten it in your hand. Put a teaspoon of filling in the center and bring up the potato mixture from all sides to cover the filling. These patties are usually made in the shape of a hand, long, flat, and oval-shaped.

Beat the eggs, dip each patty in the egg and shallow fry on both sides in hot oil until golden.

Serve with hot pickles, bread, and fresh herbs.

GROUND MEAT PATTIES
Cottlet

The Russians fleeing the Bolshevik Revolution brought these meat patties to the Caspian provinces and Tehran in the early part of this century. They were an immediate success and now make a frequent appearance on the tables of urban families all over the north of Iran. Equally delicious hot or cold, they make a convenient snack and are ideal for picnics. They also respond very well to freezing and reheating in the microwave oven.

This recipe was given to me by the late Mrs. Maria Tajadod.

....

4 slices day-old white bread (without crusts)
1³/₄ cups milk
2 tablespoons fresh parsley *or* 1 teaspoon dried
2 medium onions
1 pound ground lamb, veal, *or* beef
1 medium egg
salt and pepper
fine dried breadcrumbs

....

Put the slices of bread in a large bowl, add the milk, and leave to soak.

Wash, shake dry, and finely chop the parsley.

Grate the onions into the meat, add the beaten egg, parsley, salt, and pepper, and mix thoroughly.

Check that the bread has soaked up all the milk. It should be completely soaked, but not "standing" in the milk. (If it is, pour off excess.) Add to the meat and knead well together.

Form into oval-shaped patties in the hand, then coat them in dried breadcrumbs. Immediately slip into a plentiful amount of hot oil. Fry briskly on both sides, then reduce heat, cover, and cook gently for another 5 minutes on each side. They should be crisply firm on the outside and softly firm inside.

Serve with warm bread, fresh herbs, and lots of lemon juice. Have a bowl of pickles on the table.

TURKEY PATTIES
Cottlet Booghalamoo

This is not an ancient Persian recipe nor one that has been passed from mother to daughter down the centuries. It is quite new and is included simply to demonstrate a very Persian answer to a very alien problem: Christmas turkey leftovers.

Mrs. Maheen Fatehi, visiting her daughter in England at Christmas, was faced with lots of cold roast turkey and lots of jaded people. Fearing it might by thrown out (wasted food is a sin in Persia), she took over and made a delicious meal.

In Iran such dishes are known as *mandarâree* (self-improvisation). It is through these dishes, simple though they often are, that one becomes aware of the distinguishing features of a national cuisine. This dish, for instance, calls for lots of fried onions and chopped herbs, it involves much kneading, and is served with lemon juice, bread, and fresh herbs. It is clear, too, that the "improviser" of this dish comes from a coastal region, since it is only in such humid areas that garlic is eaten with any frequency.

....

1 large bunch fresh cilantro *or* parsley

2 tablespoons fresh fenugreek *or* 2 teaspoons dried

1 medium onion

2 cloves garlic

1 pound cooked turkey

1 teaspoon turmeric

salt and pepper

2 medium eggs

....

Wash and clean the herbs, shake dry, then chop finely. Put to one side.

Chop the onion and garlic and fry in hot oil until golden. Allow to cool.

Grind the turkey, fried onions, and garlic together, add the turmeric, salt, pepper, herbs, and eggs, and knead well together.

Make into round patties and fry in hot oil until golden. Serve with warm bread, fresh herbs, and plenty of fresh lemon juice.

STUFFED MEATS
AND FISH

The Persians have been stuffing carcasses with delicacies and roasting them whole for thousands of years. When the Macedonians returned to Greece from their conquest of Persia hundreds of years before the birth of Christ, they introduced the idea to the Athenians who in turn passed it on to the Romans. It is thought that up to then the Greeks had relied solely on grilling or spit-roasting carcasses, the oven being unknown to them. The Greeks continued for centuries to refer to stuffing and roasting as a Persian method and as late as the first century AD, Apicius, the Roman cookbook author, described his recipe for stuffed kid or lamb as being "in the Parthian manner," that is, stuffed with fruits and roasted whole. This Parthian (or Persian) recipe bears a remarkable similarity to that for the stuffed lamb and poultry in Iran today.

In the seventeenth century, Sir John Chardin noted that the Persians "dress their large Meat either in an oven or a Stove," and that "they have a way of roasting their Sheep, Lamb and Kids, whole in their own Gravy which is Delicious eating."

On special occasions, it is not unusual for whole baby lambs to be stuffed and roasted or for small boned and stuffed birds to be stuffed into larger birds which are in turn stuffed into still larger carcasses. On page 158 is a recipe for a gigantic meat dumpling, whose succulent filling is a whole stuffed chicken.

In earlier days, roast meats were necessarily confined to the kitchens of the wealthy and the imperial court, although for communal festivities, such dishes were sometimes cooked at the local bakery. Today roast dishes are returning to popularity now that most modern kitchens are equipped with an oven. The following small selection of recipes are relatively simple but they make a delightful change from the more familiar roast meats of the West. In Iran they would be served with one of the elegant dishes of *polow* (see pages 63-83).

❂ ❂

STUFFED WHOLE LAMB
Barreh Tu Por

The mere thought of a roasted whole lamb served on a great platter of rice conjures up images of the magnificent Persian banquets held in the Hall of Forty Columns in the magical city of Isfahan. Five hundred years later, roasted stuffed lambs and dishes of rice still make a frequent appearance at wedding feasts and other large celebratory meals.

The domestic kitchen and the nuclear family mean that only the most ambitious of cooks will attempt such a feat these days. But such factors should not be a deterrent. The lambs employed for this dish are quite small, between 12 and 20 pounds, so that if you have a good-sized oven or even a covered barbecue it should present no problem.

Such small lambs are only available in the spring, so it is as well to give your butcher good notice when you want one. Ask him to bone the legs for you and to let you have the organ meats.

---

1 whole lamb (about 15 pounds)
2 medium onions
salt
½ cup liquid saffron (see page 36)
½ cup unsalted butter

Stuffing
2 cups basmati long grain rice
the lamb's kidneys, heart, and liver
1 bunch scallions
1 bunch cilantro
1 bunch parsley
6 sprigs tarragon
¾ cup each walnuts and almonds
½ cup pistachios
1 cup dried apricots
5 medium onions
2 teaspoons turmeric
salt and black pepper
¼ cup dried barberries (see page 25)

First prepare the stuffing. Wash and boil the rice in lightly salted water for 15 minutes. Strain and put in a large bowl to cool.

Wash and chop the organ meats. Set aside.

Wash and chop the herbs and scallions and put to one side to dry off.

Pick over and coarsely chop the nuts. Set aside. Chop the apricots. Set aside.

Chop the onions and fry in oil until golden, add turmeric, salt, pepper, chopped organ meats, herbs, scallions, nuts, and apricots, and cook for a few minutes, stirring constantly. Remove from heat and add to the rice. Add the drained barberries and mix the stuffing well together. Leave to cool.

Now prepare the lamb. Rinse it well inside and out and pat dry.

Crush the onions (best done in a food processor), mix in some salt, then rub the lamb inside and out with the mixture.

Stuff the lamb with the cooled stuffing, and truss up the belly, using a large needle and twine.

Lay the lamb on a piece of aluminum foil large enough to fold up over it. Dab the butter over the lamb, fold over and seal the foil, and weigh the lamb.

Place in a baking pan. Put in a hot oven and roast 25 minutes per pound, basting with the saffron and cooking juices every half an hour. Open up the foil for the last 30 minutes so that the lamb may turn golden.

Serve with any of the *polow* calling for lamb. Make sure the juices and the stuffing are offered along with the slices of lamb.

STUFFED SHOULDER OF LAMB
Sardast-e Barreh Tu Por

Since we are not always giving a large party and do not need to serve a whole stuffed lamb, why not try the recipe below, which will serve a family very nicely. Ask your butcher to bone the shoulder of lamb for you—some butchers will even stuff and roll it if you prepare the stuffing in advance.

---

1 boned shoulder *or* leg of lamb, unrolled
salt
6 tablespoons unsalted butter
2 teaspoons liquid saffron (optional) (see page 36)

Stuffing
⅓ cup basmati long grain rice
⅓ cup dried apricots
½ cup chopped almonds
¼ cup golden raisins
1 medium onion
1 teaspoon *advieh* No. 2 (see page 30)
juice of 1 lemon
sprinkling of dried oregano

First prepare the stuffing. Wash and boil the rice in lightly salted water until almost cooked. Drain and put to one side. Wash and cut the apricots into six pieces each. Set aside to dry. Wash the raisins and put to one side to drain. Chop the onion and fry until soft and golden. Stir in the *advieh* and all the remaining ingredients, then set aside to cool.

Preheat the oven to 375°F. Spread out the shoulder or leg of lamb, sprinkle with salt on all sides, then fill the "pocket" with the cooled stuffing, fold over, roll, and pin together with skewers. Tie into a neat parcel and remove the skewers. Weigh the meat.

Place the meat on a piece of aluminum foil large enough to encase it completely. Smear with the butter and pour over the liquid saffron, then fold over the foil. Roast for 30 minutes per pound, then open up the foil, baste with the juices, and roast for another 20 minutes until golden and tender.

Serve with any rice dish calling for lamb as an accompaniment.

STUFFED CHICKEN, AZERBAIJAN STYLE
Morgh Tu-Por Âzarbâijâni

A tantalizingly sour stuffing that contrasts well with the bland flesh of chicken and is a perfect complement to sweet *polow*.

1 roasting chicken, 4-5 pounds
salt
4 teaspoons liquid saffron (see page 36)
½ cup unsalted butter
juice of 1 *or* 2 lemons

Stuffing
3 tablespoons dried barberries (see page 25)
8 dried peaches
5 tablespoons dried *albaloo or* Morello cherries
1½ tablespoons walnuts
2 medium onions
3 tablespoons tomato paste

Pick over and wash the barberries, peaches, and cherries. Cut the peaches into quarters and leave all the fruit to dry. Chop the walnuts coarsely.

Chop the onions and fry in a little oil until soft and golden. Add the chopped walnuts, fry briefly, then add the dried fruit and fry for another minute or so. Add the salt and tomato paste. Mix thoroughly, then put to one side to cool.

Preheat the oven to 325°F.

Wash the chicken, pat dry, and rub lightly with salt inside and out. Stuff with the cooled mixture. Using a tapestry needle and twine, sew up the cavity and tie down the legs and wings. Place on a sheet of foil large enough to fold up over the chicken to encase it.

Melt the butter, mix in the lemon juice and liquid saffron, and pour over the chicken. Fold over and seal the foil. Place into the preheated oven to roast for about an hour, then open up the foil, baste with the juices, and roast for another half hour until cooked through, tender and golden.

STUFFED TURKEY
Booghalamoo-ye Tu Por

A curious tale is related by Sir John Malcolm, British envoy to Persia in 1800, in his book, *Sketches of Persia*. It concerns the discovery of two strange creatures that "had been saved from the wreck of a vessel in the Gulf" and which were causing a great deal of wonderment among the local inhabitants of Kazeroon. They looked very like birds, it was reported, but "their head is bare" and "one of them has a long black beard on its breast."

On investigation, it transpired that the strange creatures were turkeys, but what is most remarkable about the tale is that the Persians near Kazeroon had not come across turkeys before. They were common enough in Persia at the time, having been imported from Turkey as early as 1640.

In any event, they are well enough known now throughout Persia, and are frequently stuffed and roasted for banquets and dinner parties.

---

10 pound turkey
salt
3 teaspoons liquid saffron (see page 36)

Stuffing
¼ pound lean lamb
1 medium onion
½ teaspoon each turmeric and cinnamon
salt and pepper
¾ cup short grain rice
½ cup dried apricots
¾ cup walnut halves
¼ cup barberries
⅓ cup currants
6 tablespoons unsalted butter

Trim the lamb and dice finely. Wash and leave to soak for a few minutes.

Finely slice the onion and fry in oil until golden. Add the turmeric, cinnamon, salt, and pepper, stir then add the drained lamb. Stir and fry, add a little water to just cover, and simmer gently with the lid off until meat is almost tender (about 15 minutes) and the liquid completely reduced.

Pick over and wash the rice and leave to soak in salted water for 15 minutes or so.

Cut the apricots into six pieces each and fry in a little oil for a few minutes until a rich golden color, turning constantly. Remove from heat. Add the chopped walnuts, barberries, and currants. Mix in the drained rice, cooked meat and onions, and salt and pepper to taste.

Preheat the oven to 350°F.

Wash the turkey inside and out, pat dry, and rub with a little salt all over. Stuff with the prepared mixture and tie the legs down. Place on a sheet of aluminum foil large enough to fold over the turkey. Rub the butter over the turkey and pour over the liquid saffron.

Seal the foil, and bake in a hot oven for 4 hours or until cooked through and tender. Open up the foil, baste well, then leave to bake another half an hour until golden and tender.

This may be served with the *polow* of your choice.

STUFFED CHICKEN, NORTHERN STYLE
Morgh Tu Por, Shomâli

Fry 1 chopped medium onion with 2/3 cup finely chopped walnuts, 1/3 cup lightly boiled and strained short grain rice, 1/4 cup each almond and pistachio slivers, 2 tablespoons pomegranate paste, and 2-3 teaspoons sugar. Stuff and roast the chicken as above, adjusting the cooking times.

STUFFED CHICKEN, SOUTHERN STYLE
Morgh Tu Por, Jonubi

Fry 1 chopped onion with 1/4 cup washed and drained short grain rice, 1/2 teaspoon turmeric, 1/2 teaspoon *advieh* No. 1 (or a mild curry powder), 1/3 cup currants, 1/2 cup chopped almonds, and 1 cup each washed and chopped fresh cilantro and chives (or scallions). Stuff and roast the chicken as above.

STUFFED DUCK
Ordak Tu Por

This famous Caspian dish is rich, warming and rather special on a winter's day. I am indebted to Mrs. Amini who suggested this recipe to me.

....

1 large duck
salt

Stuffing
1 bunch fresh cilantro
1 small onion
³/₄ cup walnuts
2 tablespoons pomegranate paste
¹/₂ teaspoon cinnamon
salt
2-3 teaspoons sugar

....

Wash, drain, and dry the cilantro. Chop finely and set aside.

Chop the onion and fry in a little oil until soft and golden. Chop the walnuts coarsely, add to the onions and fry briefly. Stir in the pomegranate paste, then the cinnamon, salt, and sugar to taste. Add the cilantro, stir and remove from heat. Allow to cool.

Preheat the oven to 400°F.

Wash the duck thoroughly, pat dry and rub with salt inside and out. Spoon in the cooled stuffing, and place the duck on a greased rack over a baking tray. Roast in a hot oven (basting in its own fat that will have dripped into the baking tray) for about 90 minutes until it is cooked through and crisp.

Serve with any of the sweet *polow*.

STUFFED FISH, NORTHERN STYLE
Mâhi Tu Por, Shomâli

The sweetness of the dried fruit is perfectly balanced by the sour pomegranate syrup in this strikingly different and delicious dish. It is a splendid and very Persian way to prepare a large fish for a dinner party. This recipe first appeared in Mrs. Zari Khavar's book *The Art of Cookery in Gilan.*

**1 large fish (cod, haddock, pollack), about 4-5 pounds
salt**

Stuffing
**¼ cup each dried apricots, prunes, walnut halves,
    and currants
3 tablespoons pomegranate syrup**

Basting sauce
**½ cup unsalted butter
3 tablespoons lemon juice
2-4 teaspoons liquid saffron (see page 36)
black pepper**

Have the fish merchant clean the fish, then cut a horizontal slash through to the bone from the side. Sprinkle with salt, inside and out. Preheat the oven to 350°F.

Simmer the dried apricots and prunes in a little water until tender and the water has been reduced. Chop finely and put in a bowl. Chop the walnuts finely and add to the fruit. Wash the currants, pat dry and add. Stir in sufficient pomegranate syrup to blend all the ingredients into a thick coarse paste, then stuff the fish with the mixture. Sew up the cavity with a needle and thread. Place in a well greased baking pan.

For the basting sauce, melt the butter, add the lemon juice, liquid saffron, salt, and pepper, mix well, and pour all over the fish. Bake for about 90 minutes, basting with the sauce, until the fish is crisp and golden.

Remove the fish to a warm dish and pour sauce over. Garnish with chopped herbs and quarters of oranges or lemons.

STUFFED FISH, SOUTHERN STYLE
Mâhi Tu Por, Jonubi

This recipe is typical of many from the Persian Gulf region. The rich flavors are a wondrous blend of Indian and Persian delights: red chilies and tamarind from India with the subtle fragrancy of herbs from Persia.

The recipe was given to me by Mrs. Maheen Fatehi who lived in Abadan most of her life. Here she found grey mullet, sea bass, or cod responded very well to the spicy herb stuffing. While agreeing that monkfish is also suitable, she preferred a whole fish complete with head, tail, and skin that retains its shape and flavor and makes a better appearance on the table—ever an important aspect of the Persian cuisine.

---

1 whole fish, about 4-5 pounds
salt

Stuffing
6 ounces tamarind
1 bunch each parsley and cilantro
1 medium onion
1 *or* 2 cloves garlic
1 teaspoon red chili powder
1 teaspoon turmeric
3 tablespoons fresh fenugreek *or* 4 teaspoons dried
black pepper

Slit open the fish from head to tail. Wash thoroughly and remove scales if necessary. Sprinkle lightly with salt inside and out, rubbing into skin. Close up while preparing the filling.

Leave the tamarind to soak in ³/₄ cup water. After at least 15 minutes, remove the stones and thorns and sieve through a fine strainer. Wash the herbs, removing the coarse stems, shake dry, then chop finely.

Chop the onion and garlic and fry together in a little oil until golden. Stir in the chili powder, turmeric, dried fenugreek, pepper, and a sprinkling of salt. Fry briefly, then add the herbs. Fry for 5 minutes, stirring all the time, then stir in the strained tamarind liquid.

Preheat the oven to 350°F.

Open the fish and put in the mixture. (Any mixture left over can be heated and served with the fish.) Grease a sheet of aluminum foil large enough to enclose the fish. Bring the foil up around the fish and fold over.

Place in center of oven and bake for 1 hour. Raise the heat to 400°F, open up the foil and bake for another 15-20 minutes until nicely browned.

STUFFED VEGETABLES

Stuffed vegetables (*dolmeh*) are popular all over the Middle East, from Greece and Turkey to Iran and Afghanistan as well as in all the countries of the Arab world. The origins of these dishes are lost in the mists of time. It is believed that the ancient Persians (700-500BC) and more recently the Sassanians (AD500) wrapped meat, wheat, and spices in grape leaves. Yet, the modern Persian word for stuffed vegetables is derived from the Turkish language, while it is the Greeks who claim to have invented the dish.

Suffice it to say that *dolmeh* have been around for a very long time. Nearly 500 years ago, the cookbook of the Safavid court gave recipes for stuffed zucchini, eggplant, and cucumbers as well as stuffed grape leaves, noting in passing that the Greeks also stuffed cabbage leaves. Today, everyone in the Middle East stuffs every available fruit and vegetable, and each dish is different. But for me, it is the fragrance of herbs and the delicate interest and variety of the sweet and sour sauces of the Persians that make their *dolmeh* so very special.

Every housewife has her own favorite mixture that she uses for all her *dolmeh*. But the cooking sauce will vary, each one adapted to bring out the individual flavor of the various fruits and vegetables. Indeed, two batches of stuffed grape leaves are often made at the same time, one with a sweet and sour sauce, the other with a savory sauce in order to meet all tastes. In the south, tamarind or lemon juice make a frequent appearance, while in the northern provinces, the sour juice of Seville oranges or stewed green plums are used according to the season.

Dolmeh make a fine party dish. Many can be prepared in an oven-to-table baking dish, look attractive on a buffet table, and be excitingly different to eat. In addition, the stuffing can be made the day before (it can be frozen for a large party) and the fruit and vegetables stuffed and cooked well in advance on the day of the party. They thus need little last-minute attention.

❂ ❂

BASIC STUFFING

The following recipe for basic stuffing for vegetables was given to me by my mother-in-law.

---

2 large onions
¹/₂ teaspoon turmeric
salt and black pepper
1 pound ground lamb, veal, *or* beef
³/₄ cup short grain rice
¹/₃ cup yellow split peas
1 bunch each parsley and scallions
2 tablespoons each fresh tarragon, marjoram, and dill
¹/₂ teaspoon cinnamon
pinch each of ground ginger and cloves
salt and freshly ground black pepper

Finely slice one of the onions and fry in oil until soft and golden. Add the turmeric, salt, and pepper, fry for a moment, then add the meat and fry until well cooked through, stirring well. If necessary, pour off excess fat, then put the mixture to one side to cool.

Parboil the rice in a little water with a dash of turmeric and salt. Strain if necessary. Put with the meat to cool.

Boil the split peas in a little water until tender (but not mushy), strain and leave to cool with the meat.

Finely slice half of the second onion and fry crisply golden. Add to the prepared ingredients.

Grate the other half of the onion directly into the ingredients.

Clean and chop the herbs finely, mix them with the cooled ingredients, adding the cinnamon and a sprinkling of ginger and nutmeg (and more salt and pepper if desired).

This stuffing is now ready for use in the dishes on the following pages in this section. If wished, it can be frozen and kept for up to three months.

COOKING SAUCES

NORTHERN SAUCE

¼ **cup sugar**
¾ **cup lemon juice**
4 tablespoons unsalted butter
2 teaspoons liquid saffron (see page 36)
salt and black pepper

Gently heat the sugar with the lemon juice until dissolved, then add the butter to melt, the liquid saffron, salt, and pepper.

CENTRAL REGION SAUCE

¾ **cup vinegar**
¼ **cup** *sheereh angoor* **(syrup of grapes)** *or* **cane**
  syrup
¼ **cup unsalted butter**
salt and black pepper

Gently heat the vinegar with the *sheereh angoor* or cane syrup until well blended, add butter to melt, salt, and pepper.

SOUTHERN SAUCE

4 ounces tamarind paste
¼ **cup unsalted butter**

Set the tamarind paste to soak in 1 cup warm water for 15 minutes, then strain through a fine nylon sieve. Mix with the melted butter.

STUFFED GRAPE LEAVES
Dolme-ye Barg-e Mo

This is the most famous of all stuffed vegetable dishes. Popular in all the countries of the Middle East, it has also become widely available in the West in recent years. Today, grape leaves ready for stuffing can be found on the shelves of nearly every supermarket and delicatessen in the US and Europe. They are preserved in brine and sold in cans or frozen in plastic bags. Sometimes the grape leaves are pre-stuffed, cooked, and then canned for the delectation of the adventurous but lazy diner.

From time to time, fresh grape leaves are available for sale at Middle Eastern stores and these should be snapped up, because fresh grape leaves (even if they are not freshly picked) are far superior to anything in cans or plastic bags. Best of all though is to grow your own grapevine, as recommended in other sections of this book. Vines grow easily in the Western climate, and nothing beats fresh leaves, plucked straight from the grapevine.

Pick them when they are at their best, young and fresh in early summer; try to gather them in a uniform size, not too big. They will need to be blanched before rolling and baking, unless they are very young and tender.

If you intend to freeze the leaves, they can be immediately packed in piles of about 30 leaves, wrapped in plastic wrap and put in plastic bags in the freezer. They will keep nicely for up to six months or more and will need only to be dropped into boiling water to thaw and blanch at the same time. They will then be ready for use as fresh.

Traditionally, *dolmeh* are always baked in a saucepan on top of the stove with woven "matting" or extra leaves placed in the bottom of the pan to prevent sticking and/or burning; a weighted plate is placed on top to prevent the *dolmeh* from breaking loose, bobbing about or splitting open.

Throughout the north of Iran the most common cooking sauce contains lemon and saffron, but in the southern half of the country it is more usually tamarind-based. In the central regions a sauce of vinegar mixed with *sheereh angoor* (syrup of grapes) gives a wonderful sweet-sour piquancy. High quality grape syrup is not available here but either cane *or* corn syrup is a good, if slightly oversweet, substitute. The quantities given below are for a main meal for six, or appetizers for eight to ten. Grape leaf rolls are not as a rule served as a complete meal but rather as an appetizer, a side dish, or a light summer lunch, eaten hot or cold.

---

60 fresh (*or* preserved) grape leaves
basic stuffing (see page 185)
cooking sauce (see page 186)

Prepare basic stuffing.

Trim off the stems of fresh grape leaves, and rinse in cold water. Blanch in batches of six at a time by pouring boiling water over them. Drain after three minutes, longer for older leaves, then leave to drain in another colander. If using preserved leaves, follow instructions on the package or can.

Place two or three large leaves in the bottom of an oiled saucepan.

Place a few leaves on a flat surface, with the ridged stem surface upward, and put 2-3 teaspoons of the stuffing mixture on each. Fold the sides of the leaf up over the stuffing and then roll up firmly. As you make them, pack them closely into the saucepan, folded-side down. Continue filling and rolling the leaves, packing them in firmly.

Prepare the sauce of your choice, and pour over the grape leaf rolls. Place a weighted plate on top of the rolls, cover, and simmer over a medium heat for an hour or more until tender.

Dish up on to a warmed dish. If serving cold, drain off the cooking sauce and leave in the pan to cool. In either case, garnish with whirls of sour cream or yogurt. Extra cream or yogurt should be on the table together with fresh herbs and warm bread.

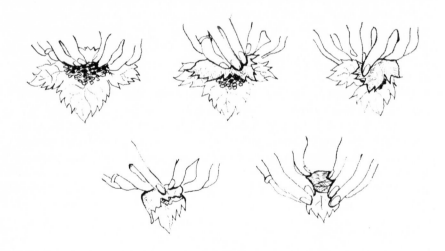

STUFFED CABBAGE LEAVES
Dolme-ye Barg-e Kalam

The cabbage most usually found in the markets in Iran is the closely-packed white cabbage. It is recommended for this recipe as its leaves are tender and easily absorb the flavors of the stuffing.

---

basic stuffing (see page 185)
1 teaspoon ground cinnamon
1 teaspoon dried dill
1 good-sized white cabbage
cooking sauce (see page 186)

Prepare stuffing, mixing in the cinnamon and dried dill.

Bring a large saucepan of lightly salted water to a boil. Trim off the broken and dried outer leaves of the cabbage and set aside. Drop the whole cabbage into the boiling water. Lift it out after 3-4 minutes and carefully peel off the softened leaves and place in colander to drain. As you reach raw hard leaves, drop the cabbage back into the boiling water for another few minutes. Repeat until you have about 35-40 leaves or until the leaves are too small and curly to bother with.

Starting with the largest leaves, lay each on a flat surface, smooth side down, and with a sharp knife cut out the lower part of the hard central stalk. Place a couple of teaspoon of stuffing on each, fold in the sides and roll up firmly.

Proceed as in the previous recipe, laying the discarded outer leaves in the bottom of an oiled saucepan, then packing in the cabbage rolls as you make them. Pour over the sauce of your choice and simmer gently for up to an hour and a half. Stuffed cabbage leaves are eaten hot with warm Persian bread and fresh herbs.

STUFFED PEPPERS
Dolme-ye Felfel

The next three vegetables may be cooked in a saucepan on the stove, or baked in the oven. They can also be prepared in a single pan or casserole dish (when each adds its own flavor to the others), or individually. If preparing them all together, allowances must be made for different cooking times required for each vegetable.

basic stuffing (see page 185, but omit split peas)
8 large green peppers
cooking sauce (see page 186)

Prepare stuffing, omitting the split peas.

Lightly butter a casserole dish large enough to take 8 green peppers standing up, and preheat the oven to 300°F.

Wash the peppers and with a sharp knife cut off the tops and keep to use as lids. Remove seeds and white membrane then blanch quickly. Fill the peppers with the stuffing. Place upright in the casserole, (leaving place for eggplants and tomatoes, if desired) and replace their lids.

Prepare the sauce of your choice and pour into the casserole around the peppers. Put on the casserole lid (or cover closely with foil) and bake covered for an hour and a half, basting from time to time.

These may be served in the casserole.

STUFFED EGGPLANTS
Dolme-ye Bâdenjân

Replace the peppers in the previous recipe with 5 or 6 small eggplants. Wash them and cut in half across, discarding the seeds. Sprinkle with salt, inside and out, and leave for 30 minutes to sweat. Pat dry, and sauté briefly in plenty of hot oil. When cool enough to handle, fill them with the stuffing and lay in a casserole side by side. Prepare the sauce as above and pour around them, cover with a lid or with foil, and bake covered for an hour, basting from time to time.

STUFFED TOMATOES
Dolme-ye Gojeh Farangi

These may be added to the above vegetables or made on their own. Take 8 large tomatoes, cut off the tops, keeping them to use as lids, and with a spoon carefully hollow out the inside. Add some of the tomato pulp to the cooking sauce instead of tomato paste. Pour sauce over and around the prepared tomatoes, replace lids, cover, and bake for 45 minutes. Served with fresh herbs and warm bread, this makes an attractive summer luncheon dish.

EGG DISHES
Omelets and Others

The Persian word *kookoo* is usually translated as "omelet," which is not an accurate description at all for it more closely resembles a savory vegetable cake than an omelet. It is very like a Spanish tortilla (not to be confused with the bread-like Mexican tortilla) and is a richly flavored, well cooked, and substantial egg-based dish. In the Middle East it is better known as *eggah*.

Once again we have a dish that is common to Iran, the Arab Middle East, and Spain, and it is interesting to speculate whether the dish went from east to west or vice versa. But whatever its history, *kookoo* is popular among all classes in Persia as a snack food that can be eaten hot or cold. The following recipes are only a small sampling of the many egg dishes eaten in Persia.

HERB OMELET
Kookoo-ye Sabzi

They have a dish they call Cookoo Challo which is dry rice and
a fritter of eggs, herbs and fishes.

John Fryer, *A New Account of East India and Persia*, 1681

This is the most famous—and the most popular—of all *kookoo* (omelets).
It is the delicious symbolic accompaniment to *Sabzi Polow* (Rice with
Herbs, see page 64) served at the Persian New Year in March.

But the herb omelet's soft and tenderly green center encased in
a crisply-cooked dark exterior is far too good to confine to spring
alone. Full of healthy goodness, fresh eggs and herbs are easily
available most of the year. Hot, the omelet can also serve as a delicious
summer luncheon or a light supper dish, while cold it makes a lovely
picnic snack.

As with all herb dishes, the weights given are only approximate,
because the longer the herbs hang about the shops, the less they will
weigh—and, it must be said, the less tasty they will be. Another way to
calculate the amount needed for ten eggs is to fill a level 4-cup bowl
with more or less equal portions of chopped parsley, cilantro, and
scallions along with a finely chopped leaf or two of lettuce and a
sprinkling of chopped fenugreek. Alternatively, one 2-ounce package of
dried herbs left to soak overnight may be used.

Some housewives add a tablespoonful of chopped walnuts
and/or barberries, mixed in with the prepared herbs, but these
additions are usually only for special occasions.

In Iran, the omelet is cooked in a frying pan and cut into eight
segments, which are carefully turned over individually. Alternatively, the
omelet can be baked in a pre-heated oven at 375°F. Place in bottom half
of oven for 20-30 minutes, then when omelet is firm to the touch, move
to top half of oven for another ten minutes. Cut into wedges and serve
immediately. If using dried herbs, though, better not make the omelet in
the oven as it can become too dehydrated.

Cut into small squares and garnished with finely chopped
walnuts, this makes an unusual and tasty cocktail snack.

....

8 ounces (1 bunch) each of parsley and cilantro*
6 ounces (1 bunch) scallions
3-4 sprigs fresh fenugreek *or* ½ teaspoon dried
1-2 lettuce leaves

---

* Or double the quantity of parsley.

> **2 teaspoons all-purpose flour**
> **1 teaspoon baking powder**
> **salt and pepper**
> **1 teaspoon dried barberries (optional) (see page 25)**
> **2-3 teaspoons chopped walnuts (optional)**
> **½ teaspoon liquid saffron (optional) (see page 36)**
> **10 medium eggs**

....

Remove the coarse stems from the herbs, wash, shake dry, and chop finely along with the lettuce leaves. Spread out to dry until all excess moisture has gone. Put in a bowl.

Add the flour, baking powder, salt, pepper, and, if using, the soaked barberries and chopped walnuts, and mix together.

Break the eggs into another large bowl and whisk thoroughly. Add the saffron, if using.

Heat oil to cover a large frying pan and at the same time beat the herbs into the eggs. While beating, pour into the hot (not smoking) oil. Immediately reduce heat, cover, and cook gently for 25 minutes until well risen.

Turn the omelet over and cook gently without a lid for another 10-15 minutes.

When cooked through, remove immediately from the pan (to prevent unnecessary absorption of fat). Serve immediately, or leave to cool for a light snack.

EGGPLANT OMELET
Kookoo-ye Bâdenjân

They have likewise a Fruit, which they call badinian, and the
same with what we call the Love Apples. It has a Taste that
comes very near the Cucumber, is as big as Apples generally
are, and as long again, and when 'tis Ripe the Skin grows quite
black; it grows as Cucumbers do, it is very good in several
different Sauces, and to be dress'd up in many Things.

Sir John Chardin, *Travels in Persia 1673-1677*

Perhaps Sir John sampled this unusual and delicious eggplant omelet
at one of the Entertainments he wrote so much about. Even today, it
still makes an appearance as one of many side dishes at formal buffet
dinners, though it is more frequently served as a light lunch and
supper dish.

4 medium onions
4 large eggplants, about 3½ pounds
4 teaspoons dried parsley
salt and pepper
3 teaspoons liquid saffron (see page 36)
4 teaspoons all-purpose flour
4 teaspoons baking powder
8 medium eggs

Garnish
crisply fried onion slices

Chop the onions and fry lightly in a little oil until soft and
pale golden.

Peel and chop the eggplant finely. Add to the onions and stir-fry
until soft, adding more oil if necessary. Remove from the heat and mix
in the parsley, salt, pepper, and liquid saffron. Leave to cool thoroughly.
When quite cool, mix in the flour and baking powder.

While the oil heats in a large frying pan, beat the eggs briskly,
and stir in the cooled eggplant mixture. Pour into the hot fat, and
immediately reduce the heat; cover and cook over gentle heat for 25
minutes until firm, then turn over and cook without a lid for another
5-10 minutes.

Garnish with crisply fried onion slices if desired and serve
immediately.

POTATO OMELET
Kookoo-ye Seebzamini

This omelet is rather like a large potato patty but with a distinctly Persian flavor. It is important that the potatoes be of a dry, floury type. I am indebted to Mrs. Pouran Ataie for this recipe.

> **2 pounds baking potatoes**
> **3 medium onions**
> **2 teaspoons turmeric**
> **1 bunch fresh parsley *or* 3 tablespoons dried**
> **2 tablespoons all-purpose flour**
> **1½ teaspoons baking powder**
> **salt and pepper**
> **10 medium eggs**

Wash the potatoes and cook them in salted water. Peel while still hot, mash, and leave to cool.

Chop the onions and fry in a little oil until soft and golden. Stir in the turmeric and put aside to cool.

Wash and chop the parsley.

When all the ingredients are quite cool, mix the potatoes, flour, baking powder, onions, and parsley together.

While the oil heats in a large frying pan, beat the eggs until frothy, then stir in the potato mixture. Pour into the hot oil, immediately reduce the heat, cover and cook over gentle heat for 25 minutes until firm. Turn over and cook without a lid for another 10 minutes.

Serve immediately with Mixed Pickles (see page 216) and fresh herbs.

CAULIFLOWER OMELET
Kookoo-ye Gol-e Kalam

Make as for potato omelet above, using one large cauliflower, 2 medium onions, and 1 cup chopped parsley.

POTATO OMELET (SWEET)
Kookoo-ye Ghand

This is another of the savory-sweet dishes so popular throughout Iran. As with the previous recipe, it is vital that the potatoes be of the floury type.

....

1 pound baking potatoes
6 medium eggs
½ teaspoon all-purpose flour
½ cup sugar
1 teaspoon liquid saffron (page 36)

Garnish
1 teaspoon mixed slivered almonds and pistachios
1 teaspoon barberries, briefly fried in butter

....

Boil the potatoes in their skins, allow to cool, then peel and put them through a grinder.

While the oil is heating in the frying pan, beat the eggs, flour, and half the sugar together, then stir into the potatoes. Mix well, and pour into the hot fat, immediately reducing the heat; cover and cook over gentle heat for 25 minutes until firm, then turn over and cook without a lid for another 5-10 minutes. Or alternatively, when it is firm, put the pan under the grill briefly until it is a light golden brown.

Dissolve the remaining sugar in a few spoons of warm water, add the liquid saffron, and pour all over the omelet. Reduce the heat to the very lowest, and leave for a few moments until the syrup has been absorbed.

Cut up the omelet before serving, hot or cold, and scatter with almond and pistachio slivers and the barberries.

YOGURT OMELET
Kookooy-e Mâst

A surprisingly delicious omelet with a wondrously exotic flavor. It is vital to use strained yogurt—either strained Greek yogurt or, if not available, then leave the yogurt to strain through a fine nylon sieve for two or three hours before using. This is excellent both hot and cold.

---

1 medium leek
2 carrots carrots
¾ cup strained yogurt
6 to 7 medium eggs
2 teaspoons all-purpose flour
1 teaspoon slivered almonds
1 teaspoon liquid saffron (see page 36)
salt and pepper to taste

Chop the leek finely and put to one side.

Peel and grate the carrots and set aside.

While heating the oil in a frying pan, beat the eggs, yogurt, flour, salt, pepper, and saffron together really well. Then stir in the carrots, leeks, and almond slivers, and immediately pour into the hot fat. Reduce the heat, cover, and cook over gentle heat for 15 minutes until firm, then turn over and cook without a lid for another 5-10 minutes. Or, alternatively, instead of turning it over, put the pan under the grill briefly until nicely browned.

This may be served hot with Persian bread and fresh herbs. Served cold, cut into bit-size pieces, it makes a delicious appetizer or a light summer snack.

GREEN BEAN OMELET
Kooko-ye Looby, Sabz

Another popular luncheon dish that makes a welcome change during the season of plenty when it can be difficult to know what to do with all the beans in the garden. Some Iranian housewives add 1 pound fried ground lamb or veal to this omelet, making it into a very substantial and tasty meal.

---

2 pounds green beans (dwarf, French, string, *or* runner)
2 medium onions
4 teaspoons all-purpose flour
2 teaspoons baking powder
salt and pepper
10 medium eggs

Wash and chop the beans finely and boil in a little lightly salted water until the water has been reduced to a scant amount and the beans are just tender. Add oil and sauté briefly. Leave to cool.

Chop the onions and fry in a little oil until soft and golden. Add to beans and leave to cool. Mix the beans and onions together with the flour, baking powder, salt, and pepper.

While the oil heats in a large frying pan, beat the eggs briskly and stir in the bean mixture. Pour into the hot oil, immediately reduce the heat, cover, and cook over gentle heat for 25 minutes until firm. Turn over and cook without a lid for another 5-10 minutes.

Serve immediately with pickles (see page 216), fresh herbs, and bread.

EGGPLANT WITH EGGS
Mirza Ghâssemi

Mirza ghâssemi is the Mazandarani name given to this dish from the Caspian region. As will be seen it is very different from the cake-like eggplant omelet given earlier in this section.

As in so many recipes from the northern provinces, garlic is an important ingredient. The following recipe is a favorite of Mrs. Shamsi Rasti, who always serves it with bread, herbs, and yogurt on the table. In *The Art of Cooking in Gilan*, however, Mrs. Zari Khavar recommends serving it with *katteh* (plain white rice).

The eggs may be cooked and mixed carefully into the eggplants and tomatoes, or they may be fried and served as a garnish over the vegetables. Either way, it is a tasty dish that is quick to prepare.

3¼ **pounds eggplant**
1 **whole garlic bulb**
½ **teaspoon turmeric**
3 **medium tomatoes**
salt and pepper
3 **large eggs**

Slit the eggplants open and bake in the oven at 400°F for 20 minutes until cooked through. When cool enough to handle, remove the tops, peel, and mash into a purée with a wooden spoon.

Peel the garlic, pound in a little salt, then sauté in oil with the turmeric until golden. Add the mashed eggplant and fry over medium heat, stirring constantly, until liquid is reduced.

Peel and chop the tomatoes, stir into the eggplant, and continue to fry until all is well blended.

Push the mixture to one side, add a little oil to the pan and break in the eggs. When the eggs are just set, stir in the eggplant.

Immediately, dish up into a warm bowl and serve with bread and fresh herbs.

SWEET OMELET, SHIRAZ STYLE
Khâgineh Shirâzi

The Persian name for this dish is derived, like *khâveeyâr* (caviar), from the Old Persian word *khâyeh*, meaning eggs. This is another dish that traveled with the Moghuls from Iran to India in the sixteenth century.

The authentic Persian *khâgineh* is a sweet omelet flavored with sugar. It is a favorite breakfast dish.

¼ **cup unsalted butter**
3 large eggs
2 teaspoons sugar
1 teaspoon flour

Melt the butter in a pan. Beat the eggs, sugar, and flour all together and pour into the hot butter. As the eggs begin to set, turn over and cook for a moment or two longer.

Serve immediately with fresh *barbari* bread (see page 48) and jam.

Sweet Omelet, Azerbaijan Style
Khâgineh Âzarbâijâni

This sweet egg dish is customarily considered a breakfast dish, but it can also occasionally be found served as a dessert in the northern provinces.

....

3 tablespoons vegetable oil
3 medium eggs
3 tablespoons all-purpose flour
3 tablespoons water

Syrup
1 cup sugar
½ cup water
½ teaspoon liquid saffron (see page 36)

....

First prepare the syrup by boiling the water and sugar for 3 minutes. Add the liquid saffron and boil for another 3 minutes. Keep in a warm place.

While the oil heats in a frying pan, beat the eggs, flour, and water together, then pour into the hot fat. Immediately reduce the heat, cover and cook gently until risen and firm. Turn over and cook without a lid for another few moments.

Remove from the pan, cut into wedges, and pour the syrup over the omelet.

YOGURT DISHES
AND SALADS

It is said that the beautiful Queen Pourandokht, a monarch of the pre-Islamic Sassanian dynasty who ruled over Iran in AD626, was exceedingly fond of yogurt dishes. In this she showed great wisdom, as yogurt is excellent for both the complexion and the digestion. The chefs of the royal kitchens lost no time in creating a number of new dishes that were refreshing and visually attractive. These dishes became known as *poorâni* after the queen herself.

When the Arabs conquered Iran, they found these dishes very appealing and rapidly adopted them. The Arabs, however, did not have the soft letter "p" in their alphabet, so the dishes became known as *boorâni*.

Whatever the truth of its origins, *boorâni* makes an unusual and delicious appetizer and in the summer can be eaten with bread for a cooling lunchtime snack. Traditionally, it is served as an accompaniment to a main course.

In Persian cookbooks of the early nineteenth century, *boorâni* was described as "Persian salad," a somewhat free translation of a word for a limited number of dishes whose only similarity to salad is that they are cold and frequently served as an accompaniment.

To make all the *boorâni* recipes in this section, the yogurt must be strained. This is best done through a cheesecloth, although a fine plastic strainer is also very effective for the amounts required for these recipes. The remaining liquid may be used in place of water or stock for Persian soups and stews to give a rich and pleasantly tart flavor. The Greek yogurt sometimes available in supermarkets is already strained and makes an ideal base for *boorâni*.

YOGURT WITH SPINACH
Boorâni-ye Esfenâj

The most popular of all the Persian *boorâni*, this dish can now be found in many parts of the Middle East. It is traditionally served as a side dish in Persia, but it makes an unusual appetizer for a formal dinner, or a delicious light summer lunch. Serve with fresh Persian bread.

---

2 medium onions

2 pounds fresh spinach *or* **1 10-ounce package frozen chopped spinach**

¼ teaspoon turmeric

salt and freshly ground black pepper

1 cup strained yogurt

Garnish

2 teaspoons liquid saffron (optional) (see page 36)

Slice the onions finely and fry in oil until soft and dark golden.

Wash the spinach thoroughly, shake dry, and chop finely. Add to the onions with the turmeric, salt, and pepper, cover and cook gently until the spinach is soft. Beat the spinach and onions together until well blended. Leave in a strainer to drain and cool.

Mix into the strained yogurt. Garnish with liquid saffron and serve very cold.

YOGURT WITH BEETS
Boorâni-ye Laboo

The delicate color of this attractive *boorâni* dish adds unusual interest to the delights of a Persian banquet.

1 pound cooked beets
1 cup strained yogurt
salt

Garnish
½ teaspoon crushed dried mint

Peel the cold cooked beets and cut into ¼-inch cubes. Sprinkle with salt.

Stir lightly into the strained yogurt immediately before serving. Sprinkle with crushed dried mint.

Yogurt with Eggplant
Boorâni Bâdenjân

This delicious and surprisingly satisfying *boorâni* is a very pleasing summer luncheon dish. Serve with fresh herbs and Persian *taftoon* bread (see page 52).

---

2 large eggplants, about 10-12 ounces each
2 cloves garlic
salt and freshly ground black pepper
1 cup strained yogurt

Garnish
chopped walnuts

Peel the eggplant and cut into rounds, 1/4-inch thick. Sprinkle with salt and leave to sweat for at least 30 minutes.

Chop and fry garlic in oil. Keep on one side.

Dry off the eggplant slices with a paper towel and fry them in the same oil until golden brown on both sides. Leave to drain and cool in a colander over a bowl.

When cold, cut the eggplant into small cubes and sprinkle with the garlic and pepper. Carefully stir in the strained yogurt, adding salt to taste. Cover and chill.

Garnish with chopped walnuts.

YOGURT WITH SHALLOTS
Mâst-o Mooseer

A favorite dish in the Caspian region for centuries, this has always been considered an effective relief for people suffering with malaria. Although the disease has long since been eradicated in Iran, *mâst-o mooseer* still makes an appearance at every meal in the northern provinces.

---

8 shallots
1 cup strained yogurt
salt and freshly ground black pepper

Peel and chop the shallots and put to soak in cold water overnight.
Strain, making sure they are thoroughly drained. Sprinkle with salt and pepper, and stir into the strained yogurt. Serve well chilled.

Yogurt with Cucumber
Mâst-o Kheeyâr

The cucumbers are very tiny and tasty in Iran. Almost seedless, they are in season from March to December and have such a delicate flavor that they are often served as a fruit. Peeled and salted, they make a refreshing snack on a hot summer's day. In the West, these tiny cucumbers can be found in Middle Eastern and Indian stores. If using the more familiar long ones, remove the seeds from them first.

The addition of about 1 cup iced water results in a very popular and refreshing summer soup known as *âb-doogh-kheeyâr*.

2-3 small cucumbers, *or* **1 long with seeds removed**
salt and freshly ground black pepper
¼ cup golden raisins
¼ cup each chopped walnuts and chives (*or* scallions)
4 sprigs each of fresh dill and mint
¾ cup strained yogurt
¼ cup sour cream

Garnish
crushed dried rose petals *or* crushed dried mint

Peel and finely chop the cucumbers. Sprinkle with salt and pepper. Wash and chop the golden raisins. Coarsely chop the walnuts. Wash and chop the dill, mint, and chives finely.

Stir the cucumbers, golden raisins, walnuts, dill, mint, and chives into the strained yogurt with the sour cream and chill.

Just before serving, garnish with the dried rose petals or crushed dried mint.

EGGPLANT WITH YOGURT PASTE
Mast-e Bâdenjân

The next two recipes are different versions of the same thing—a very popular appetizer, snack, or supper dish eaten with fresh bread and Persian pickles. I am very grateful to Mary Behnam who gave me her delicious recipe.

---

6 medium eggplants (about 2 pounds)
2-3 crushed cloves garlic
½ cup strained yogurt
salt and pepper

Garnish
1-2 teaspoons sour cream
1 onion, thinly sliced
2 teaspoons *na'nâ dâgh* (see page 42)

Peel the eggplant, slice, salt, and leave to sweat for half an hour to remove bitterness. Wipe dry and fry in oil until golden brown.

Put the eggplant and garlic in a pan, and add water to barely cover and cook together for twenty minutes or so until tender. Set aside to cool.

Mash the eggplant, stir in the yogurt, and add seasoning to taste.

Spread on a plate and garnish with a teaspoon or so of sour cream, crisply fried onions, and *na'nâ dâgh*. Serve with warm Persian bread.

EGGPLANT AND BUTTERMILK PASTE
Kashk-e Bâdenjân

In this dish, it is vital to use dried and reconstituted buttermilk. This is available from Iranian stores, but if you cannot find it, then add sour cream and a dash of lemon juice. I am grateful to Simin Mirshamsi for passing on her lovely recipe.

---

6 medium eggplants (about 2 pounds)
1 large onion
1 small package prepared buttermilk *kashk* (see page 26)
salt and pepper

Garnish
1 onion, thinly sliced
2 teaspoons *na'nâ dâgh* (see page 42)

Peel the eggplant, slice, salt, and leave to sweat for half an hour to remove bitterness. Wipe dry and fry in oil until golden brown. Chop the onions and fry until golden. Set aside to cool.

Put the eggplant and fried onions in a pan, add water to barely cover, and cook together for 20 minutes or so until tender. Set aside to cool.

Mash the cooked eggplant and onions together, and stir in the *kashk* and seasoning to taste.

Spread on a plate and garnish with crisply fried onions and *na'nâ dâgh*. Serve with warm Persian bread.

CUCUMBER AND POMEGRANATE SALAD
Salad-e Dezfuli

A delightful salad from Dezful, this unusual combination is both pretty and refreshing. The ingredients are all easy to find in the autumn months when pomegranates make their first appearance. Traditionally, lemons were peeled and the segments skinned, chopped, and added to the salad, but below I suggest a simple dressing of lemon juice. I am indebted to Mrs. Shahnaz Karimianpour for giving me her lovely recipe.

4 pomegranates
1 long English cucumber
1 medium onion
juice of 2 small lemons
salt and pepper
1 teaspoon crushed dried mint

Break open the pomegranates and separate the seeds from the membrane.

Wash the cucumber and peel the onion, then chop both finely (so that all the ingredients are of a uniform size).

Mix all the ingredients together, add lemon juice, salt, and pepper to taste. Finally, sprinkle the crushed dried mint over all. Leave for 30 minutes before serving.

GREEN SALAD WITH POMEGRANATES
Salad Irani

An attractive salad with an exciting, crunchy texture. Dress a salad of mixed lettuce leaves with the dressing of your choice (in Iran, they would blend lemon juice with oil, salt, and pepper) and garnish with a sprinkling of pomegranate seeds and chopped fresh mint. If possible, get Iranian pomegranates, which have a tart flavor and a ruby red color.

Yogurt and Cheese Spread
Poloor

This recipe, given to me by my sister-in-law, is thought to come from ancient Assyria. It is delicious with freshly baked *barbari* (see page 48) or any crusty bread and makes a tasty supper dish.

---

2 cups mixed fresh herbs, mint, dill, chives, cilantro,
  ***and/or* parsley**
½ cup strained yogurt
½ cup crumbled feta cheese
4 tablespoons unsalted butter
salt

Clean and wash the herbs. Spread to dry, then chop finely.

Blend the yogurt, cheese, butter, and salt, if necessary, together, then mix in the chopped herbs. Serve with fresh Persian bread.

✸ ✸

CHICKEN AND POTATO SALAD
Salad Olivieh

This is an immigrant dish. It came to Iran earlier this century with the White Russians, and quickly became a firm favorite. It is much in evidence in Tehran hotels and cafeterias and is often found on the dining tables of modern hostesses, both as an extra dish at a buffet dinner or as a summer luncheon dish.

Inevitably it has altered in flavor and appearance from the original Russian salad. The ingredients are more finely chopped and the diced vegetables have disappeared, though some people still add peas and carrots. But perhaps the most striking difference is the absence of olives, except in the olive oil for the mayonnaise. And even the mayonnaise has lemon and cream added to give it an extra piquancy and richness.

The recipe below is an unashamedly Tehrani interpretation that is unlikely to be found anywhere else in the world—or even anywhere else in Iran. It is made with gherkins in brine (*kheeyâr-shoor*) (see page 223), which are always available from Iranian stores in big cities in the West and can sometimes be found in delicatessens and enterprising supermarkets. The dill pickles found in Jewish delicatessens, though larger and less crisp, will serve as well if the tiny *kheeyâr-shoor* are not available. It is important that the gherkins are preserved in brine, not pickled in vinegar. The ingredients are given by weight to indicate that they are of equal proportion.

....

> **4 medium eggs**
> **2-3 small potatoes (red-skinned *or* new)**
> **½ pound cooked chicken *or* turkey breasts**
> **½ pound gherkins in brine**
> **salt and pepper**
> **juice of 2 lemons**
> **1 cup mayonnaise (preferably homemade)**
> **¼ cup sour cream (optional)**
>
> *Garnish*
> **strips of tomato and gherkins**

....

Hard boil the eggs. Cool, shell, and chop finely.

Boil the potatoes in their skins until firm. Cool, peel, and chop finely.

Remove skin from the cooked chicken breasts, chop finely.

Remove stalks from gherkins, chop finely.

Mix all the ingredients together with the salt, pepper, and lemon juice, then stir in the mayonnaise (reserving 3 tablespoons for garnish) and sour cream, if using. Pile onto an oval dish in a symmetrical mound and spread the remaining mayonnaise over the top of the salad. Garnish with strips of tomatoes and gherkins. Chill thoroughly before serving with fresh bread.

Opposite: Stuffed Peppers (*dolme-ye felfel*) and Stuffed Tomatoes (*dolme-ye gojeh farangi*)

PICKLED PLEASURES

Pickles and preserves feature strongly in the Persian cuisine. As in so much Iranian cooking, herbs play an important part. Persian vinegar is made from dates (in the southern regions) or grapes, apples, and other fruits (in the cooler climes), but I find cider vinegar works very well in the recipes given in the following pages.

While many of the ingredients are local and difficult to find outside of Iran, others are easier to come by. On the other hand, some look the same but taste very different. Tiny green peppers, for instance, are much used in Persian pickles (*torshi*) and are sometimes pickled on their own, but the small green peppers available here are too hot and fiery for the Persian palate.

Many of the following recipes were given to me by Mrs. Pouran Ataie from Azerbaijan who is famed for her fine pickles and preserves. It is believed in Iran that a "green thumb" is the first necessity for making good pickles. Some women are thought to have a special affinity for them, but I suspect it is mostly due to close care and attention in the making. All the ingredients must be thoroughly dry before being put into sterilized and dried jars.

A wide variety of seeds and herbs are used to flavor Persian pickles including angelica seeds, nigella seeds, coriander seeds, peppercorns, garlic, and cinnamon as well as fresh peppermint or spearmint leaves, green peppers, fresh tarragon, dill, cilantro, and parsley.

Opposite: Fresh fruit, the traditional Persian dessert

MIXED PICKLES
Torshi-ye Makhloot

There are as many varieties of mixed pickles as there are vegetables. This recipe gives one simple combination, but each one of the vegetables may be replaced by any other. Preparations should start the day before you wish to make the pickles. The quantities suggested here will fill about four 1-pint jars.

---

1 medium eggplant

3 tablespoons salt

2 cups cauliflower florets

2-3 stalks celery

1 large green pepper

4-5 small green peppers

3 carrots

1 cup each fresh cilantro *and/or* parsley

2 teaspoons crushed dried mint

1 tablespoon each whole nigella seed and whole coriander seed

2 tablespoons crushed angelica seed

1 quart cider vinegar *or* tarragon vinegar

Prick the eggplant all over with a fork and bake in a hot oven 400°F for about 20 minutes until tender. Allow to cool, then peel. Put in a colander and place a weighted bowl on top, and leave to drain for a day. Lay pulp between two layers of paper towel and leave overnight. Cut up into small cubes, put in a large bowl and sprinkle with one tablespoon salt and a spoonful or two of vinegar.

Sterilize the jars, drain, and leave to dry.

Wash the cauliflower and break into tiny florets. Wash the celery thoroughly, discard any coarse leaves and outside stalks, then dice, reserving any small leaves. Wash, stem, remove seeds, and dice the peppers. Peel and dice the carrots. Spread all the vegetables out to dry.

Wash and clean the herbs, removing any coarse stems, shake dry, and chop finely along with the small celery leaves. Spread out to dry.

When vegetables and herbs are quite free of moisture, add to the eggplant. Sprinkle with the remaining salt, mint, nigella, coriander and angelica seeds, and mix well together.

Pack into the dry jars to about $1/2$ inch from top. Pour in sufficient vinegar to cover. Seal the jars well and label. Keep at least 40 days before eating.

PICKLED RELISH
Torshi-ye Leeteh

As in the previous recipe, the choice of vegetables is entirely optional. Green beans, young turnips, or zucchini could as well be used in place of those listed below, while the same ingredients as for the mixed pickles could also be used. However, for this type of pickle, the total weight of vegetables should be matched by half their weight in herbs. The quantities suggested below will make about seven or eight 1-pint jars of relish.

This relish is traditionally eaten with Ground Meat Kebab (see page 149) and is delicious with Rice with Fava Beans (see page 66). I am grateful to Mrs. Maheen Fatehi for giving me this recipe.

----

2 cups each chopped onions, white cabbage, leeks, and celery

3 carrots

1 medium eggplant

1 large green pepper

5-10 cloves garlic

2 bundles parsley, about 12 ounces

2 tablespoons each fresh tarragon, mint, dill, and oregano *or* 1 teaspoon each dried

4 tablespoons salt

1 teaspoon freshly ground black pepper

2 teaspoons each whole nigella seed and whole coriander seed

1 teaspoon whole black peppercorns

about 1 quart cider *or* wine vinegar

Sterilize the jars and leave to dry.

Peel and chop the onions coarsely. Wash and clean the cabbage, leeks, celery, carrots, and pepper, then chop coarsely, reserving fresh young celery leaves. Spread them out to dry.

Clean and wash the herbs, shake dry and spread out with the celery leaves to dry off. Peel the garlic cloves.

Cut off eggplant top and, without peeling them, chop into cubes. Put into a pan, add some of the vinegar just to cover, bring to a boil, and boil for 20 seconds. Remove from heat, and add eggplant and vinegar to all the vegetables in a large bowl. Mix thoroughly, adding salt and spices.

Put the vegetables through the large-holed grater, then spoon into the dry jars to within ½ inch of the top. Fill up with vinegar. Seal and label.

This relish may be eaten immediately, but is best left for two weeks.

PICKLED STUFFED EGGPLANT
Torshi-ye Bâdenjân

Another old favorite, this pickle is best made with very small eggplants no bigger than 5 inches long. They are seedless and can sometimes be found at Iranian stores. If using larger ones, remove the seeds.

1½ pounds small seedless eggplant

1 large bunch each fresh parsley and cilantro

4 teaspoons each dried crushed mint and dried crushed basil

5-10 cloves garlic

8 teaspoons salt

4 small green peppers

2 teaspoons whole nigella seed

1 teaspoon whole coriander seed

2½ cups cider *or* wine vinegar

Sterilize the jars and leave to dry.

Remove the eggplant tops, then steam them, unpeeled, until soft. Place in a colander and put a weighted bowl on top to drain and dry thoroughly. Leave for 24 hours, then spread between two layers of paper towel for another hour.

Wash and clean the herbs, removing coarse stems, shake dry, and chop finely. Spread out on a paper towel to dry.

When dry, put herbs in a bowl and stir in the mint, basil, crushed garlic, and two teaspoons salt.

Split open the eggplants lengthwise and fill with the herb mixture. Seal by rolling the eggplants gently closed. Sprinkle with salt and pack into the jars, interspersed with whole green peppers and sprinklings of nigella and coriander seed. Top up with vinegar to cover completely.

Seal, label, and leave for at least 40 days before serving.

PICKLED SHALLOTS
Torshi-ye Mooseer

In this popular pickle, the shallots are treated to whiten them. They are then cut into vertical slices, so that despite the familiar-sounding name, they make an interesting change.

Allow five days for preparation.

1½ pounds shallots
8 teaspoons salt
1 tablespoon crushed dried mint
2½ cups cider *or* wine vinegar

Peel the shallots and put in a bowl. Pour boiling water over them, leave to cool, then drain. Repeat twice more. When cool and drained for the third time, pour cold water over them and leave for 3 days, changing the water every 5 or 6 hours. Strain again and spread out to dry thoroughly for 24 hours.

In the meantime, sterilize the jars and leave to dry.

Slice the shallots, downward into quarters, sprinkle with salt and mint, then pack into sterilized jars. Cover with vinegar.

Seal and label. Keep for at least 40 days before serving.

PICKLED GARLIC
Torshi-ye Seer

This is another popular pickle from along the Caspian littoral, and when the color of the fresh pink cloves is captured, it is also the prettiest.

12 whole garlic bulbs
10 teaspoons salt
2½ cups white malt vinegar

Sterilize the jars and leave to dry.

Bring the vinegar and salt to a boil and pour into a sterilized jug to cool.

Peel the garlic and remove the skins from each clove. Pack into the dry jars.

Pour the cooled vinegar into the jars, covering the garlic completely.

Seal and label. Keep for at least 40 days before serving.

PICKLED FRUIT
Torshi-ye Meeveh

This unusual blend of fruits and vegetables combines to make a delicious pickle full of late summer flavors.

---

1 large apple
1 large quince
2 medium carrots
3 stalks celery
16-20 cherry tomatoes
20 green beans
2 heaping tablespoons salt
1 tablespoon whole nigella seed
2 tablespoons tomato paste
1-2 pieces of cinnamon stick
about 6-7 cups cider *or* wine vinegar

Sterilize the jars and leave to dry.

Wash and peel the apple and quince and cut into cubes. Peel and dice the carrots. Wash and string the celery and cut into 1/2-inch lengths. Wash the tomatoes. Spread all the ingredients on paper towels to dry.

Wash and string the beans, cut into short lengths and blanch in salted water. Strain and spread to dry.

Mix all the fruit and vegetables in a large bowl together with the salt and nigella seeds. Cover with vinegar. Drain the vinegar into a saucepan, add the cinnamon sticks and tomato paste, bring to a boil and boil for 30 seconds. Remove from heat and leave to cool.

Pack the fruit and vegetables into the jars and cover with the cooled vinegar. Seal and label, and store for at least 40 days before serving.

PICKLED GRAPES
Torshi-ye Angoor

During the autumn months when the harvest of grapes is at its peak in the northwestern province of Azerbaijan, housewives put by some of the largest and finest black and green grapes to preserve for the festival of the longest night, *Shab-e Yaldâ*, on December 21. These huge, fleshy grapes are preserved in a cool shady corner of the courtyard, where the early snows cover the jars, keeping them cool and dark.

Mrs. Pouran Ataie, who gave me this recipe, well recalls the excitement when the jars of black and green grapes, symbolizing night and day, were pried out of the drifted snow, to accompany the celebration meal marking the longest night of the year. Everyone would stay up throughout the whole of the night, eating, talking, and keeping vigil so as to be able to greet the birth of the new sun in the morning.

> 1 pound each large thick-skinned black grapes and large thick-skinned green grapes
>
> 6½ cups white wine vinegar
>
> 3 tablespoons grape syrup (*sheereh angoor*) *or* cane syrup *or* corn syrup
>
> 2 teaspoons salt

Sterilize the jars and leave to dry.

Separate the grapes, wash and spread out to dry.

Bring the vinegar, syrup, and salt to a boil, then boil for a minute. Pour into a sterilized jug to cool.

Pack the grapes into jars, arranging in alternating colors. Fill the jars with the cooled vinegar.

Seal and label. Keep in a cool dark place for 40 days before serving.

PICKLED CUCUMBERS
Torshi-ye Kheeyâr

Whenever I find tiny cucumbers, I snap them up to make this delicious pickle.

....

1 pound tiny cucumbers

1 cup each fresh parsley and fresh dill *or* 1 teaspoon dried parsley and dill

4 teaspoons salt

1 teaspoon each whole coriander seed and whole nigella seed

about 1 quart tarragon vinegar

....

Sterilize the jars and leave to dry.

Wash and clean the parsley and dill, removing coarse stems, shake dry and chop finely. Spread out to dry. Wash and chop the cucumbers into cubes (if necessary) and spread out to dry.

When dry, put in a bowl with the herbs, salt, coriander seed, and nigella seed. Mix well, then pack into the sterilized jars. Fill up with the tarragon vinegar.

Seal and label, and store for 40 days before serving.

GHERKINS IN BRINE
Kheeyâr Shoor

A most popular accompaniment in Iran is *kheeyâr shoor* or dill pickles. The fresh gherkins are very tiny, not more than 2-3 inches long, and are hard to find outside Iran. Cans of Persian gherkins in brine can be found in Iranian and Middle Eastern stores in the West.

2 pounds tiny gherkins
4 small hot green peppers
1 cup fresh dill
6 peeled cloves of garlic
about 1 quart water
4 tablespoons salt

Sterilize the jars and leave to dry.

Wash and thoroughly dry the gherkins and green peppers. Wash the dill and shake dry.

Bring the water and salt to a boil, remove from heat, and leave to cool.

Pack the gherkins, dill, peppers, and garlic into sterilized, dry jars and fill with the cooled brine. Seal and keep in a cool place for a month.

JAMS AND PRESERVES

Sugar preserves and candied sweetmeats have a very long and noble history in Iran. Sugar had already arrived in Persia from India at least 2,500 years ago. The Sanskrit *sarkara* became *shikar* in Old Persian and sugar in English, while the Persian *qand* for lump sugar became candy in English. Even today, the confection shops of Persia are called *qanâdi*.

It was, however, the Arabs who spread the cultivation and the vocabulary of sugar along the North African coast and up into Spain and Europe in the eighth and ninth centuries. Prior to that time, honey had been the sweetening agent in the West.

The jams and preserves (*morabbâ*) of Persia are quite different from the thick, set jams of the US and Europe. They have a translucency and aromatic delicacy that belie the name of jam. One of the joys of visiting the small towns and cities of Persia is to see the dark interiors of small grocery shops lit up by shelf upon shelf of jars of whole fruits or transparent blossoms preserved in syrup. Such preserves are not intended to be spread on slices of bread and butter, rather they are used as a dip for bread, the fruit sliced and served with the syrup, or as a sauce over ice cream or creamy rice dessert, or sometimes even stirred into tea for sweetness and fragrance.

Many of the jams and preserves are made from familiar fruits (apricots, plums, oranges, and so on) but here I have chosen only those that are very different from our own fruit jams. Ranging from vegetables to blossoms, they are a sample of the diverse methods and produce that form Iran's preserves.

A speciality from the Caspian littoral is a preserve of Seville orange blossoms. The tiny flowers are washed and soaked in limewater, a solution of water and calcium hydroxide (or slaked lime), then well rinsed and washed again, and soaked in hot water for 24 hours before being added to a syrup of sugar and water. The blossoms become quite transparent and are a most delicate and delicious preserve to eat with bread or to serve over simple puddings.

As far as I know, limewater is never used in Western cooking. It has the effect of making treated fruits and vegetables quite transparent and thus more able to absorb beautifully the flavors of the preserving syrups. The name limewater has inevitably led to some confusion, and suggestions that water and lime juice may replace it are of course entirely misleading. Slaked lime is a white powder and a constituent of plaster of Paris. In Persian it is call *âhak*.

Very great care must be taken in the preparation and use of slaked lime. After mixing the powder well with water, it must be left for at least an hour for the sediment to settle. When the solution is quite clear, it can be poured over the fruits, but the sediment must be discarded.

In all other respects, the usual rules of jam-making should be followed. Use a copper pan or a good preserving pan. Also use preserving sugar if available, as it obviates the need for skimming or straining. Sterilize the jars and warm them before filling with the hot preserves. Seal as quickly as possible, and label when cool enough to handle.

CARROT JAM
Morabbâ-ye Haveej

Traditionally, this jam was made of carrot "rings," i.e., thin slices of carrots with the central core removed by use of a small round cutter. Today, it is more usually made of slivers and actually looks rather like an orange marmalade. The delicate flavoring of cardamom, rosewater, and orange peel gives this preserve a wondrous air.

---

3 orange peels
4 pounds carrots
6 cups sugar
4-5 teaspoons rosewater
2-3 teaspoons lemon juice*
1 teaspoon ground cardamom
½ cup each pistachio slivers and almond slivers

Peel the oranges thinly, cut the peel into thin slivers, and boil up and strain three times to remove bitterness. Drain and put to one side.

Peel the carrots, cut into quarters lengthwise, then cut out the central core and slice into thin slivers. Wash and pat dry.

Bring the sugar and 2½ cups water to a boil, then boil gently for 5 minutes. Add the carrots and orange slivers and boil until the carrots become tender and soft and the syrup begins to thicken. Add rosewater, lemon juice, ground cardamom and nuts and boil for another few minutes or until the jam reaches 225°F.

Remove from heat, pour into warm, sterilized jars, and seal immediately. Label when cool enough to handle.

---

* If possible, use the peel and juice of Seville oranges in preference to sweet oranges and omit the lemon juice. If using sweet oranges, add more lemon juice.

CUCUMBER JAM
Morabbâ-ye Bâlang

When Dr. Wills, an English doctor living in Iran in the late nineteenth century, visited a village near Hamadan, he was fascinated by the way cucumber jam was made and gave the following description:

> The cucumber having been cut into long slices the thickness of an inch, and the peel and seeds removed, had been soaked in lime-water some months; this was kept frequently changed, and the pieces of cucumber were now quite transparent. They were carefully put in a simmering stewpan of strong syrup, which was placed over a wide fire, and, after cooking for a quarter of an hour, the pieces of cucumber were carefully laid in an earthenware jar, and the syrup poured over them, spices being added.

The recipe below was first published in 1960 in Rosa Montazami's *The Art of Cooking* and it is clear that the method had changed very little. Hamadan is still famous for its cucumber preserves.

4½ pounds tiny cucumbers
4½ pounds slaked lime (see page 225)
13½ pounds sugar
¼ cup rosewater
2 teaspoons lemon juice
1-2 tablespoons whole cardamoms

Peel the cucumbers and cut lengthwise into quarters. Discard any seeds, and pat dry.

Stir the slaked lime into 4 quarts water. Mix thoroughly, then let stand until the powder settles to the bottom of the bowl.

Put the cucumber in a bowl and carefully pour over the lime-water, keeping back and discarding the sediment. Leave for 12 hours.

Drain and rinse thoroughly several times, removing all traces of limewater, then cover with fresh cold water and let stand for another 12 hours. Drain and rinse again.

Bring the cucumbers and rosewater to a boil. Immediately add the sugar, stirring until dissolved and boil for another 25 minutes or until setting point is reached and the cucumbers are tender and transparent.

Remove from heat, pour into warm sterilized jars, and seal immediately. Label when cool enough to handle.

QUINCE JAM
Morabbâ-ye Beh

It is a rare occasion indeed when the golden quince makes an appearance in our local shops. And when it does, it is difficult to decide which delectable dish to make with it, whether to stew it with lamb and split peas, or whether to stuff and bake it, or whether, after all, to make a simple sherbet. Its lovely color and sweet aromatic flavor can be a rapturous treat in the dying days of autumn.

In this recipe, the flavors can be captured and preserved for the winter months. If possible, make this jam in a copper pan, which really does enhance its stunning color. Mrs. Fatimeh Khorsandi gave me this simple recipe.

....

4 large quinces
4 cups granulated sugar
1 quart water
3 *or* 4 whole cardamoms

....

Wash and cut the quinces into two halves, remove the seeds and core, then slice into thin segments (there is no need to peel them).

Put the sugar, water, and quinces into a copper pan, cover and bring to a boil, then simmer gently until transparent, tender, and richly colored (this will take at least an hour and a half).

Add the cardamoms, simmer for a few moments more, then remove from heat.

Pour into warm sterilized jars and seal immediately. Label when cool enough to handle.

ORANGE PEEL JAM
Morabbâ-ye Khalâl Nâranj

The following preserve is extraordinarily beautiful and aromatic. It takes a little time and patience to prepare, but is especially lovely served as a sauce over the simple creamy rice puddings given in the desserts section (see page 254). Seville oranges are preferable, but if using sweet oranges, add half as much lemon juice again as orange juice and reduce the amount of water accordingly. Preparations should start the day before.

---

8 Seville *or* other large oranges
1½ cups sugar
2 teaspoons whole cardamoms

Thinly peel each orange in a continuous wide strip, cut each strip into four or five lengths, then roll each into the shape of a rosebud and pack neatly into a container, so that the orange "roses" hold each other together. Carefully cover with cold water and leave to soak for 12 hours.

Squeeze the oranges and keep juice to one side.

Drain the orange rolls, put in a pan, cover with water, and bring to a boil. Simmer gently for an hour. Drain and rinse with cold water.

In the meantime, bring the sugar and 1½ quarts water to a boil and boil gently for 5 minutes. Add the cardamoms, orange rolls, and juice, then simmer on a low heat until the peel is transparent and tender and the syrup thick.

Remove from heat and pack the "roses" into warm sterilized wide-mouthed jars and pour over the syrup, discarding the cardamoms. Seal immediately. Label when cool enough to handle.

Orange Blossom Jam
Morabbâ-ye Bahâr Nâranj

This preserve comes from the Caspian region in the north and is traditionally made from the blossoms of the sour *nâranj* (Seville orange).

....

1 pound orange blossoms
2 cups preserving *or* granulated sugar
½ cup water
1-2 tablespoons rosewater

....

Pour boiling water over the orange blossoms and strain.

Bring the water and sugar to a boil. Boil for ten minutes, then add the rosewater. Boil for a minute or two more, then add the blossoms. Boil for another 10 minutes until the syrup is thick.

Remove from heat and pour into warm sterilized jars. Seal immediately. Label when cool enough to handle.

Eggplant Preserve
Morabbâ-ye Bâdenjân

This recipe comes directly from Rosa Montazeri's *The Art of Cookery*. She recommends using tiny young eggplant, "freshly formed from the blossom and still seedless." These may be difficult to find in the West, but are sometimes available in Iranian and Middle Eastern stores.

---

2 pounds tiny eggplants
2 cups preserving *or* granulated sugar
3 *or* 4 whole cardamoms
1-2 tablespoons rosewater
2 tablespoons lemon juice

Bring a pan of water to a boil and keep on a steady simmer. Top, tail, and peel the eggplants one at a time and drop immediately into the simmering water to prevent discoloring.

In the meantime, bring the sugar to a boil in 3 cups water. When the sugar is dissolved, strain the eggplant and add to the syrup along with the cardamoms, then boil gently until the syrup thickens. Add the rosewater and lemon juice and boil for a minute more.

Remove from heat, pour into warm sterilized jars, and seal immediately. Label when cool enough to handle.

APPLE PRESERVE
Morabbâ-ye Seeb

The next two delightful recipes were given to me by Mrs. Pouran Ataie who comes from Azerbaijan, a region famed for its preserves.

4¹/₂ pounds even-sized apples
¹/₂ cup vinegar
about 9 cups sugar
juice of 1 lemon
2 tablespoons rosewater

Garnish
¹/₂ teaspoon each almond and pistachios

Wash, peel, and carefully core the apples (keeping the stem in place if possible). Drop them immediately into a bowl of water and vinegar to prevent discoloring.

When all the apples have been prepared, drain, dry, and weigh them. Then place in a pan, cover with cold water, bring to a boil, and simmer for a minute. Strain the apples, reserving half the water.

Weigh out sugar pound for pound of peeled and cored apples and add to the reserved water in the pan. Bring back to a boil and simmer for a minute, then carefully drop in the apples. Simmer gently for half an hour or more, until the apples become clear and almost transparent and the liquid a little sticky. Finally, add the lemon juice and the rosewater. Bring to boil once more, then remove from heat.

Immediately pack the apples, stem up, into large preserving jars and cover with the syrup. Seal and store.

Serve cold with a little syrup and garnish each apple with slivered almonds and pistachios.

PEAR PRESERVE
Morabbâ-ye Golâbi

Replace the apples with small even-sized firm pears.

ORANGE PRESERVE
Morabbâ-ye Nâranj

If possible, use Seville oranges; if not, then use the ordinary sweet oranges and add the juice of two lemons instead of one.

---

3 Seville *or* other large oranges
4 cups sugar
juice of 1 lemon (*or* 2 if using sweet oranges)

Garnish
½ teaspoon almond and pistachio slivers

Wash the oranges and scrub the skins (to release the essence). Carefully remove the central core and seeds from top and bottom without damaging the shape or peel of the orange.

Cover in water and bring to a boil; strain and repeat once more. Strain, cover in cold water, and leave for 24 hours, changing the water every 3 to 4 hours. Test to ensure there is no bitter flavor to the water. If there is, bring to a boil and strain again.

Bring 2½ cups water and the sugar to a boil and simmer until sticky. Add the lemon juice, then slip the oranges into the warm syrup and leave for 24 hours. Remove the oranges and boil up the syrup until thick.

Put the oranges into a large-mouthed preserving jar and pour the syrup over them. Seal and keep for at least ten days.

Cut the oranges into quarters, garnish with slivers of almonds and pistachios, and serve with a little syrup.

BEVERAGES
Cooling Refreshments

Noah's first act, when the Great Flood abated, was to plant a vineyard in the Persian foothills of Mount Ararat in northwestern Iran (now in Turkey). Grape leaves, grapes, and wine abounded in Persia for centuries thereafter.

According to Persian legend, wine was first discovered by the mythical King Jamsheed who, sitting with his courtiers in the palace gardens, saw a beautiful bird struggling to free itself from a coiling snake. Summoning his finest archer, he instructed him to shoot the snake. With one arrow, the archer killed the snake and the bird soared joyfully up into the clear blue sky.

Turning back, the bird swooped down to the monarch, dropping some seeds at his feet. The king instantly ordered that they be planted and tended. They grew into fine plants, which bore clusters of translucent berries bursting with juice. They were so delicious that the king commanded the juice be kept in a cool place. But when the king drank it later, the juice had become bitter and foul-tasting. He declared it poisonous and ordered it to be destroyed.

His courtiers, however, kept the poison in a safe place. Many months later, when one of the king's wives contracted a painful illness for which the doctors could find no cure, she called to her eunuch to bring her a cup of the poison hidden by the courtiers, to drink so that she could die peacefully. She fell into a deep slumber. When she awoke, she was cured of her illness and the true gratitude for the bird was finally and fully appreciated.

Thus was the wonder of wine revealed to the ancient Persians. Several centuries later, when Herodotus visited Persia in about 450BC he was intrigued by the way the ancient Persians decided on important matters of state:

> It is their general practice to deliberate upon affairs of weight when they are drunk; and then on the morrow, when they are sober, the decision to which they came the night before is put before them by the master of the house in which it was made; and if it is then approved of, they act on it; if not, they set it aside. Sometimes, however, they are sober at their first deliberation, but in this case they always reconsider the matter under the influence of wine.

Clearly wine was an important part of life for the ancient Persians.

But, over a thousand years later, when the Arabs brought Islam to Iran, they also brought the prohibition of wine and spirits. Islam firmly discourages excessive consumption of alcohol, believing that the subsequent loss of physical control is demeaning.

The transition from wine-drinking to abstinence was not easy nor was it quick. More than 400 years after the advent of Islam, Omar Khayyam was still occasionally drinking himself into a philosophical stupor that resulted in some of the finest—and most famous—Persian poetry ever to be translated. His yearning for a "loaf of bread beneath the bough, a flask of wine, a book of verse, and thou beside me singing in the wilderness" is familiar to many who know little else of Persia or its poetry.

> Drink! For you know not whence you came, nor why;
> Drink! For you know not why you go, nor where!

Despite Omar Khayyam's mystical exhortations, the Persians finally and somewhat reluctantly accepted a more sober way of life, although many European visitors over the centuries continued to comment on the public abstinence and the private indulgence of many of their hosts.

Even in the thirteenth century, Marco Polo noted that the Persians quieted "their conscience on this point by persuading themselves that if they take the precaution of boiling (wine) over the fire by which it is partly consumed and becomes sweet, they may drink it without infringing the commandment; for having changed its taste, they change its name and no longer call it wine, although it is such in fact." And well into the seventeenth century, Sir John Chardin wrote that the Iranians made "the strongest Wine in the World and the most Luscious."

Drinking was nevertheless officially frowned upon and the majority of people complied with the ban. But the hot dry climate in most of Iran for most of the year meant that wine had to be replaced with something. The water was often brackish and unhealthy, particularly toward the end of summer. And so was born the *sharbat* of Persia. *Sharbat* (or sherbet in English) is derived from *sharab*, the Arabic for drink, and is a glittering example of Persian ingenuity and adaptation. Wondrous blends and balances of fruit syrups and ice quench the thirst in a most refreshing way. Evidence of their extraordinary appeal is that the names of some of these non-alcoholic drinks found their way into the pubs, bars, restaurants, and shops of the US and Europe—punch, syrup, sorbet, and sherbet are all derived from various Persian drinks.

The use of *golâb* (rosewater) (*gol* means flower, *âb* water), mint, and other herbs to give some interest to the cooling drinks of the new Muslims in Persia attracted the attention of the Crusaders. They came to know *golâb* through the Arabs who, not having a hard "g," called it *jolab*, which was promptly Westernized to julep. As the name changed, so did the rosewater. It was diluted and sweetened, but despite this it became indispensable in the apothecaries and kitchens of medieval England.

In the sixteenth century, the poet John Milton praised the julep cordial as having "spirits of balm and fragrant syrups mixt." The herbalist Nicholas Culpeper had rather less regard for it, describing it in an offhanded manner as "a pleasant potion, as is vulgarly used by such as are sick and want help, or such as are in health, and want no money to quench their thirst." The pilgrims took it to America where it acquired great popularity, especially when laced with rum or other spirits, as a breakfast beverage. Today it makes a regular appearance in the Southern US, especially at the Kentucky Derby, as mint julep.

At about the same time, the Portuguese traders, stopping off for refreshment and provisions at Hormuz (now the port of Bandar Abbas in the Strait of Hormuz) found their thirst in the intense heat of the Persian Gulf, well quenched with a drink called *panj* (five) that consisted of five ingredients: grape juice, rosewater, sugar, lemon, and crushed ice. The grape juice, inevitably, was replaced with rum, and *panj* became "punch" with little more than a momentary hiccup.

The English travelers of the eighteenth and nineteenth centuries were also entranced by Persia's sherbets:

> The sherbets were worthy of notice, from their peculiar delicacy: these were contained in immense bowls of the most exquisite workmanship, made of the pear tree. They consisted of common lemonade, made with superior art; of the "sekenjebin" or the vinegar, sugar and water, so mixed that the sour and sweet were as equally balanced as the blessings and miseries of life; the sherbet of sugar and water, with rose-water to give it a perfume, and sweet seeds to increase its flavour; and that made of the pomegranate; all highly cooled by lumps of floating ice.

James Morier, *The Adventures of Hajji Baba of Isphahan*, 1824

News of the blissful refreshment of Persia's cooling fruit drinks laced with snow and crushed ice filtered back to Europe, and it wasn't long before the European version, the cleansing fruit sorbet, made an appearance on the tables of high society. To spread the delights to all levels of society, sherbet was eventually produced in powder form for the easy preparation of lemon and other effervescent drinks.

By the first half of this century, sherbet in this form was being sold in English sweet shops. It comes in small sealed paper containers into which a liquorice "straw" is inserted so that the fizzy powder can be sucked up. The sherbet immediately dissolves in the mouth, creating a tart mouth-watering fizziness and is naturally very popular with children. Made of bicarbonate of soda, tartaric acid, sugar, and flavorings, such sherbet has clearly come a long way from the refreshing fruits of Persia.

In recent years in Iran, the traditional sherbets have largely been replaced by mass-produced bottles of fizzy drinks. Every teahouse, hotel, and caravanserai on the highways of Iran has ice chests filled with sodas. But a wide range of delicate and refreshing sherbets are still made and served in the home. Poured over ice, diluted with water and served in tall frosted glasses, they are an elegant reminder of traditional Persian hospitality.

Upon his auspicious arrival, let him drink fine sherbets of lemon and rosewater, cooled with snow; then serve him preserves of apple, watermelon, grapes, and other fruits, with white bread, just as I have ordered.

For this royal guest, prepare each drink with sweet attars and ambergris; and each day prepare a banquet of five hundred rare and delicious and colorful dishes...Give a feast, tremendous and enticing, of meats and sweetmeats, milk and fruits, to the number of three thousand trays.

Decree of Shah Tahmasp (sixteenth century)

CHERRY SYRUP
Sharbat-e Âlbâloo

If you are unable to get Persian sour cherries (sometimes available in May and June), morello cherries are the next best thing. This delightful sherbet preserves the flavors of summer into the months of winter and spring.

1 pound sour cherries
4 cups sugar
1 cup water

Wash and pit the cherries. Place in a bowl and cover with the sugar. Leave for an hour or so.

Add the water and bring to a boil. Simmer gently for 10 minutes, then strain through cheesecloth.

Return the strained juice to the pan and boil gently until the syrup is thick. Remove from the heat, leave to cool, then pour into sterilized bottles. Seal and store in a cool place. Once opened, keep in the refrigerator.

To serve, pour a couple tablespoons over some ice cubes in frosted glass and stir in cold water to taste.

RHUBARB SYRUP
Sharbat-e Reevâs

Replace the cherries with 6 long stalks rhubarb, cut into 1-inch chunks.

QUINCE AND LIME SYRUP
Sharbat-e Beh-Limoo

Replace cherries with 1 large quince, peeled, cored, and chopped into small cubes. (While preparing, keep the cubed quince in a bowl of cold water laced with a tablespoon of lime juice.) Add ½ cup lime juice when the strained juice is returned to the pan.

LEMON SYRUP
Sharbat-e Limoo

The tart lemons and limes of Persia were an obvious choice to make into a sherbet. Poured over ice, it makes an inviting drink throughout the year.

1 cup fresh lemon *or* lime juice
2 cups sugar
3 cups water
1-2 tablespoons rosewater (optional)

Place the freshly squeezed lemon or lime juice in a pan with the sugar and water. Bring to a boil and simmer gently, uncovered, for 20-25 minutes.

Allow to cool. Stir in the rosewater, if desired. Pour into a bottle and seal. Once opened, keep in the refrigerator.

To serve, pour over ice and stir in chilled water.

ORANGE SYRUP
Sharbat-e Nâranj

Replace the lemon juice with the freshly squeezed juice of Seville oranges (or juice of 3 sweet oranges and 1 lemon).

POMEGRANATE JUICE
Âb-e Anâr

In addition to sherbets, the Persians are also fond of serving *afshoreh* or cold freshly squeezed fruit juice. Known today as *âb-e meeveh*, these are quick and easy cool drinks.

Persian pomegranates make a most satisfying drink that is beautiful, tasty, and beneficial. Rich in iron, it purifies and strengthens the blood and is highly recommended for anemia and for pregnant women. Its color and piquant flavor also make it a sheer pleasure to drink.

Cut the pomegranates in half, split open and separate the small jewel-like seeds from the bitter white inner casing. Crush the seeds in a fruit press. (Be careful of spills; pomegranate stains are difficult to remove.)

MINT AND VINEGAR SYRUP
Sharbat-e Sekanjebeen

This is one of the earliest sherbets known to the Persians, and the unique blend of vinegar and sugar was clearly an early attempt to replace the forbidden wine.

In Khuzistan, a special delight of the *Seezdah Bedar* picnic (on the thirteenth day of the Iranian New Year) is to eat fresh young romaine lettuce leaves (the first of the season) dipped in *sekanjebeen* syrup. In fact, this dish is popular all over Iran in early summer—but summer comes very early in the southern province of Khuzistan and coincides with Picnic Day.

As a drink, this unusual blend of flavors seems to work best when served very cold. It also makes a pleasant non-alcoholic punch when garnished with thin cucumber slices and almond slivers.

---

1 cup water
1 cup sugar
4 tablespoons white vinegar
juice of 1 lemon
6 leaves of mint

Boil the water and sugar together for 10 minutes.

Stir in the vinegar and lemon juice. Boil for 10 minutes, adding the mint leaves during the last 5 minutes.

Remove from the heat, leave to cool, strain, and pour into sterilized bottles. Seal and store in a cool place.

To serve, pour one or two tablespoons over a couple of cubes of ice in a frosted glass, stir in cold water, and add a sprig of fresh mint for garnish.

YOGURT DRINK
Doogh

The antiquity of this beverage is so great that Plutarch mentions
it as part of the ceremony at the consecration of the Persian
Kings, to quaff a large goblet of this acidulated mixture.

F. Shoberl, *Persia*, 1818

This yogurt drink has been known in Persia since ancient times. Its
name is derived from the Old Persian verb *dooshidan* (to milk), as is the
name of the young maids who did the milking: *dukhtar* in Persian and
daughter in English.

Today, *doogh* is known throughout the Middle East and the
Indian subcontinent in many forms. In Iran, however, it never has a
sweet flavor as in the subcontinent, but is only ever salty and sour.
Yogurt is considered at its best when slightly sour.

In Iran, the yogurt is always live. In the West, pasteurization kills
off the bacteria and prevents any increase in lactic acid or further
souring. In the recipe below, this loss is compensated for by the
addition of ascorbic acid. The lemon juice also combines with the sour
cream to give a hint of the rich sour yogurt drink of Persia. The coarsely
chopped fresh mint leaves further give an authentic touch.

Served over crushed ice, it is a most satisfying and refreshing
drink at any time of the year, but on a hot summer's day it is
incomparable. It succeeds in truly quenching the thirst without
immediately creating a new one.

In Iran, this is the perfect accompaniment for *chelow kabâb* (a rice
with lamb kebab dish, see pages 144-145). Such is its popularity that it
has been mass-produced over the last thirty years or more. Known as
doogh Âbali, it is reputedly made with the pure, aerated spring waters
from Ali's Spring situated some seventy miles northeast of Tehran in
the valleys of the Elborz mountains. The recipe below produces only an
approximation of the rich character of the unbeatable *doogh Âbali*, but it
is by the far best I have come across. I am indebted to Dr. Fazlollah Sadr
for giving me his special recipe.

....

2 cups yogurt
5 tablespoons sour cream
juice of 1 lemon
1-2 level tablespoons salt
about 1 quart carbonated mineral water
2 sprigs fresh mint

....

Whisk the yogurt, sour cream, lemon juice, and salt together until smoothly blended.

Gently whisk in the mineral water, and add the washed and coarsely chopped mint. Chill and serve over ice.

This will keep bottled in the refrigerator for several weeks, but it is best to strain and replace the sprigs of mint with fresh if serving more than 12 hours later.

> About half a pint (of yogurt) is added to a quart of water to form a buttermilk or *doogh*. A little cut mint is added, and a few lumps of ice, and a cooling drink is made. It is without question a capital thirst-quencher in hot weather.
>
> J. Wills, *The Land of the Lion and Sun*, 1891

TEA
Châi

It is thought that tea arrived from China with the early Persian caravans more than 1,500 years ago, but it made little impression until well after the Mongol conquests of the thirteenth and fourteenth centuries. Before then, the most popular hot drink had been the stimulating coffee that had arrived from Arabia in the ninth century. Coffee was already common enough to have its merits listed in Razi's medical encyclopedia of the tenth century. Razi was a Persian born in the city of Ray, just south of present-day Tehran, and like many Persians he wrote his scholarly works in Arabic.

Coffee had the advantage of the blessing of Islam and was much favored at religious ceremonies. For several centuries, it was as popular in Persia as it is in Arabia and Turkey today. Coffee houses sprang up all over the country and became the focal point of every community. Sir John Chardin describes the coffee houses of Persia with great warmth:

> Spacious and Large rooms...generally in the finest Parts of the
> Cities, because there is the Rendezvous, and place of Diversion
> for the Inhabitants...They serve you very exactly there with
> Coffee, very quick, and with abundance of Respect; there they
> converse; for there is the Place for News, and where the
> Politicians criticise upon the Government, with all the Freedom
> in the World, and without being disturb'd: the Government not
> troubling it self with what the World says: Here they play those
> innocent Games I have been speaking of, which are like
> Draughts or Chess; and besides this, there are your Repeaters in
> Verse and Prose, which the Mollas, Derviches, or Poets, take
> their Turns to perform.

Despite Chardin's glowing description in the seventeenth century, successive Iranian governments over the next 300 years frequently suspected both coffee and the coffee houses of fostering degeneration and political dissent. In this, they were not alone—coffee houses were being banned all over the Middle East and Europe for inciting vice and discord.

Finally, and only as recently as the 1920s, the former Shah's father decided to discourage the coffee house and its activities. He banned the "innocent games" and sought to convert its devotees to tea drinking. He even imported new strains of tea from China as well as some fifty Chinese families to oversee and upgrade tea production in Iran. He was successful in his aims.

Today, coffee has been largely relegated to a mourning drink, offered only to the bereaved at memorial services, while tea has taken over completely. It is now the most popular drink in Iran, and is the only beverage, apart from the ubiquitous soft drinks, offered in the many thousands of Persian "coffee houses" that still exist under that name.

Tea is also the first drink to be offered to guests on their arrival in both the wealthiest of homes and the poorest. It is served at breakfast, after meals, between meals, and last thing at night. It is served in the city bazaars, in shops, and in offices; no serious transactions can be concluded without an accompaniment of numerous glasses of tea.

When the first samovars were imported from Russia, they were greeted with relief by everyone in charge of the endless job of preparing tea, and today they are as much a part of the Persian household as they are of the Russian. Every home has a well-used samovar.

In Iran, tea is served in tiny glasses called *estekân*. Neither milk nor sugar are added. The fragrance and the color of the brew are thus both of great importance. Sugar lumps are served but are not added to the tea. They are placed on the tongue, and the tea is drawn through them. Frequently, accompanying sweetmeats, dried fruit or fruit syrups take the place of sugar.

Iran still grows most of its own tea in the Caspian littoral, but is obliged to import to satisfy all the needs of its growing population. The finest Caspian tea is fragrant and very expensive and consumed entirely in Iran, but many people find a blend of Earl Grey and Darjeeling to be a good approximation to Iranian tea. For formal entertaining, the tea will be flavored with cinnamon or garnished with crushed rose petals.

Half a teaspoon of Earl Grey blended with half a teaspoon of a cinnamon or rose tea will make a dozen small glasses of light amber tea. Serve with a bowl of sugar lumps or sugared almonds or a mixture of dried fruits, as well as with a selection of pastries and sweetmeats.

> The waterpipe gives pleasure at your lips, And in your mouth
> its reed has turned to sugar. 'Tis not tobacco smoke which
> wreathes about your head, But clouds which turn about the
> moon, and turn again.
>
> Anonymous

Opposite: Syrup Fingers (*bâmieh*) and Syrup Threads (*zoloobiyâ*)

DESSERTS AND DELICACIES

Puddings and desserts as we know them in the West play an insignificant role in the cuisine of Persia. The name itself, *dessert*, is of course the French word for the sweet course and was adopted in Iran only in the early part of this century to describe these dishes. In Iran many people complete their meal with bread, cheese, and herbs, and the traditional dessert on offer is a bowl of fresh fruit, followed by tea (see page 245) and sweetmeats (see page 260).

> I have been at some Entertainments in Ispahan, where they have had above fifty sorts of Fruit at Table, some of which grow three or four hundred Leagues off. France, or Italy, can't afford any Thing like it.
>
> Sir John Chardin, *Travels in Persia 1673-1677*

The Persians eat a great deal of fruit throughout the year. From April and throughout the summer months come a wide variety of melons: first the small and sweet *garmak* (like a honeydew or cantaloupe) to ones the size of footballs (which are white inside and taste like "one entire lump of pure sugar," as Sir John Chardin famously noted) and on to the huge watermelons in late summer.

The famously sweet apricots arrive in early summer, followed by black cherries from Meshed, and white cherries from Isfahan, nectarines and peaches. Then come the first of the grapes. There are more than a dozen varieties that are commonly available for the dining table, but whether they are large, small, long, round, black, red pink, or white, seedless or juicy, they are all without exception, sweet and fleshy. Sir John Chardin wrote:

> In Persia they keep their Grapes all Winter, leaving them half the Winter hanging upon the Vine, each Bunch being folded in a Linnen Bag, to hinder the Birds from getting at them; they pick just the quantity they intend to eat; this is the Advantage of the dry serene Air, which the Persians breathe, that it preserves every Thing.

Autumn heralds the arrival of apples, pears, quinces, figs, and a large variety of plums, as well as the first of the winter fruits: sweet and sour pomegranates, medlars, persimmons, dates, sweet and sour oranges, tangerines, and sweet and sour lemons.

The fruit is piled high on to a large tray in a carefully arranged confusion of glorious choice. Tiny clusters of grapes are cut, and the

Opposite: Baklava (*bâghlavâ*)

hostess sees that each guest is given a selection of fruit. Melons are always cut up and chilled before serving and the jewel-like seeds of the pomegranate are pried from their leathery casing and poured into a bowl to be eaten with a spoon.

Since desserts do not form a part of the traditional Persian meal, many of the sweet rice creams given in this section are not really desserts at all. Many of them are nourishing dishes ideal to tempt a flagging appetite caused by ill health or bereavement. Others are nursery dishes, and others are simply iced refreshments served to welcome newly arrived guests on a hot summer's day.

It seems the Persian have never lacked for ice, and that, given the extreme heat of an Iranian summer, is little short of a miracle.

Three hundred years ago, Sir John Chardin reported with some astonishment that:

> They use abundance of Ice in Persia. In Summer especially
> every one drinks with Ice: But that which is most remarkable, is,
> That tho' at Ispahan, and even at Tauris (Tabriz), which is
> further North, the Cold is dry and penetrating more than it is in
> any part of France or England, yet the greatest part of the
> People drink with Ice as well in the Winter as the Summer.

He gave a detailed description of how the ice is made and kept into the summer months, adding,

> What is very Remarkable, as well as Agreeable in their Ice, is its
> beauty and clearness; you can't see the least Dirt, nor
> gloominess; Rock-water is not clearer, nor more transparent
> than it is.

In 1891, Dr. Wills, a resident English doctor, was also impressed by the abundance and quality of the ice, commenting that "the Persians well understand the art of making water-ices and ice-creams." He too described how ice (*yakh*) was made and stored in a special pit (*châl*). He went on to explain that in Shiraz, ice was available from May to October and that no one would think of drinking anything uncooled.

> So common is the use of ice that the poorest are enabled to have
> it, a big bit being sold for a farthing, and even the bowls of
> water for gratuitous drinking at the shop doors are cooled by it.
> Ripe fruit is generally also cooled prior to being eaten.

Despite the introduction of the modern refrigerator (which is called a *yakhchâl*), mountain-stored ice is still available in great blocks in Iran today. It can be purchased very reasonably to fill ice boxes and to cool drinks and fruit for picnics and parties.

Cooled fruit and iced dishes make an appearance at any time of the day, not only because they are undoubtedly sweet and pleasant, but because many of these cooling refreshments have come to be viewed by modern Iranian hostesses as useful dishes to serve when a dessert is expected.

When they are presented at the end of a Persian banquet, though, they must be viewed as an extravagant extra, more usually served in hospitable deference to Western custom. Happily, the traditional bowls of fresh fruit are never omitted, nor are the pastries and sweetmeats and the numerous tiny glasses of fragrant tea.

> Among its fruits, the grapes, melons, pomegranates and figs are
> excellent. As for its inhabitants, they are hospitable to strangers,
> inclined towards good and charitable deeds, and fond of
> making the pilgrimage to Mecca.
>
> Hamdollah Mostowfi (fourteenth-century poet describing
> Khawaf, a village in the northeastern province
> of Khorassan)

PERSIAN ICE CREAM
Bastani Sa'labi

An ice cream maker or simply a freezer and some patience are all that are needed to make this wonderful ice cream. Of all the ices, *sa'labi* ice cream, or that made with *sa'lab* (salep, a white powder from the *Orchis mascularis*) is the best known. This ice cream, sprinkled with pistachios and laced with rosewater, was first produced commercially in Tehran some forty years ago by a certain Akbar Mashdi. His ice cream was so delicious that everyone aspired to make their own ice cream like his. Today, all such ices are known simply as *"Akbar Mashadi."*

I was given this recipe by my sister-in-law, Batul. It is not difficult to make, though salep can be hard to find (and it is not really possible to make without salep). Some people add 1/3 cup small chips of frozen heavy cream about five minutes before the freezing time is finished instead of salep, but it does not give the same elastic and satiny consistency that is the hallmark of this ice cream.

Salep is occasionally available in Iranian or Middle Eastern shops in the West, and ready-made Persian ice cream can always be found in Iranian stores. It is delicious on its own, or it may be served with sweet noodles (see following recipe).

---

2 cups milk

1 cup sugar

1-1½ tablespoons rosewater

1 level teaspoon salep

1 teaspoon liquid saffron (optional) (page 36)

1 teaspoon coarsely chopped pistachios (optional)

Turn on the ice cream maker to chill. And put a bowl in the freezer to chill.

Beat the milk, sugar, and rosewater together. While beating, sprinkle in the powdered salep until the sugar and salep are completely dissolved. If desired, stir in the liquid saffron at this stage.

Pour into the ice cream maker and freeze, turning for 25 minutes (or according to instructions). If wished, chop the frozen heavy cream into small pieces and add to the ice cream five minutes before the end of the freezing. (See above.)

When softly firm, pile the ice cream into the chilled bowl and keep covered in the freezer. Garnish with chopped pistachios.

SWEET NOODLES
Pâloodeh

This is a recipe dating back to the days of ancient Persia. Originally, it was made into small rice-like grains, which were served with fruit syrups, and indeed this version of *pâloodeh* can still be found among the Zoroastrian community in the great salt desert of southeastern Iran. But throughout the rest of Persia it more usually appears in noodle form, frequently served with the wondrous Persian ice cream or as a cooling refreshment laced with lime or sour cherry syrup. Traditionally, these noodles were made in a manual paste-making machine.

---

1 cup cornstarch
2½ cups water

Slowly blend the cornstarch with one third of the water until smooth, then add the rest of the water.

Stir continuously over medium heat until the water is completely reduced and the mixture is a smooth, thick, and very white paste.

Have a bowl of iced water ready. When cool enough to handle, put the paste into an icing bag, and using the finest nozzle, force the paste directly into the iced water.

Strain and serve with lime or sour cherry juice, or serve with Persian ice cream and lemon juice.

Or you can buy fine Chinese rice noodles, dip into boiling water for a moment, then strain and stir into a bowl of ice.

ICED MELON
Pâloodeh Garmak

This crushed melon dessert is sometimes diluted with ice as a refreshing drink, but it is also delicious served thoroughly chilled as a dessert. The small honeydew melons are the first of the season and are surely the most fragrant and refreshing melons of all. While it is never necessary to add sugar in Persia, it may not come amiss to sprinkle a little superfine sugar in with the rosewater if the melons are not quite sweet enough.

----

2 melons (honeydew, musk, *or* cantaloupe)
2 teaspoons rosewater (optional)
superfine sugar (if necessary)

Garnish
sprinkling of crushed rose petals (optional)

Working over a bowl to catch the juice, cut the melons in half, remove the seeds, and scoop out the flesh. Chop coarsely (or put into a food processor for half a minute) and add the rosewater (and sugar if necessary) to taste.

Chill in the refrigerator. If liked, sprinkle lightly with crushed rose petals just before serving ice-cold.

> The Melons...are the most excellent Fruit in all Persia. They
> reckon in that Country above twenty different sorts of them; the
> first are called Guermec, as much as to say, the hot ones; they
> are round and small. This is the sort of Melon that the Spring
> Produces;...in the Month of April, They will eat at that time a
> matter of ten or twelve Pound of Melon a-Day, for a Fortnight or
> three Weeks together; and this is as much for Health's sake as it
> is to please their Palates, for they look upon it as a great
> refresher and cooler of their Blood; and if a Man is fallen away,
> it will restore him again.
>
> Sir John Chardin, *Travels in Persia 1673-1677*

DRIED FRUIT SALAD
Miveh Khoshkbâr

In winter, when fresh fruit is limited, this popular dessert makes a frequent appearance. The choice of dried fruit varies from kitchen to kitchen and the following selection is merely a suggestion.

---

2 cups dried fruit (apricots, peaches, figs, prunes, golden raisins, and currants)
$\frac{1}{2}$ cup each almond and pistachio slivers
the peel of 1 orange and 1 lemon
sugar to taste
2 teaspoons orange blossom water
some tiny sprigs of mint

Wash and drain the dried fruit, then place in a bowl with 2 cups warm water and leave to soak, overnight if possible.

Peel the orange and the lemon finely, and cut into fine julienne strips. Put in a small pan of cold water, bring to a boil and strain. Do this twice more to remove bitterness.

Place the fruit, the soaking water, the slivers of pistachios and almonds, and the strips of peel into a saucepan and bring slowly to a boil. Simmer until fruit is tender, but not overly soft. Add sugar to taste.

Remove the fruit with a slotted spoon, and reduce the syrup until thickening. Remove from heat, stir in the orange blossom water, and pour over the fruit.

Chill thoroughly before serving, garnishing with tiny sprigs of mint leaves.

SAFFRON RICE PUDDING
Shollehzard

This dish has a very special place in the hearts of our family. As a child, my husband was stung by a scorpion and he nearly died. During the severe and dangerous illness that followed, my mother-in-law vowed that should he survive, she would make saffron rice pudding each year, on the occasion of the martyrdom of Imam Hassan, to share with her relatives, friends, and neighbors, and all who had prayed for her son's swift recovery. This she continues to do today, nearly sixty years later, and far from her home in Persia.

Such pledges are not uncommon in Iran, and serve as a delightful reminder of the miracle and joy of life. Not surprisingly, I became very fond of this dish, and I frequently serve it as a dessert, in addition of course to the fresh fruit, tea, pastries, and sweetmeats.

½ cup short grain rice
about 7 cups water
¾ cup sugar
1 teaspoon liquid saffron (see page 36)
1 tablespoon solid vegetable shortening
2 tablespoons rosewater

Garnish
ground cinnamon
almond and pistachio slivers (optional)

Pick over, wash, and put the rice to boil in the water in a large saucepan over medium heat until very soft, adding more water if necessary and stirring from time to time. (Be careful it doesn't boil over.)

When rice is completely soft, stir in the sugar, rosewater, and saffron and simmer until sugar is dissolved.

Reduce heat, melt the vegetable shortening, and stir in. Cover and simmer for three minutes.

Dish up into a serving bowl. When set decorate with powdered cinnamon and, if desired, almond and pistachio slivers.

RICE CREAM
Fereni

Fereni is a simple rice cream, smooth and delicate, that can be eaten hot or cold. In my opinion, its light fragrance is greatly enhanced when it is served well chilled. This dessert often calls for the addition of half a teaspoon of ground cardamom seed, but my mother-in-law (whose recipe this is) prefers not to risk discoloring its smooth, creamy appearance.

This dish needs continuous stirring over gentle heat. It must be neither hurried nor neglected for a moment. But if by any chance the cream does go a little lumpy for lack of constant attention, a quick whizz in the food processor can partly remedy the situation.

....

½ cup superfine sugar
1½ tablespoons rosewater
1 cup rice flour
1 quart milk

Garnish
chopped pistachios

....

Measure out the sugar and set aside. Have the rosewater and a tablespoon handy.

Mix the rice flour with some of the cold milk to a smooth paste. Bring the rest of the milk to a boil, stir into the paste, then return it all to another (cold) saucepan, and stir over low to medium heat. Stir continuously for 10 minutes or so until it begins to thicken, then stir in the sugar and rosewater. Stir over low heat for another 3 minutes until it is well mixed, smooth and shiny. Pour into a glass serving bowl and leave to cool.

Garnish with chopped pistachios and serve well chilled.

RICE PUDDING WITH MILK
Sheer Berenj

A far cry from our own traditional baked rice pudding, this light and flavorsome version makes a delightful alternative. It is always served refreshingly chilled in Persia.

....

½ cup short grain rice
1 quart milk
2 cups sugar
½ teaspoon ground cardamom
1½ tablespoons rosewater

Garnish
pistachio slivers

....

Pick over and wash the rice, then leave to soak in a large saucepan in water standing 1 inch above level of rice for half an hour.

Bring to a boil and cook until soft, then add the milk, sugar, cardamom, and rosewater, and continue cooking until the liquid has all been absorbed, stirring from time to time and being careful it doesn't stick (especially toward the end of the cooking time).

When the consistency has become thick and creamy, pour into a serving bowl and leave to cool.

Serve well chilled and garnish with pistachio and almond slivers.

ICE IN HEAVEN
Yakh dar Behesht

As with the previous two desserts, this rosewater-flavored cream must be cooked very gently indeed. Its delicate flavor is best appreciated after it has been thoroughly chilled.

The cooking starch used in Iran is derived from wheat and can be found on sale in Iranian shops in the West. But cornstarch may be used with equal success. This and the following recipe are best made in a heavy-bottomed saucepan.

1 cup cornstarch
$2\frac{1}{2}$ cups water
1 cup rice flour
$2\frac{1}{2}$ cups milk
1-$1\frac{1}{4}$ cups sugar
$\frac{2}{3}$ cup rosewater

Garnish
chopped pistachios

Soak the cornstarch in the water and leave for 10 minutes.
Blend the rice flour with the milk.
Put the cornstarch and the rice flour in a pan and bring to a boil slowly on a low heat, stirring constantly.When it comes to a boil, add the sugar and rosewater, and continue to cook gently on a very low heat for 5-10 minutes more, until it is smooth and glossy.
Pour into a serving bowl (or individual bowls) and decorate with chopped pistachios. Serve well chilled.

HALVAH
Halvâ

Halvah was originally made in pre-Islamic Persia as a celebratory dish. Known as *sen*, it was a fudge made of sprouting wheat, dates, walnuts, fennel seeds, turmeric, and oil, and it was prepared on the last day of the New Year festival to sustain the ancestors on their heavenward journey following their annual visit to earth.

The conquest of Islam in the seventh century crushed many of the ways of the ancient religion, but it was less easy to alter people's eating habits. They continued to make *sen* (and still do in southeastern Iran), but gradually another form of this fudge came to be made on the departure of loved ones to heaven. Today it is called *halvâ*, the Arabic derivative of "sweet," and it is a plain sweet dish, made only on the occasion of the death of a close relative to be offered to mourners at the memorial service.

Other, more festive and sweeter versions of halvah have come down to us. Quite different from this fudge-like sweet of ancient Iran, they are made of the precious sesame seed, plain or flavored with pistachios, and are popular all over the Middle East. They can be purchased ready-made at any Greek or Middle Eastern store in the West.

---

1 cup sugar

½ cup water

4 tablespoons rosewater

4 teaspoons liquid saffron (see page 36)

1 cup unsalted butter

2 cups all-purpose flour

Boil the sugar and water together until the sugar is dissolved, then add the rosewater and saffron. Remove from heat but keep warm.

Melt butter in a pan and gradually stir in the flour to a smooth paste. Cook over a low heat until golden in color.

Over a very low heat, slowly add the syrup to blend into a smooth paste. Remove from heat immediately.

While still warm, spread on to a plate and press down with the back of a spoon, making a pattern with the spoon.

Serve cold, cut into small wedges, accompanied by toast and tea.

HALVAH CREAM
Kâchee

This dish is a creamier thinner version of the fudge-like halvah of the previous recipe. Made with extra water, it is usually served warm.

Another traditional dish with a long history, *kâchee* is thought to have great restorative powers, and is frequently served to newly married couples during their honeymoon and also to nursing mothers.

---

2 cups sugar
2½ cups water
2 cups unsalted butter
2 cups all-purpose flour
4 tablespoons rosewater
1 tablespoon liquid saffron (see page 36)

Bring the sugar and water to a boil. Remove from the heat as soon as the sugar has dissolved.

Melt the butter in a saucepan, then over a low heat stir in the flour to a smooth paste. Stirring continuously, slowly add the syrup, rosewater and liquid saffron. Cook very gently for a few minutes more, stirring constantly, until the mixture is a thin smooth cream. Add a little warm water if it becomes too thick.

Dish up into individual bowls and serve warm.

SWEETMEATS AND OTHER CONFECTIONS

The Oxford English Dictionary defines sweetmeats as follows: "Sugared cakes or pastry, confections, preserved or candied fruits, sugared nuts, also globules, lozenges, drops or sticks made of sugar with fruit or other flavouring." This is a fulsome yet perfectly accurate translation of the Persian word *shireeni*, which simply means sweet things, so despite the fact the OED notes that the use of "sweetmeats" today is "chiefly archaic," it nevertheless remains the most apt description of the delicacies that appear in this section.

The Persians have long had a taste for sweet things. When Herodotus visited Persia in about 500BC he commented on the sweetmeats served after the meat course, and the aspiring page of the Sassanian King Khosrow gave a glowing description of sweet pastries stuffed with almonds.

The regions of Persia all have their specialities, but the Yazd region in the southeast of the country is the most famous for its wide and delicious range of cakes and sweet pastries. It will be recalled that it was to Yazd that the ancient Persians, the followers of Zoroaster, fled before the Muslims in the seventh century, and it is in this region that many of the ancient ways still survive.

It must be said, however, that generally the Persians partake of sweetmeats only on special occasions, the most special being of course the Iranian New Year in March. At that time, tables are laden with sweet pastries, sugared nuts, confections, and "lozenges" of all kinds. *Lowz*, incidentally, is Arabic for diamond shapes and most particularly for diamond-shaped sweets. It is the origin of our lozenge. Many of the Persian sweets are cut into this rhombus-diamond shape, the most famous being baklava (see page 269).

The sampling of sweetmeats that follows is very limited, and representative only of some of the most popular. Any one (or any number) of them may be offered whenever tea is served.

SUGARED ALMONDS
Noghl

Strikingly different from our own pink and white sugar almonds, these tiny sugar almond slivers give little resistance before melting in the mouth. *Noghl* are served at all festive occasions. They are offered to friends and relatives during the first moments of the New Year so that their mouths and their lives will remain "sweet" for the entire year. And at wedding receptions they are proffered to guests so that the ceremony (and the future of the young couple) may be filled with sweetness and happiness.

Noghl are also served at formal tea parties as an elegant replacement for the sugar lumps usually served with the tiny glasses of tea.

While not difficult to make, the task becomes easier if two people undertake the sugaring of the almonds. Unless you are ambidextrous, it is very hard to perform the different actions required, and in any event, it is more pleasant to work with a partner. I am grateful to Miss Sobhani for giving me her recipe.

....

> **2 cups sugar**
> **2½ cups water**
> **½ cup rosewater**
> **1 cup almond slivers (see page 25)**

....

Boil the sugar and water in a pan until it reaches 237°F, or when a drop of syrup firms up immediately on a cold saucer, and add the rosewater. Bring back to a boil, then immediately remove from heat.

Put almonds in a saucepan (preferably nonstick) and tossing and shaking them constantly, add the syrup a drop at a time. Continue to toss and roll the almonds while adding the syrup drop by drop until the almonds are thickly coated. They will whiten as they cool and more syrup can be added. When the syrup is finished, pour the sugared almonds on to a baking sheet to cool.

When they are cold, white, and separated, they may be stored in an airtight container and kept for up to a month.

STARCH FUDGE
Masghati

This fudge, known as *Masghati* in Persian, comes from Muscat on the Arab shores of the Persian Gulf, most of which were part of the Persian Empire until 300 years ago. It is made of cooking starch, which in Iran is usually derived from wheat. Cornstarch will serve as well.

3 tablespoons cornstarch
2 cups water
¾ cup sugar
¼ cup unsalted butter
1 teaspoon rosewater

Blend all the ingredients together and stir over medium heat until thick and sticky.

Grease a 7- x 11-inch pan lightly with butter and pour in the mixture. Leave to cool and set. Cut into strips lengthwise, about ¾-inch wide, then diagonally also ¾-inch apart into neat diamond-shaped pieces.

DATE FUDGE
Ranginak

The sweetly moist dark dates of Iran are some of the best in the world and a far cry from the more familiar pale dry dates that make an appearance in Western supermarkets each Christmas time. Iranian dates are packed in cans to keep them fresh and can be found at most Middle Eastern and Iranian stores in the autumn and early winter.

They are so delicious that they are in little need of culinary expertise to improve their flavor. For special occasions, the pit is removed and replaced with a split almond or walnut or a sliver of molded rose-flavored marzipan. In the dish below, the plain "fudge" mixture serves to balance the sweetness of the dates. In Shiraz, the dates and walnuts are chopped together, spread in a shallow dish and the fudge mixture poured over it. In the imperial court in seventeenth-century Isfahan, once the dates and fudge mixture had set, *sheer berenj* (see page 256) would be poured all over the dish. When cool it would be garnished with a pretty display of powdered pistachios and almonds, hence its name, *ranginak*, meaning colorful.

---

1 pound dates
³⁄₄ cup walnut halves
1 cup butter
2 cups all-purpose flour

Garnish
1 teaspoon each ground pistachios and almonds

Pit the dates, insert a quarter of a walnut in place of the pit, and close up the date again. Stand each date up in a shallow serving dish.

Melt the butter and stir in the flour. Cook gently until golden, then pour closely over the dates, being sure to fill all the crevices.

Leave to set, then garnish with pistachio and almond slivers. Cut into squares and serve with tea.

> As for the Dates, which I take to be the best Fruits in the World, they are no where so good as they are in Persia. They grow in Arabia in greater Quantities than they do in Persia; but besides, being much less in Size, they do not come near those of Persia for Goodness; and that both at the Time you gather them, and a long time after, are cover'd with thick Juice, like a Sirrop, which is more soft, and more delicately sweet to the Taste than Virgin-Honey.
>
> Sir John Chardin, *Travels in Persia 1673-1677*

Syrup Fingers
Bâmieh

These syrupy delicacies are known as *bâmieh* in Persian, as is the vegetable, okra. The only similarity is in their ridged shape. It would thus appear that despite their syrupy, Eastern aspect, these sweetmeats are fairly new to Persia. The African okra has not been common in Iran for many years, and even today, it is better known in the Persian Gulf than in the northern regions of Iran.

The nature of the pastry too is identical to choux pastry in the making (if not in the baking) and gives one further reason to suppose that these sweet "ladies' fingers" made an appearance on the Persian scene at about the same time as the vegetables, possibly over a hundred years ago, when the French influence was great.

In any event, they are now a permanent feature among the range of sweetmeats served at Persian celebrations and banquets, and so they must be included here. They are frequently found in two shades: a dark golden color and a pale yellow shade. The following recipe will result in pale yellow *bâmieh*. If you wish to make them darker, simply add an additional tablespoon of butter before you boil the water and butter together, and before you add the flour. The sugar will then caramelize when you fry the *bâmieh*. They are usually served together with *zoloobiyâ*, syrup threads (see following recipe). I am grateful to my sister-in-law who gave me these two recipes.

Syrup
1 cup sugar
½ cup water
½ dessertspoon fresh lemon juice
2 dessertspoons rosewater

Fingers
½ cup water
4 tablespoons butter
1 cup all-purpose flour
2 medium eggs

First prepare the syrup. Dissolve the sugar in the water by bringing it to a boil. Immediately add the lemon juice and boil for five minutes. Remove from heat, add rosewater and leave to cool completely.

Heat oil for deep-frying the fingers to 350°F.

To make the fingers, bring the water and butter to a boil in a saucepan, reduce the heat, and add the flour all at once, beating until it is a smooth paste. Then beat in the eggs one at a time until the mixture is smooth and shiny.

Pipe the mixture through a large rosette, making the fingers no longer than 3 inches, straight into the hot oil. When golden, remove with a slotted spoon and slip straight into the cold syrup. Turn until well coated, remove from the syrup and leave to cool on a wire rack over a plate to catch the excess syrup. When cool, arrange on a plate and serve with tea.

These can be stored in an airtight container for a week or ten days.

✸ ✸

SYRUP THREADS
Zoloobiyâ

In his book, *The Land of the Lion and Sun*, Dr. Wills, an English doctor resident in Iran in the nineteenth century, described these syrupy threads as "a curious form of eatable" that are prepared during the fasting month of Ramadan. And he noted that they were "delicate-looking and rather appetising."

Today, *zoloobiyâ* are considered far too "appetizing" to eat during only one month in the year, and they are frequently served on special occasions. A very similar sweetmeat is popular in India, where it is known as *jelebi*.

Syrup
1 cup granulated sugar
½ cup water
1 teaspoon lemon juice
4 teaspoons rosewater

Threads
1 cup tepid water
1½ cups self-rising white flour
2 tablespoons arrowroot
juice of half a lemon

First prepare the syrup. Dissolve the sugar in the water by bringing it to a boil. Immediately add the lemon juice and boil for five minutes. Remove from heat, add rosewater, and leave to cool completely.

Heat oil for deep-frying the fingers to 350°F.

Blend the water, flour, arrowroot, and the lemon juice into a smooth thin batter. (This can be mixed in a food processor if wished.)

Pipe the mixture through a ⅛-inch nozzle* straight into the hot oil in rose or pretzel shapes.

Turn over in the oil and remove with a slotted spoon when evenly golden. Drop immediately in the cold syrup. Turn until well coated, remove from the syrup, and leave to cool on a wire rack over a plate to catch the excess syrup. When cool, arrange on a plate and serve with tea.

---

* A standard piping set (or a clean plastic ketchup dispenser) will do.

RICE SHORTBREADS
Nân-e Berenji

Nân-e berenji is another melting sweetmeat that is very popular on the New Year table. The shortbread should remain creamy white in color and is garnished with a sprinkling of black poppy seeds. Preparation needs to be started a day earlier as the mixture improves with overnight chilling.

---

1 teaspoon finely ground cardamom
3 cups fine white rice flour
1 cup unsalted butter
1½ cups powdered sugar
2 medium eggs
1 tablespoon rosewater

Mix the cardamom and flour together and put to one side.

Cream the butter and sugar together, then add the eggs one at a time, beating constantly. Beat in the rosewater.

Gradually beat in the rice flour and continue beating until the mixture is stiff and smooth.

Cover and chill for six hours or overnight.

Preheat the oven to 375°F.

Take a teaspoon of the mixture, roll into a ball, press on to a greased baking sheet. Imprint a pattern with a thimble and sprinkle with a few poppy seeds.

Bake for 12-15 minutes. They should be firm but should not change color.

Remove from the baking sheet, and store like cookies. These keep very nicely for a week or ten days.

CHICKPEA SHORTBREADS
Nân-e Nokhodchi

These tiny shortbreads are served at the New Year festival in March. They have a long history as part of the ancient festival of *No Rooz*, and are traditionally made in a four-leafed clover shape. They simply melt in the mouth and are quite delectable at any time of the year. If you cannot find a four-leaf clover pastry cutter, rosette cutters will do very well.

---

1 cup chickpea flour
½ cup superfine sugar
½ teaspoon ground cardamom
¼ cup unsalted butter

Sift the flour, sugar, and cardamom together on a pastry board.

Place the butter in the center and carefully knead the flour into the butter until the mixture holds together. (This is a very short mixture but it will eventually hold together after some kneading. An egg yolk may be used to help bind the mixture but the shortbread will be softer without.)

Carefully roll out to a thickness of ¼ inch and cut out into tiny shapes and place on a sheet of wax paper on a baking sheet. Leave to cool and firm for 30 minutes.

In the meantime, preheat the oven to 300°F.

Bake in the oven for 5-7 minutes. Allow to cool.

Decorate with finely chopped pistachios, and arrange carefully on a plate. They will keep very well for a week or ten days in an airtight container.

BAKLAVA
Bâghlavâ

Baklava is no longer a mysterious Eastern dessert, known only by exotic reputation. Nowadays, it has become almost common and can be found in every Turkish and Greek restaurant in every town and city in the West, and in a good many other restaurants too. Made with filo pastry, nuts, and honey syrup, these large square syrupy sweets, sometimes served with cream, have taken over the name of baklava.

Persian *bâghlavâ*, however, is a very different type of sweetmeat. Smaller and less syrupy, made with finely-ground almonds and pistachios, and faintly flavored with cardamom, it is crisper and more refined altogether. It is never served with cream; small glasses of fragrant amber tea are the only accompaniment.

In this recipe, the *bâghlavâ* is made in two layers of different colored nuts. The ingredients are sufficient for a 7- x 11-inch baking pan and will result in about 40 pieces.

Filo pastry can be bought ready-made in most supermarkets and all Middle Eastern stores. Follow the instructions on the package, i.e. have all the ingredients ready before you open the package; and once opened, work quickly. I find it best to separate six sheets of pastry (rewrapping the rest and returning it to the package), then cut them with scissors to the required size, keeping them covered with a lightly damp cloth until you use them.

If you do not have a candy thermometer, put a drop of syrup on a cold saucer and allow to cool—it should not be runny but slightly resistant when pressed with a finger, as for jam.

Filling
1 cup each ground almonds and pistachios
1 teaspoon ground cardamom
3/4 cup granulated sugar
2 ounces filo pastry (about 6 large sheets)

Syrup
3/4 cup sugar
6 tablespoons water
2 tablespoons rosewater

Garnish
1½ tablepoons finely chopped pistachios

Preheat the oven to 375°F, and melt the butter.

Prepare two sets of filling: mix the almonds with half the sugar and cardamom, and the pistachios with the remaining sugar and cardamom. Put to one side.

Brush a shallow baking pan with butter and line with one layer of filo pastry, brush with melted butter, then another layer of filo pastry also brushed with butter. Then pack in the almond mixture firmly and evenly and put a layer of pastry on it, brush with butter. Pack in the pistachio mixture and cover with another two layers of pastry, each brushed with butter.

Prick holes all over, put into the preheated oven and bake until golden brown (20-30 minutes).

Heat the sugar and water together and boil gently for 15 minutes to 220°F. Remove from heat immediately and carefully stir in the rosewater.

Remove *bâghlavâ* from oven and with a sharp pointed knife immediately cut lengthwise into strips about ¾ inch apart then across at an angle, also ¾ inch apart into neat diamond-shaped pieces. (Make sure you cut through to the bottom layers of pastry.) While still warm in the baking pan, pour the syrup all over, sprinkle over the chopped pistachios, then leave to cool.

When quite cold, cover with aluminum foil, and keep in the pan until ready to serve.

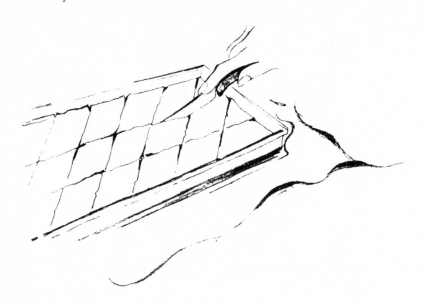

MARZIPAN MULBERRIES
Toot

Simply called mulberries (*toot*) in Persian, these delicate little marzipan rolls are softly firm and made to look like white mulberries. They make an appearance on the New Year table and are equally popular at other festive occasions.

------

2 cups ground almonds
1 teaspoon ground cardamom
1 cup powdered sugar
4 tablespoons rosewater
3/4 cup superfine sugar
2-3 tablespoons pistachio slivers

Mix the ground almonds, cardamom, and powdered sugar together in a bowl, then slowly stir in the rosewater, and knead lightly to make a soft dough.

Take a teaspoonful of the mixture and mold into the shape of a mulberry. Roll lightly in superfine sugar and put a pistachio sliver in the "stem end" of each "mulberry."

Store in an airtight container. To serve, arrange in circles on a plate with the stems out.

Persian Waffles
Nân-e Panjaere'i

This is another recipe using cornstarch. These light and fragrant rose-shaped waffles are a pure delight to eat.

3/4 cup cornstarch

1/2 cup milk

2 teaspoons rosewater

3 small egg yolks

1 tablespoon all-purpose flour

Garnish

1/2 cup powdered sugar

1/4 teaspoon ground cardamom

Stir the milk into the cornstarch, add the rosewater, and leave to dissolve for 10 minutes.

Heat oil for deep frying to 350°F.

Beat the egg yolks thoroughly, then beat in the flour, and the cornstarch mixture to make a smooth batter.

Heat the waffle iron by holding it in the hot oil. Remove, shake off excess oil and half dip the hot iron into the batter. (Do not coat completely. The batter should come up to the top edge of the iron only, not over the top, thus allowing the waffle to slip off the iron during cooking.)

Plunge straight into the hot oil. Shake after a few moments, and the waffle will separate easily from the iron. Turn the waffle while cooking so that it becomes evenly golden.

Remove waffle from hot oil when crisp and golden, and lay on a paper towel to drain and cool.

Repeat the process until all the batter has been used.

Arrange the waffles on a dish and sprinkle liberally with the cardamom-flavored powdered sugar.

ELEPHANT'S EARS
Goosh-e Feel

These light and delicate little pastries are made from filo pastry, and, provided you keep the pastry well covered, any leftovers from the Baklava (see page 269) may serve very well. If the filo dries out, the pastry sheets become impossible to hold together, so keep the pastry moistly covered. Such fragrant little morsels are too good to miss.

Syrup
1 cup granulated sugar
½ cup water
1½ tablespoons rosewater

Pastries
2 ounces filo pastry

Boil the sugar and water together for 20 minutes. Add the rosewater, remove from heat, and leave to cool. The syrup should be quite cool before being used.

Heat the oil for deep frying to 350°F.

Cut the filo into 2-inch squares, place two together, one on top of the other, and pinch together along the sides only. Drop into the hot oil. They should puff out and turn golden within seconds.

Remove from the oil with a slotted spoon and drop into the syrup for a moment. Take from the syrup with a slotted spoon and drain on a wire rack over a plate to catch the syrup. Serve with tea.

ALMOND PASTRIES
Ghotâb

Small stuffed pastries, known in Iran as *sanbuseh*, have been featured in Persian cuisine for many centuries. The Sassanian King Khosrow found them most delicious in the seventh century; and a number of recipes for both sweet and savory pastries appeared in the seventeenth century cookbooks from the kitchens of the royal Safavid court. Over the centuries, the meat-filled pastries have been adopted by many countries throughout the Middle East (called *sambusak*) and also by India (*samosa*), but in Iran they are now only found in some regions and have little national recognition any more.

The sweet almond-stuffed pastries, however, are found all over Iran and are very popular, served with tea, as after-dinner snacks. This mixture should make about 30 almond pastries.

½ cup unsalted butter
½ cup natural live yogurt
2 medium egg yolks
1½ cups all-purpose flour
½ teaspoon baking powder

Filling
½ cup powdered sugar
¾ cup ground almonds
1 teaspoon ground cardamom

Garnish
½ cup powdered sugar
¼ teaspoon ground cardamom

Beat the softened butter, yogurt, and egg yolks together until creamy. Mix the baking powder and flour together and gradually beat into the creamed mixture. Knead well until smooth and the dough no longer sticks to the fingers. Leave in a covered bowl in a warm room for 2-3 hours to rise.

To prepare the filling, mix together the powdered sugar, ground almonds, and ground cardamom.

Roll out the dough on a well-floured board, fairly thinly, and cut out in 3-inch rounds. Put 2 teaspoons of the filling on each round. Damp the edges and seal together, curving them rather like tiny croissants.

Deep fry in hot oil 385°F for about 4 minutes until golden brown. Drain on a paper towel, then while still warm dredge in cardamom-flavored powdered sugar. When quite cold, sprinkle again with the powdered sugar.

TINY CREAM BUNS
Nân-e Khâmeh-i

I suspect that the idea for these delicious little delights was introduced into Iran during the last hundred years or so. They are the Persian version of the French *profiterole* or the English cream bun. It seems unlikely that they are indigenous to Persia since cream never appears in traditional Persian desserts.

I have included them in this group of Persian sweetmeats because they are very popular in Iran today, and although the recipe is similar to that for *profiteroles*, the end result is quite different. While the English bun is larger than the French *profiterole*, the Persian *nân* is slightly smaller than both. Delicately flavored with rosewater and cardamom, these tiny buns appear reassuringly familiar yet have a haunting aura of the East.

Pastry
1 cup water
½ teaspoon salt
½ cup unsalted butter
1 cup all-purpose flour
4 large eggs

Filling
1¼ cups heavy dream
2 tablespoons powdered sugar
3 tablespoons rosewater

Garnish
4 tablespoons powdered sugar
⅓ teaspoon ground cardamom

Preheat the oven to 350°F.

Bring the water and butter to boiling point in a saucepan, reduce heat, and immediately pour in the flour and salt at one go, beating until the mixture becomes a smooth paste and leaves the side of the pan (about a minute). Remove from heat and leave for a minute or two, then beat in the eggs, one at a time until the paste is smooth and shiny.

Take a teaspoonful of the paste and push it off with your finger (so that the mixture becomes a small ball) on to a baking sheet. Leave 2-3 inches between each ball to allow for expansion when cooking.

Put into the hot oven and bake until puffed and golden (about 10 minutes). Remove from oven. Turn off the oven and leave the door ajar.

Make a small slit in the under side of each bun to release the steam. Put back into the cooling oven for five minutes. Remove and leave to cool on a wire rack.

For the filling, beat the powdered sugar into the cream until mixture is stiff, then slowly add the rosewater spoonful by spoonful (do not beat once the rosewater has been added).

Mix the ground cardamom with the powdered sugar and set aside for garnish.

When the buns are quite cool, pipe the whipped cream through the small slit that was made to release the steam. Pile buns in a pyramid and sprinkle liberally with the cardamom-flavored powdered sugar.

PASTRY TONGUES
Zabun

The extent of French influence in Persia at the beginning of the last century is clearly revealed in the confection shops where French pastries and cakes are displayed along with Persian sweetmeats and confections. Many of the *shireeni-tar*, wet (or creamy) cakes, and the *shireeni khoshk*, dry (or pastry) cakes, are European in style. Interestingly, however, the "French pastry" offered at modern hotels in Tehran is usually a selection of Danish pastries, while the pastries given below have been completely absorbed into the Persian cuisine.

In Iran, such pastries were never made in the home, unlike the Persian confections given in earlier pages. Nevertheless, the following three recipes are simple enough to make, especially in a Western kitchen with its complement of pastry boards, rolling pins, refrigerators, and ovens, and yet are sufficiently different and exotic to make the effort worth while.

---

1 sheet (8 ounces) puff pastry*

Glaze
1 teaspoon flour
1 teaspoon baking soda
1 teaspoon superfine sugar
3-4 teaspoons water

Preheat the oven to 450°F.

To make the glaze, mix the flour with a little water to make a smooth paste, add the baking soda and sugar and a little more water if necessary to produce thick creamy liquid.

Roll out the pastry to a thickness of a little under ¼ inch and cut out long shapes, about 1 inch wide and 5 inches long and rounded at both ends.

Paint the "tongues" with the glaze and place them on a baking sheet, leaving 2 inches between each, and bake them until well risen and golden.

Cool on a wire rack.

---

* The ready-made frozen puff pastry works quite nicely for these pastries. My favorite recipe for homemade pastry appears on page 286.

PASTRY TWISTS
Peechak

....

1 sheet (8 ounces) puff pastry (see previous recipe)
½ cup powdered sugar
¼ teaspoon ground cardamom

....

Preheat the oven to 450°F.

Roll out the pastry to a thickness of a little under ¼ inch and cut out narrow strips, about ¼ inch wide and 3 inches long. Twist each strip so that the top of one end is twisted around to face down.

Lay on a baking sheet leaving 2 inches between each, and bake until well risen and pale golden.

Sprinkle with cardamom-flavored powdered sugar and leave to cool on a wire rack.

CREAM FLAKES
Napoleon

The origins of this popular pastry cake are indisputable. Known as *Napoleon* in Persian, they are in fact a version of *millefeuille*. But such is their popularity among modern Iranians that not to include them in this pasty section would be a sad omission.

---

1 sheet (8 ounces) puff pastry (see page 286)

Filling
1¼ cups milk
1 cup cornstarch
2 egg yolks
1 tablespoon sugar
1 teaspoon rosewater

Preheat the oven to 450°F.

Divide the pastry into two, and roll out each piece into two equal-sized squares to a thickness of ⅛ inch. Rinse the baking sheet in cold water, place pastry on the damp surface, prick all over with a fork, and put in the hot oven to bake for about 10 minutes or until puffed up and golden. Place carefully on to a wire rack and leave to cool.

In the meantime, make the filling by blending the milk and cornstarch together, then beating in the egg yolks and sugar. Cook over a low heat, stirring constantly until thickened. Beat in the rosewater. Put to one side to cool.

When the pastry squares are cool and crisp, trim them to an equal shape, keeping the pastry bits. Spread most of the custard (keeping back 2-3 tablespoons) on one of the squares and carefully lay the other square on top. Spread the remaining custard over the top of the pastry, then sprinkle the crusted pastry bits all over the top to cover it completely.

Cut into four equal squares.

MASTER RECIPES

POACHED LAMB

---

12 ounces boned leg of lamb, knuckle end
1 medium onion
½ teaspoon turmeric
salt and pepper
2-3 teaspoons liquid saffron (see page 36)

Wash the meat thoroughly and leave to soak in fresh water for 3-4 minutes.

Slice the onion finely, put in a pan with the turmeric, salt, and pepper. Add the drained meat and a little water (no more than 1 inch). Simmer gently on a medium-low heat for at least two hours or until the meat is completely tender. Turn off heat and add the liquid saffron, turning the meat and onions over in it.

When the meat is cool enough to handle, strip off the fat and membrane, and pull the meat apart into 4 or 5 pieces.

Arrange the meat around the dish at the base of the rice; or intersperse it in among the rice; or serve it on a separate plate with a tablespoonful of saffron rice sprinkled over as a garnish; or in a bowl with the saffron stock.

If not using immediately, wrap and store in the fridge or freezer. To warm it through, place around the sides of the saucepan on top of the rice during the steaming process.

FRIED FISH

½ **cup all-purpose flour**
½ **teaspoon turmeric**
salt and pepper
½ **teaspoon crushed dried fenugreek leaf (optional)**
4 fillets of fish (flounder, haddock, *or* cod)

Mix the flour, turmeric, salt, pepper, and crushed fenugreek (if using) together.

Dip the fillets in the seasoned flour, covering them completely, and fry them immediately in hot oil.

Serve with *sabzi polow* (rice with herbs) and have extra lemon quarters available.

SAFFRON CHICKEN

1 medium onion
salt and pepper
3-4 chicken breasts
3 teaspoons liquid saffron (see page 36)

Cut the chicken breasts into three or four "mini breasts." Mince the onion into a pan, add the salt, pepper, and three tablespoons of water, then lay the chicken breasts on top. Cover and bring to a simmer on a low heat. Simmer for another 15 minutes, or until the chicken is soft and tender.

Add the liquid saffron and turn the chicken pieces over to coat thoroughly in the saffron sauce.

The chicken breasts may be served in a shallow bowl with the saffron-flavored cooking juices poured over them; or they may be arranged around the dish at the base of the rice or interspersed with the *polow* when dishing up the rice.

FRIED CHICKEN

4 drumsticks *or* other chicken pieces
salt and pepper
3 tablespoons all-purpose flour
½ teaspoon turmeric
salt and freshly ground black pepper

If using any chicken breasts, cut them into three or four "mini breasts." Mix flour, turmeric, and black pepper together in a shallow dish. Roll the chicken pieces in the seasoned flour, then brown in hot oil, turning and rolling the pieces until golden all over.

Serve on a separate plate, or interspersed with the rice, or on the dish around the base of the rice.

NOODLES
Reshteh

....

1 cup all-purpose flour
½ teaspoon salt

....

Mix the flour and salt together, then slowly add water and knead until a smooth pastry-like dough has been formed. If it becomes too sticky, add more flour.

Lightly flour a pastry board and roll out the dough very thinly into a long rectangle. Turn, sprinkle the pastry with flour and roll up into a long roll. With a sharp knife, cut across the roll into narrow strips.*

These noodles may be separated and spread out to dry in a warm room to be kept for future use.

---

* For *reshteh polow* (rice with noodles), make the strips as fine as possible (as for spaghetti), but for *âsh-e reshteh* (noodle soup), the strips should be a little wider, as for linguine or tagliatelli.

Puff Pastry

....

2 cups all-purpose flour
½ teaspoon salt
1 cup, plus 2 tablespoons, unsalted butter
1 teaspoon lemon juice
about ½ cup iced water

....

Sift the flour and salt and rub in the 2 tablespoons of butter with the fingertips. Add lemon juice to the flour and mix to a smooth dough with iced water. Work the mixture into a fairly stiff, smooth dough, adding a little more water if necessary. Make into a ball, sprinkle lightly with flour, wrap in a plastic bag, and put in refrigerator for 1 hour.

Form the remaining butter into a square and putting it between 2 sheets of wax paper, roll it out with a rolling pin to make a 2-inch square. Remove the paper, sprinkle the butter lightly with flour, wrap it in fresh paper, and refrigerate until the butter is firm.

Lightly flour a board and roll out the dough to a strip wider than the butter and more than twice its length. Put the butter at one end and fold the dough over it as if making an envelope. Make sure the butter is completely sealed in. Turn the "envelope" over.

For the first fold, lightly flour the board and the dough and roll out dough gently and evenly into an oblong. Do not roll to the edges, but keep the butter and air within the parcel. Fold one third of the pastry over to the center, then the other third over that. Seal at the sides by pressing lightly, then place the dough into a plastic bag, and refrigerate for another half hour.

Repeat the "folds" 5 or 6 times, refrigerating between each fold. Refrigerate before using.

This dough may be kept wrapped in the refrigerator for a week, or in the freezer for 3-6 months.

"HOT" AND "COLD" FOODS

Almonds	hot
Apples	hot
Apricots	cold
Barberries	cold
Barley/barley flour	cold
Basil	hot
Bayleaf	hot
Beef	cold
Beet	cold
Cabbage	cold
Cardamom	hot
Cardoons	cold
Carrots	cold
Cauliflower	cold
Celery	cold
Cheese (feta)	–
Cherries, sour	cold
Cherries, sweet	hot
Chickpeas/chickpea flour	hot
Chives	hot
Cinnamon	hot
Citrus fruits	cold
Cloves	hot
Cockerel	cold
Coffee	cold
Cilantro (coriander leaf)	cold
Corn/cornstarch	cold
Costmary	hot
Cucumbers	hot
Cumin	cold

Currants	hot
Curry powder	hot
Dates	hot
Dill	hot
Duck	hot
Eggplant	cold
Eggs	hot
Fenugreek leaf	hot
Figs	hot
Fish, all types	hot
Garlic	cold
Ginger	hot
Grapes	hot
Hen	hot
Honey	hot
Kidney beans	cold
Lamb/mutton	hot
Lentils	cold
Maize	hot
Mangoes	hot
Marjoram	hot
Milk	cold
Mint	hot
Mung beans	hot
Mushrooms	hot
Nigella seed	hot
Nutmeg	hot
Okra	hot
Onions/shallots	hot
Oregano	hot
Parsley	hot
Peaches	cold

Pears	–
Peppers	hot
Pinto beans	cold
Pistachios	cold
Pomegranates	cold
Plums	cold
Prunes	cold
Quinces	hot
Radishes	cold
Raisins	hot
Rice/rice flour	cold
Rosewater	hot
Saffron	hot
Salt	hot
Split peas	hot
Sugar	cold
Sumac	cold
Tamarind	cold
Tarragon	hot
Tea	–
Tomato paste	cold
Turkey	cold
Turmeric	hot
Vanilla	hot
Veal	cold
Verjuice	cold
Vinegar	cold
Walnuts	hot
Watermelon	cold
Wheat/flour	hot
Whey	hot
Yogurt	cold

GLOSSARY

Âbishen	oregano
Bâlâghoti	watercress
Barg-e boo	bay leaf
Dârcheen	cinnamon
Felfel	pepper
Gard-e limoo	dried lime powder
Geshneez	coriander/cilantro
Golpar	angelica
Hel	cardamom
Ja'fari	parsley
Jowz-ve hind	nutmeg
Keshmesh	golden raisins
Khalâl bâdâm	almond slivers
Khalâl nâranj	orange peel slivers
Kashkhâsh	poppy seed
Limoo amâni	dried limes
Marzeh	marjoram
Maveez	raisins
Meekhak	cloves
Namak	salt
Na'nâ	mint
Neshâsteh	cornstarch
Piâzcheh	scallions
Pooneh	water mint
Rayhân	basil
Seer	garlic
Shâhi	costmary
Shambaleeleh	fenugreek
Sheveed	dill
Siâhdâneh	nigella seeds
Soomâgh	sumac
Tahteezak	costmary
Tarkhoon	tarragon
Tarreh	garlic chives
Torâbcheh	radishes
Za'farân	saffron
Zanjebil	ginger
Zardchoobeh	turmeric
Zeereh sefeed	caraway seed
Zeereh siâh	cumin seed
Zereshk	barberries

Almond slivers	*khalâl bâdâm*
Angelica	*golpar*
Barberries	*zereshk*
Basil	*rayhân*
Bay leaf	*barg-e boo*
Caraway seed	*zeereh sefeed*
Cardamom	*hel*
Cinnamon	*dârcheen*
Cloves	*meekhak*
Coriander/Cilantro	*geshneez*
Cornstarch	*neshâsteh*
Costmary	*shâhi, tahteezak*
Cumin seed	*zeereh siâh*
Dill	*sheveed*
Fenugreek	*shambaleeleh*
Garlic	*seer*
Garlic Chives	*tarreh*
Ginger	*zanjebil*
Golden raisins	*keshmesh*
Lime, dried	*limoo amâni*
Lime, dried, powder	*gard-e limoo*
Marjoram	*marzeh*
Nigella seed	*siâhdâneh*
Nutmeg	*jowz-ve hind*
Orange peel slivers	*khalâl nâranj*
Oregano	*âbishen*
Parsley	*ja'fari*
Pepper	*felfel*
Poppy seed	*khashkhâsh*
Radishes	*torâbcheh*
Raisins	*maveez*
Saffron	*za'farân*
Salt	*namak*
Scallions	*tarreh*
Spearmint	*na'nâ*
Sumac	*soomâgh*
Tarragon	*tarkhoon*
Turmeric	*zardchoobeh*
Watercress	*bâlâghoti*
Water mint	*pooneh*

BIBLIOGRAPHY

Anon, *The Modern Traveller* Vol. 2, James Duncan, 1827

Apicius, *The Roman Cookery Book*, A Critical Translation by Barbara Flower and Elizabeth Rosenbaum, Harrap, 1958

Arnold, Arthur, *Through Persia by Caravan*, 1877

Batmanglij, Najmieh, *Persian Cookery*, Mage, Washington, 1987

Bradley-Birth, F.B., *Through Persia from the Gulf to the Caspian*, Smith Elder, 1909

Brown, E.G., *A Literary History of Persia*, Fisher, Unwin, 1902

Byron, May, *Jam Book*, Hodder & Stoughton, 1913

Chardin, Sir John, *Travels in Persia 1673-1677* (reprinted by Dover Publications, 1988)

Culpeper, Nicholas, *Complete Herbal*, c.1650 (reprinted by Dover Publications, 1988)

Curzon, George, *Persia*, Longmans, 1892

David, Elizabeth, *Italian Food*, Macdonald, 1954

Fryer, John, *A New Account of East India and Persia*, Chiswell, 1698

Ghanoonparvar, Mohammad, *Persian Cuisine*, Books 1 and 2, Mazda, 1982

Glasse, Hannah, *The Art of Cookery Made Plain and Easy*, 1747 (reprinted by SR Publications, 1971)

Grigson, Jane, *Vegetable Book*, Michael Joseph, 1978

Hekmat, F., *The Art of Persian Cooking*, Doubleday, 1961

Herbert, Thomas, *Famous Empires of Persia and Hindustant*

Herodotus, *The Histories*, translated by George Rawlinson, University of Chicago, 1952

Jaza'eri, *Khorâk-e Senâkhteh* (in Persian) 1981

Johnson, Samuel, A Dictionary of the English Language, 1819

Khavar, Zari, *Honar-e Âshpazi dar Gilan* (in Persian), Ashianeh Ketab, 1987

Khayyam, Omar, *The Rubaiyat*, translated by Edward Heron-Allen, Nicholas, 1898

Leyel, C.F., *Herbal Delights*, Faber & Faber, 1937

Malcolm, Sir John, *Sketches of Persia*, J. Murray, 1828

Mallos, Tess, *The Complete Middle East Cookbook*, Grub Street, 1995

Mazda, Maideh, *In a Persian Kitchen*, Tuttle Co. 1975

Montazami, Rosa, *Honar-e Âshpâzi* (in Persian), Offset Publishing, 1961

Morier, James, *The Adventures of Hajji Baba of Isphahan*, 1824, Macmillan, 1895

Mounsey, Augustus, *A Journey through the Caucasus and the Interior of Persia*, Smith Elder, 1872

Perry, Charles, *Shorba: A Linguistic Chemico-Culinary Inquiry*, Petits Propos Culinaires (PPC) 7, 1981

———, *Notes on Persian Pasta*, PPC 10, 1982

———, *A Mongolian Dish*, PPC 19, 1985

Ramazani, Nesta, *Persian Cooking*, University Press of Virginia, 1974

Reid, Mehry Motamen, *Gourmet Cooking Persian Style*, M.M. Reid, 1989

Rodinson, Maxime, *On the Etymology of 'Losange'* (translated by Charles Perry, PPC 23, 1986)

Roden, Claudia, *A New Book of Middle Eastern Food*, Viking, 1968

Ryder, M.L., *Sheep and Man*, Duckworth, 1983

Safavid Cookery Book (in Persian) (reprinted by Islamic Republic of Iran Radio and Television Publications, 1981)

Shoberl, Frederick, *Persia*, John Grigg, 1828

Simmons, Shireen, *Entertaining in the Persian Way*, Lennard, 1988

Soyer, Alexis, *Pantropheon*, 1853 (facsimile reprint, 1977)

Spurling, Hilary, *Elinor Fettiplace's Receipt Book*, Penguin, 1986

Stewart, Katie, *Cooking and Eating*, Hart-Davis, 1975

Sykes, Ella, *Persia and its People*, Methuen, 1919

Sykes, Percy, *A History of Persia*, Macmillan, 1930

Tilsley-Benham, Jill, *Is that Hippocrates in the Kitchen? A Look at Sardi/Garmi in Iran*, Oxford Symposium on Food & Cookery, 1985

Wills, Dr. J., *The Land of the Lion and Sun*, Ward Lock, 1891

INDEX

NOTES

NOTES